AS: USE OF MATHS

Algebra & Graphs

JUNE HAIGHTON • ANNE HAWORTH • GEOFF WAKE

...e rates of female marathon runners

Speed (m/s)	Average stride rate
15.9	3.1
16.9	3.1
17.5	3.2
18.6	3.3
20.0	3.4
21.1	3.5
22.1	3.6

Speed (metres per second)

Published in 2003 by:
Nelson Thornes Ltd
Delta Place
27 Bath Road
CHELTENHAM
GL53 7TH
United Kingdom

03 04 05 06 07 / 10 9 8 7 6 5 4 3 2 1

A catalogue record for this book is available from the British Library

ISBN 0 7487 6976-5

Illustrations by Oxford Designers and Illustrators
Page make-up by Tech Set Ltd

Printed and bound in Great Britain by Scotprint

Acknowledgements

The authors and publishers would like to thank Lawrence Wo for his help and
assistance in checking and compiling the manuscript.
The publishers wish to thank the following for permission to reproduce copyright
material:
Digital Vision 6 (NT): 1; Digital Vision 20 (NT), 3,6; Creativ Collection/EWI (NT), 5,20;
Corel 772 (NT); Photodisc 66 (NT); Digital Vision XA(NT), 28; Corel 604 (NT), 20;
Digital Vision XA (NT), 19; Photodisc 31 (NT), 35,39; Photodisc 22 (NT), 39;
Peter Adams/Digital Vision BP (NT), 39; Corel 522 (NT), 48; Digital Vision 9 (NT), 51;
Photodisc 54 (NT), 72; Corel 681 (NT), 81; Photodisc 31 (NT), 111;
Digital Vision PB (NT), 114; Corel 578 (NT), 114; Corel 542 (NT), 115;
Stockbyte 6 (NT), 118; Elektravision 1 (NT), 121; Photodisc 40 (NT), 125;
Corel 781 (NT), 151; Corel 790 (NT), 140; Corel 62 (NT), 140; Photodisc 54 (NT), 168;
Photodisc 44 (NT), 187; Photodisc 50 (NT), 192; Stockbyte 9 (NT), 194;
Photodisc 54 (NT), 201; Activity Games, 52; AKG London, 170;
Bodleian Library (Collection Archiv F Kunst & Geshichte, Berlin); Hulton Getty (Hulton
Deutch), 140; NASA, 69; NOAA, 49; Photo RMN (H. Lewandowski); Science Museum
(Science and Society picture Library); Science Photolibrary (A.B. Dowsett), 101;
(Jeurgen Berger, Max-Planck Institute); Topham Picturepoint (Pressnet), 73,130.
All other photographs Nelson Thornes Archive.

The publishers have made every effort to contact copyright holders but apologise if
any have been overlooked.

Contents

UoM4

UoM4

UoM4

Using this book

This book will support you in learning the mathematics you will need for the two compulsory units of the AS Use of Mathematics:

- *Working with algebraic & graphical techniques*
- *Applying mathematics*

These units will help you appreciate that mathematics can be a very powerful tool that you can use to help you make sense of the world about you. This will involve you in considering mathematical models of the situations you investigate, using algebraic and graphical techniques, recurrence relations or simulations. It is important that at all stages you consider how effective your mathematics is at describing the situation you are investigating. For example, you will need to consider whether the assumptions on which the model is based are realistic. You will constantly refer back and forth between your mathematics and the real world. This diagram attempts to summarise the mathematical modelling process.

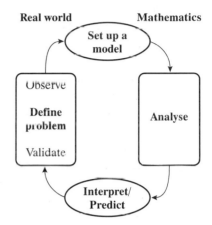

Throughout your work you will need to have access to technology – in particular a graphic calculator. On some occasions you may find a spreadsheet or graph plotting software on a computer useful. See the section 'Using Technology' for some advice.

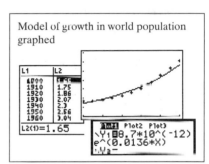

Model of growth in world population graphed

The activities of each chapter introduce you to the mathematical content for either one or both of the units *Working with algebraic & graphical techniques* and *Applying mathematics*.

At the end of each chapter there are sections:

- Revision summary
  – giving the key mathematical points you will have learned
- Preparing for Assessment
  – giving advice about how to develop your coursework portfolio and some practice exam questions to work through.

There are four comprehension articles in the book to help you prepare for that assessment component (Paper 1 of *Applying mathematics*). These are in the coloured section in the centre of the book and you should make sure you understand the mathematical content of the appropriate chapter before attempting them.

Other features include:

| Discussion point

You should discuss these with your teacher and other students.

Resource Sheet

When you are working on an activity that has this symbol your teacher may have a sheet that will help you – for example there may be a ready-scaled graph for you to use or a simulation table to complete.

This icon indicates that there is an Excel activity available that the authors have developed to help you understand or practise a particular mathematical technique.

Practice Sheet

When you see this box in the margin, your teacher may have a sheet of questions that you can work through for more practice on a technique that you are finding difficult.

Nuffield resource

This box indicates that there is an additional activity available on the Nuffield website – *http://www.fsmq.org/resources/index.asp* – that your teacher might ask you to do.

UoM1

This symbol is used to indicate that a particular part of the book is useful only for the Free-standing Mathematics Unit *Working with algebraic & graphical techniques*.

UoM4

This symbol is used to indicate that a particular part of the book is useful only for the terminal unit *Applying mathematics*.

This symbol indicates that a question is difficult.

1 Rules, Laws and Models

You can use mathematics to analyse situations, solve problems and make predictions. To do this, you have to use or construct mathematical descriptions – **rules**, **laws** or **models** – of the situations. This may involve making numerical calculations, drawing graphs and using algebra. In this course you will learn how to apply some mathematics that you already know, together with some new mathematics that you will learn, to use mathematical rules, laws and models effectively. If the rule, law or model is good, it will provide realistic answers to the problem in hand. If it is not good, any answer may be misleading or even completely useless.

Sometimes the rule, law or model you use will be exact. For example, when you **convert** from one system of measuring length to another, such as converting from inches to millimetres, you use the rule

$$1 \text{ inch} = 25.4 \text{ mm}$$
$$\text{number of millimetres} = 25.4 \times \text{number of inches}.$$

This is straightforward and an easy rule to use, which works in all cases.

On other occasions a mathematical model may be developed to describe **empirical data** as accurately as possible. For example, a description of how a population grows is useful to those who have to plan for housing, health-care, roads and so on.

World Population Growth, Actual and Projected, 1950–2050

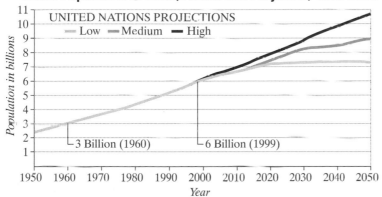

In this chapter, you will investigate a variety of rules, laws and models in different forms and you will consider carefully their usefulness. You will also learn in depth about **linear models** and models of **direct proportion**.

NASA's Mars Climate Orbiter

NASA's Mars Climate Orbiter was lost in space... because engineers failed to make a simple conversion from Imperial to metric units. This was an embarrassing lapse that sent the $125 million craft fatally close to the surface of Mars.

Discussion point
Can you find examples of other embarrassing mathematical errors?

Empirical data is that found by observation or experiment.

1.1 Models of direct proportion

Key web search terms

direct proportion
constant of proportionality
unit conversions
imperial metric
gradient of a line

mobile phone tariffs
currency conversions
euro dollar yen

A Welsh journey

Mobile phone tariffs 1

More direct proportion models

Converting currency (UoM4)

The importance of units

A Welsh journey

The distance from Cardiff in south-east Wales to Bangor in
north-west Wales is about 180 miles and the journey takes about
four and a half hours by car. The table shows the distance from
Cardiff to a number of towns on the way and how long it took to
reach them on one journey.

Place	Distance from Cardiff (miles)	Time from Cardiff (minutes)	Time from Cardiff (hours)
Cardiff	0	0	0.0
Merthyr Tydfil	23.4	31	0.5
Libanus	40.1	54	0.9
Llyswen	54	72	1.2
Builth Wells	65.3	88	1.5
Newbridge on Wye	70.8	96	1.6
Rhayader	79	108	1.8
Caersws	101.1	139	2.3
Mallwyd	124.2	172	2.9
Rhyd	154.9	220	3.7
Bangor	182.4	267	4.5

Activity 1.1A

Resource
Sheet
1.1A

a Draw a graph to show this journey. Put time from Cardiff,
  t hours, on the horizontal axis and distance from Cardiff,
  d miles, on the vertical axis and plot the (time, distance) point
  for each town.

b Draw a straight line of best fit on your graph.

c Your line should go through the origin – why?

d Find the equation of the line.

e The gradient of your line represents the speed of the journey.
  Explain why this is the case.

f What are the units used to measure speed in this case?

(UoM4) g How would your graph be changed if the journey was faster or
  slower? Sketch a graph to illustrate these situations.

Discussion point

How do you convert a time in
minutes to a time in hours?

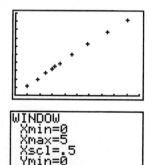

```
WINDOW
 Xmin=0
 Xmax=5
 Xscl=.5
 Ymin=0
 Ymax=200
 Yscl=20
 Xres=1
```

Discussion point

The points on the graph lie more-or-
less on a straight line. Why is this?
Can you describe a car journey
where the points would not lie on a
straight line?

☞ Variables x and y are in **direct proportion** if $y = kx$, where k is a constant. The graph of y against x will be a straight line that passes through the origin (where $x = 0$, $y = 0$).

For all direct proportion relationships, **the constant k is called the constant of proportionality**. It is equal to the gradient of the graph.

The units of k are $\dfrac{\text{units of } y}{\text{units of } x}$.

k often gives a significant measure, e.g. in the case of the Welsh journey k gives speed.

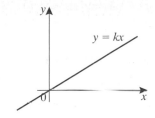

Activity 1.1B

Find two further examples of direct proportion models of your own. Find these from other areas of your studies if you can.
In each case:

a draw a graph

b find the constant of proportionality (remember to give its units) and state what it tells you.

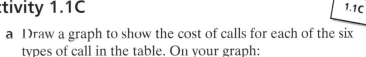
Mobile phone tariffs 1

There are many different tariffs that you will need to consider when choosing a mobile phone. The most straight forward – but not necessarily the cheapest – charge all calls at the same rate per minute (you will actually be charged by the second).
The table shows the charges for a particular network, for a 'pay-as-you-go' mobile phone for different types of calls.

Call charges per minute	Standard tariff	Off-peak tariff
Standard calls to non-mobiles	25p	5p
Calls to mobiles – same network	20p	10p
Calls to mobiles – other networks	50p	30p

Resource Sheet 1.1C

Activity 1.1C

1 **a** Draw a graph to show the cost of calls for each of the six types of call in the table. On your graph:
   i plot time (0–30 minutes) on the horizontal axis
   ii plot cost in pounds on the vertical axis
   iii draw a straight line graph for each tariff showing the cost of up to 30 minutes of calls
   iv label each line clearly.

  b Find the gradient of each line. What does this tell you in each case?

2 For each type of call, write down an equation that gives cost £C, for a call lasting t minutes. What is the constant of proportionality in each case?

The importance of units

Many conversions such as currency conversions and conversions between different units (e.g. from kilometres to miles) are **models of** direct proportion.

Activity 1.1D

One pint is 0.57 litres.

1   Draw a graph to convert from p pints to l litres.

Plot p on the horizontal axis and l on the vertical axis. Choose a range of values useful to someone shopping in a supermarket.

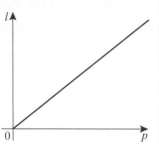

2   **a** Write down a formula connecting p and l. Remember your formula should have the form $y = kx$, as the relationship is one of direct proportion.

   b What is the value of your constant k?

Discussion point

What is the connection between the constant of proportionality for conversion from pints to litres and that for conversion from litres to pints?

NASA's Mars Climate Orbiter fatally crashed into the planet Mars because engineers did not convert from **imperial** to **metric** units. NASA engineers used metric units but the company that built the spacecraft provided data in the imperial system of inches, feet and pounds.

The engineers who built the Mars Climate Orbiter measured the thrust force of the rockets in foot-pounds – meanwhile the NASA engineers thought that this data was in the metric units of Newtons.

$$1 \text{ foot-pound} = 4.448\,222 \text{ Newtons}$$

This difference was not spotted and the spacecraft approached the planet at too low an altitude resulting in its destruction.

Activity 1.1E

1   Write a formula, in the form '$N =$', that NASA engineers could have used to convert F foot-pounds to N Newtons.

2   **a** Use a graphic calculator to draw a graph that the engineers could have used to convert F foot-pounds to N Newtons.

   b What is the gradient of your graph? How is it related to the formula?

More direct proportion models

Activity 1.1F

Here are some more direct proportion models.
For each of these sketch a graph of the relationship and find the constant of proportionality.

1   For each £100 of business sponsorship that a school can attract, the government will provide £50.

2   When making pastry, the weight of fat needed is half the weight of flour.

3   A mail order computer outlet adds 17.5% VAT to the price of everything before it is sold.

Discussion point

Your results will depend on what you choose for your axes. For example, in the pastry example, you could show weight of fat against weight of flour, or the other way round, or the weight of either fat or flour against the total weight of the pastry. Compare results and make sure you can reconcile any differences.

UoM4 Converting currency

Activity 1.1G

Resource
Sheet
1.1G

1 Euro = 0.9 United States dollars
1 Euro = 110 Japanese Yen

1   Use the currency conversion factors to draw two lines on a copy of the grid below. Notice that you use the left-hand vertical scale for Japanese Yen and the right-hand vertical scale for US dollars.

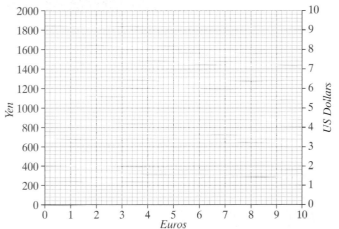

2   Find a formula giving Y, the number of Japanese Yen for E Euros.

3   Find a formula giving S, the number of US dollars for E Euros.

4   Find a formula giving Y, the number of Japanese Yen for S US Dollars.

5   Find a formula giving S, the number of US dollars for Y Japanese Yen.

1.2 Linear models

Key web search terms

mobile phone line rental
linear models
oil-fired boiler
gradient of a line
shoe sizes
intercept line axis
Olympic games results (history of)
rates of change
economics supply and demand models

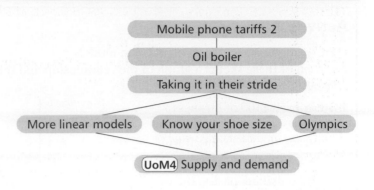

Mobile phone tariffs 2

In Section **1.1** you considered the most straightforward type of mobile phone tariffs where all calls are charged at the same rate per minute.

Sometimes a mobile phone tariff also includes a line rental cost. This is charged even if you make no calls. The table shows the costs of two mobile phone tariffs each including a monthly line rental plus an extra charge for the calls.

Tariff name	Line rental (£/month)	Call time (pence/min)
Just chat	12	8
Talk time	16	6

Resource Sheet 1.2A

Activity 1.2A

1   Work out the total charge using each tariff for a month in which a customer made
    a 60 minutes of calls   **b** 600 minutes of calls.

2   **a** Draw a graph to show the cost, £C, of t minutes of calls for each tariff. Use a horizontal axis for times from 0 to 600 minutes. Remember to identify each line clearly.

    b Find the gradient of each line. What does this represent?

    c Find the value of C where each line meets the vertical axis. What do these values represent?

    d What are the values of t and C where the lines meet?
    What is the significance of these values?

3   **a** For each tariff, find a formula that gives the cost, £C, for a month in which the total call time was t minutes.

    b Solve these as simultaneous equations.

4   How are your answers to **2** and **3** related?

If the relationship between variables x and y is **linear** it can be written in the form $y = mx + c$, where m and c are constants (**Direct proportion models** are special cases of this in which c is zero, so $y = mx$.)

The graph of y against x is a **straight line**.

For all linear relationships, the constant m is the gradient of the graph and c is the intercept on the y axis.

The units of m are $\dfrac{\text{units of } y}{\text{units of } x}$.

The units of c are the same as those of y.

Both m and c usually give significant measures, e.g. in the case of the mobile phone tarrifs £m/minute is the charge per minute and £c is the monthly line rental cost.

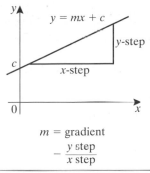

m = gradient
$= \dfrac{y \text{ step}}{x \text{ step}}$

Nuffield resource
UoM1
Starter
Interactive Graphs

Activity 1.2B

Excel Activity

Use a spreadsheet or graphic calculator to explore graphs of the form $y = mx + c$ for different values of m and c.

a First of all, investigate the effect of altering m on the graph. Set $c = 0$ and see what happens as you vary m from -5 to $+5$. Now set $m = 1$ and see what happens as you vary c from -5 to $+5$. Try other values of m and c.

b What conclusions can you draw? Check by predicting what will happen for a specific case, e.g. $y = 5 - 2x$.

c Write some notes about what you find out – illustrate these with some sketch graphs.

Oil boiler

A hotel uses an oil-fired boiler to produce hot water. The table and graph show the way in which the quantity of oil in the storage tank fell during an eight-week summer period after the tank was filled.

The points do not lie on a perfect straight line because the relationship between the variables is not exactly linear.

t (weeks)	g (gallons)
0	400
1	360
2	339
3	315
4	261
5	234
6	185
7	170
8	115

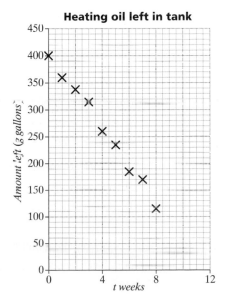

Heating oil left in tank

Discussion points
How would the graphs of a summer period and a winter period differ? Sketch a graph of quantity of oil used against time for a full year. Do you think a linear model would be appropriate in this case? What other variables could have an effect on the amount of oil used?

Activity 1.2C

Resource
Sheet
1.2C

1 How much oil did the tank hold when full?

2 **a** Draw a graph of the data and, on this, draw a line to model the data. Make sure it passes through the point (0, 400) as this is the most accurate reading.

   b Find the gradient of the line.

   c What information is given by the gradient?

3 **a** Write down a linear formula that gives the relationship between the amount of oil, *g* gallons, in the tank after *t* weeks.

   b Use your formula to calculate an estimate of the time taken to *use* 300 gallons of oil. Check your answer using the graph.

Taking it in their stride

The stride rate of a runner is the number of steps made per second. Researchers studied the stride rates of 21 female marathon runners at different speeds.

The results are shown in the table and graph.

Speed (m/s)	Average stride rate
15.9	3.05
16.9	3.12
17.5	3.17
18.6	3.25
20.0	3.36
21.1	3.46
22.1	3.55

Stride rates of female marathon runners

Average stride rate (steps per second) vs *Speed (metres per second)*

Discussion point

If you extend the graph, it will not pass through the origin. Why? Should the graph pass through the origin? Why?

Activity 1.2D

1 Show calculations to confirm that the gradient of the line, m, is approximately 0.08.

In this case it is not possible to read the intercept with the vertical axis, c, directly from the graph. Instead you can calculate c by substituting the co-ordinates of a point on the line into the formula $y = mx + c$ (where x m/s is the speed and y strides/s is the stride rate).

2 **a** Find c using $m = 0.08$ and substituting the values for the point (17.5, 3.17) into $y = mx + c$.

    b State the model giving stride rate, y, for any speed, x, in the form $y = mx + c$.

Discussion points
Do other data points give the same value of c? If not, why not?
In this case what would be the interpretation of the value of the intercept c?
Is it realistic?

More linear models

Activity 1.2E

Find two examples of linear models of your own. Find these from other areas of your studies if you can. In each case:

a draw a graph

b find the gradient, m, and the intercept with the vertical axis, c, and write down a linear model in the form $y = mx + c$.

Activity 1.2F

For each of the following linear relationships:
- define the two variables and write down a linear model in the form $y = mx + c$
- sketch a graph
- explain what information the gradient and intercept with the vertical axis give
- discuss whether or not the linear model is good and whether it can continue in the long term.

a A plumber charges £25 for a call-out plus £20 per hour.

b Sam borrows £120 from his father and pays back the loan at £18 per week.

c A car joins a motorway at a speed of 25 m s^{-1} and accelerates at a rate of 0.5 m s^{-2}.

d After a 20 cm candle is lit, it burns at a steady rate of 1.6 cm per hour.

e A joint of meat is taken from a freezer at a temperature of $-18\,°C$ and defrosts at a rate of 1.5 °C per hour.

Know your shoe size

The table below shows different systems for measuring shoe sizes.

British	2	3	4	5	6	7	8	9	10	11	12	13
European	34	35.3	36.75	38	39.25	40.5	42	43.25	44.6	46	47.3	48
US male	3	4	5	6	7	8	9	10	11	12	13	14
US female	4	5	6	7	8	9	10	11	12			
Japanese	21	22	23	24.8	25	26	27	28	29	30	31	32
Mexican				4.5	5.5	6.5	7.5	8.5	9.5	10.5	11.5	12.5
Foot length in cm	21.4	22.4	22.9	23.8	24.9	25.7	26.6	27.6	28.3	29.3	30.1	
Foot length in inches	8.4	8.8	9.1	9.4	9.8	10.1	10.5	10.9	11.2	11.6	11.9	

Activity 1.2G

Use a graphic calculator or a spreadsheet.

a Find some linear relationships between the sets of data for different countries – use graphs to help you identify them.

b For those you find write a formula to describe the relationship. Define your variables carefully.

Olympics

Activity 1.2H

Resource Sheet 1.2H

The table gives the times and distances achieved by gold medallists in three events in the Olympic games from 1928 to 2000.

1 For each event:
- draw a graph showing the results
- draw a straight line to model the data
- find the equation of your linear model
- explain why a linear model is not likely to be appropriate in the long run.

2 For each event sketch a graph showing what you think will happen to the winning result in future Olympic games. Explain your reasoning.

Year	Men's high jump (m)	Women's 100 m (s)	Women's javelin (m)
1928	1.94	12.2	not held
1932	1.97	11.9	43.68
1936	2.03	11.5	45.18
1948	1.98	11.9	45.57
1952	2.04	11.65	50.47
1956	2.12	11.82	53.86
1960	2.16	11.18	55.98
1964	2.18	11.49	60.54
1968	2.24	11.08	60.36
1972	2.23	11.07	63.88
1976	2.25	11.08	65.94
1980	2.36	11.06	68.40
1984	2.35	10.97	69.56
1988	2.38	10.54	74.68
1992	2.34	10.82	68.34
1996	2.39	10.94	67.94
2000	2.35	10.75	68.91

Supply and demand · UoM4

Economists use different models to explain how prices are determined in the market place. **Demand** is the term used to describe the quantity of goods that consumers are willing to buy at a particular price.

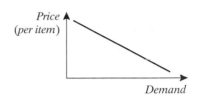

This simplified graph illustrates how the price of a particular type of graphic calculator may be linked to demand.

Activity 1.2I(a)

Resource Sheet 1.2I

1   Write a brief interpretation of the graph explaining how the price and demand are related.

2   On a copy of the graph draw and label new lines to show the likely effect of the following events:

   a   graphic calculators being made compulsory in exams

   b   a decrease in the population of school pupils

   c   a competitor's graphic calculator being halved in price.

3   Briefly explain your reasoning in each case.

This simplified graph illustrates how the **supply** of the particular type of graphic calculator by its manufacturer may be linked to price.

Activity 1.2I(b)

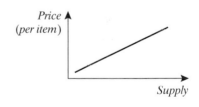

1   Write a brief interpretation of the graph explaining how the price and supply are related.

2   On a copy of the graph draw (and indicate clearly) new lines to show the likely effect of the following events:

   a   the use of a new more efficient manufacturing plant

   b   a reduction in the pay of the manufacturer's workforce

   c   an increase in the price of components used by the manufacturer

   d   the removal of VAT from electronic goods.

3   Briefly explain your reasoning in each case.

The **supply and demand models** may be combined to give this supply and demand diagram.

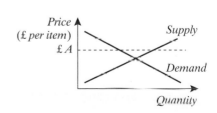

At price £A the quantity of graphic calculators supplied is more than that demanded. There will be a surplus of graphic calculators. The price is likely to fall.

Activity 1.2I(c)

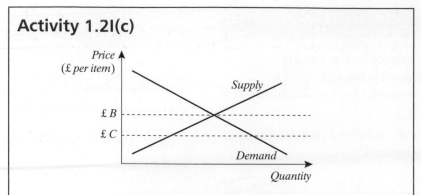

Interpret the situation at prices £B and £C.

Activity 1.2I(d)

1 The graph below shows possible supply and demand models for a particular type of graphic calculator.

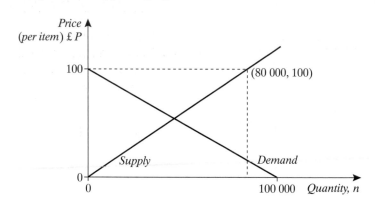

Write down a formula relating P and n for

a the supply model

b the demand model.

2 Solve your equations simultaneously to find the price at which supply is in equilibrium with demand.

Practice sheets:
Solving linear equations
Finding equations of straight lines

1.3 More complex linear models

Key web search terms

income tax bands
cooling liquid models
Newtons law of coding
stamp duty
acceleration
0–60 mph

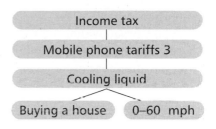
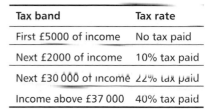

Income tax

The table shows different rates of income tax that may be used for different incomes These rates tend to be changed slightly in each annual government budget. The graph is based on the data in the table – it is a series of straight lines.

The data given here is not real data. It is just used to illustrate how income tax is usually calculated.

Tax band	Tax rate
First £5000 of income	No tax paid
Next £2000 of income	10% tax paid
Next £30 000 of income	22% tax paid
Income above £37 000	40% tax paid

Discussion point

Describe what happens to the amount of tax you pay as your income increases.

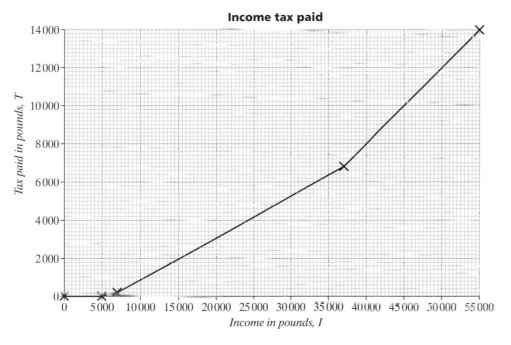

Income tax paid

Tax paid in pounds, T (y-axis)
Income in pounds, I (x-axis)

Activity 1.3A

1 Find a formula relating tax paid, £T, to income, £I, for each of the lines on the graph.

2 Use a graphic calculator or a spreadsheet to recreate the graph.

Mobile phone tariffs 3

The monthly line rental charged for a mobile phone often includes some 'free' minutes. The table shows the two mobile phone tariffs that you worked with in **1.2** together with another tariff called Talk 400. The monthly line rental for Talk 400 is £40 but this gives you 400 'free' minutes before you begin to pay for your calls at the rate of 5 pence per minute.

The graph shows all three phone tariffs.

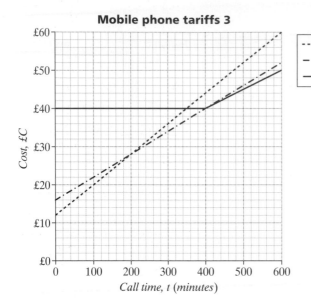

Tariff	Line rental (£/month)	Call charge (pence/min)
Just chat	12	8
Talk time	16	6
Talk 400	40*	5

*includes 400 minutes

Activity 1.3B

1   The Talk 400 graph is made up of two line segments.
    In the first part of the graph the cost, £C, is a constant, not related to the call time, t minutes.
    Write down an equation for the first part of the Talk 400 graph (i.e. for $0 \leqslant t \leqslant 400$).

2   **a** Find the gradient, m, of the second part of the Talk 400 graph.

    b The formula for this line segment is of the form $C = mt + c$. Since the line segment does not meet the cost axis you cannot use the intercept on the cost axis to give the value of c.

    i Find c by substituting the values $t = 400$ and $C = 40$ into $C = mt + c$.

    ii State the formula for the second linear section of the Talk 400 tariff.

UoM4   3   Write a brief paragraph advising potential customers about which tariff is best value and when.

$0 \leqslant t \leqslant 400$ means that t is between 0 and 400, because $0 \leqslant t$ means 0 is less than or equal to t (so t is greater than or equal to 0) and $t \leqslant 400$ means that t is less than or equal to 400.

Cooling liquid

The graph shows the temperature, $T\,°C$, plotted against time, t seconds, for a cooling liquid. The data is in the table on the right.

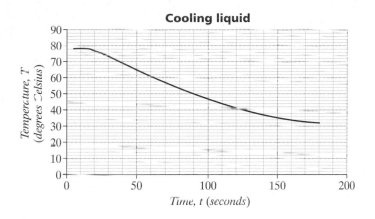

Cooling liquid

As you can see the graph is not a straight line. However, if you consider part of the time for which the liquid was cooling, it may be possible to use a straight line model.

Activity 1.3C

1. Use the data in the table to recreate the graph using either a graphic calculator or a spreadsheet.

2. Model the data by one straight line for $20 \leqslant t \leqslant 60$ and one for $140 \leqslant t \leqslant 180$.
    For each section find a formula that links T and t.

3. **a** Test how good the models are by comparing the values they predict at the end- and mid-points of the range (i.e. at $t = 20, 40, 60$ and $t = 140, 160, 180$) with the actual data at these points. Write a sentence or two about what you find.

    b Find what each model predicts for extreme values (when $t = 0$ and when $T = 0$). Write a sentence or two about what you find.

    (UoM4)

4. **(UoM4)** Suggest how to find a linear model for the whole data set.

5. **(UoM4)** Find a linear model for the whole data set. Evaluate when this model is most useful.

Time (seconds)	Temperature (degrees Celsius)
5	77.9
10	78.2
15	78.0
20	76.7
25	75.2
30	73.6
35	71.5
40	69.4
45	67.4
50	65.3
55	63.1
60	61.0
65	59.0
70	57.0
75	55.0
80	53.1
85	51.3
90	49.6
95	48.0
100	46.5
105	45.1
110	43.8
115	42.3
120	41.2
125	40.1
130	39.0
135	37.9
140	37.0
145	36.2
150	35.3
155	34.5
160	34.0
165	33.3
170	32.7
175	32.1
180	31.6

Buying a house

If you buy a house you have to pay a tax called **stamp duty** if the house is above a certain price. The table gives some likely rates of stamp duty.

House price	Stamp duty
£60 000 or less	0%
Over £60 000 but not more than £250 000	1%
Over £250 000 but not more than £500 000	3%
Over £500 000	4%

Discussion point

Find current rates of stamp duty. Find out about other taxes such as inheritance tax, capital gains tax, etc.

Activity 1.3D

Use the data to:

1 draw a graph that will give you the amount of stamp duty paid, £S, for a house of any cost, £H;

2 find formulae relating H and S for the different phases of stamp duty.

0–60 mph

Car manufacturers often quote the time a car takes to reach 60 mph from a standing start.

The graph below shows the speed, v miles per hour, against time, t seconds, for a particular car accelerating from 0 mph to 60 mph.

The time this car took to reach 60 mph was 10.75 seconds.

Discussion point

Interpret the 'blips' (small almost horizontal sections) of the graph.

Checkpoint

Use the graph to check that this statement is true.

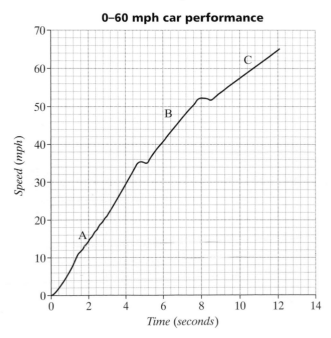

0–60 mph car performance

Activity 1.3E

1 Find three distinct linear functions of the form $v = u + at$ to model three phases of the motion where

    A $0 \leqslant t \leqslant 4$

    B $5 \leqslant t \leqslant 7$

    C $9 \leqslant t \leqslant 11$.

2 **a** For each phase of the motion state the value of a.

    b What does this measure?

3 **a** For each phase of the motion state the value of u. What does this measure?

    b Explain why the values of u for phases **B** and **C** of the motion inform you that these linear models are unsuitable for phase **A** of the motion.

4 Use your model for phase **A** of the motion to predict when the speed of the car would reach 60 mph if this model were used throughout the car's motion.
Say what this tells you about the motion of cars.

5 Why are all of these models inappropriate for the long term motion of a car?

1.4 Representing rules, laws and models in different ways

Key web search terms

temperature conversion
Celsius
annual interest rates
cooking times

Fahrenheit
temperature scales
Boyle's law

Temperatures
|
More models

Temperatures are rising

Temperatures in different parts of the country are often shown using different shades on a map.

The key below the map shows what the shades mean. You can also use the key as a conversion diagram for **Celsius** and **Fahrenheit** temperatures.

Sometimes an approximate or rough rule is useful because it allows you to calculate values easily and the values it gives are accurate enough for the purpose.

An **approximate rule** for converting from temperatures in Celsius to temperatures in Fahrenheit is

in words: 'double the Celsius temperature and add thirty'

using algebra: $F = 2C + 30$

as a graph:

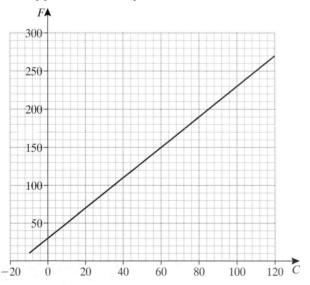

Approximate temperature conversion

as a diagram:

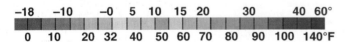

TUESDAY 1300

Temperature scales are developed by dividing the temperature between two fixed points into a number of equally spaced divisions. The two fixed points usually used are the temperature at which water freezes and the temperature at which water boils at sea level.

The Celsius scale divides the gap between the two temperatures into 100 equal divisions and takes the freezing point of water as $0\,°C$.

The Fahrenheit scale divides the gap between freezing and boiling point into 180 equal divisions and takes the freezing point as $32\,°F$.

Checkpoint

Check whether the different ways of representing the rule are consistent with this model.

Activity 1.4A

The exact algebraic rule for converting from temperatures in Celsius to temperatures in Fahrenheit is: $F = \frac{9}{5}C + 32$.

1 Write the exact conversion rule in words and draw a graph of it using a graphic calculator or spreadsheet.

2 Investigate the approximate rule by finding the values it gives for F when $C = 0$ (freezing point) and $C = 100$ (boiling point). Make sure you are clear about the differences between the approximate and exact rules in the different formats.

3 **a** Rewrite the approximate rule $F = 2C + 30$ in the form '$C =$',

   b Show that the exact rule can be rearranged to give

   $$C = \frac{5(F - 32)}{9}.$$

4 Find the one value of C for which the approximate and exact rules give the same value of F. Do this by putting $2C + 30$ and $\frac{9}{5}C + 32$ equal to each other.

   Check your answer by substituting the value you get for F back into each original rule.

5 The **Kelvin scale** of temperature, like the Celsius scale, divides the gap between freezing point and boiling point into 100 equal divisions but takes freezing point as 273K. Write a rule to convert from C to K.

Discussion point
What are the advantages and disadvantages of using the approximate and exact rules?

When giving temperatures using the Kelvin scale we do not use a degree '°' symbol

More models

Here are some more mathematical rules, laws and models. Each is given either in words, algebraically, graphically or as a diagram.

Cost of petrol

The formula for the total cost, £C, of V litres of petrol:
$C = kV$ where £k is the cost of one litre of petrol.

Price and demand

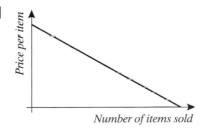

Price per item (vertical axis), *Number of items sold* (horizontal axis)

Skydiver

The formula for the distance, d metres, fallen in time t seconds is $d = 4.9t^2$.

Currency conversion

The exchange rate for euros to US dollars is
1 euro = 0.9 US dollars
€1 = $0.9.

Savings

The amount of money, £A, in the bank t years after investing
£1500 at an annual interest rate of 2.4% is given by the formula
$A = 1500 \times 1.024^t$.

Boyle's law

Boyle's law states that for a fixed mass of gas at a fixed temperature
the product of the volume and the pressure is constant.

Cooking

The time needed to cook a well-done roast joint of beef is 30
minutes plus 20 minutes per pound.

Concorde flight

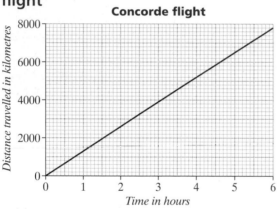

> **Practice sheet:**
> **Rearranging equations**

Simple code

> **Maths → Qexlw**

To put words into code, each letter is replaced by the letter four
further on in the alphabet.

Ticket prices

For the month of August, an airline cut the prices of tickets by 10%
and gave another £5 off for booking online.

Activity 1.4B

1   For each rule, law or model show each one in as many different
    formats (words, algebra, graph, diagram) as you can.

2   Which of the rules, laws or models are linear models?
    For each of the linear models in the form $y = mx + c$, find the
    values of m and c, and say what they represent.

Checkpoint
Check that your work is correct by
comparing the results for the
different representation(s) of each
example.

Discussion point
Which representations are most
useful in each case? Think about
using them in different
circumstances such as in a
spreadsheet, in an e-mail, as
instructions on packaging, in a
presentation, etc.

1.5 How good is the model?

Key web search terms

Thomas Malthus Population models
Rule of twelfths   Tide times
100 m sprint times

A simple population growth model

Rule of twelfths

The fastest men in the world

In the previous section you looked at some rules, laws and models. Some of them, such as the formula $F = \frac{9}{5}C + 32$, for converting between Celsius and Fahrenheit temperatures, are exact rules and work for all values of F and C.

Others, such as the straight line graph showing the connection between the price of an item and how many are sold, are simplified models of complex situations which are difficult or impossible to analyse exactly.

Some models may be unrealistic in the long term – often because the model is too simple to always give good results.

A simple population growth model

In this section you will look critically at some models and consider just how good they are.

In 1798, in Britain, Thomas Malthus wrote *An Essay on the Principle of Population, as it Affects the Future Improvement of Society* in which he predicted how many people would be living in years to come. The model he used was that the population would double every 25 years; this was based on data of the population of the United States.

Malthus also suggested that food did not grow rapidly enough to feed the population, but he pointed out that if wheat each year produced six grains for every one planted then a single acre of wheat could expand to cover the entire surface of the Earth's land mass in just fourteen years.

Year	Population (millions)
1900	76.1
1910	92.4
1920	106.4
1930	123.1
1940	132.1
1950	152.2
1960	180.6
1970	205.1
1980	227.2
1990	249.4
2000	270.3

Activity 1.5A

1 In Malthus' time, the UK population was about seven million. The population now is about 60 million. Use Malthus' model to find what his prediction of today's population would have been.

2 The data shows the population of the United States for the period 1900–2000. Use a graphic calculator or spreadsheet to plot the data for the population of the United States together with what would be predicted by Malthus' model.

3 Use your answers to **1** and **2** to comment on the suitability of Malthus' model for population growth.

4 Investigate Malthus' claim that an acre of wheat could spread in fourteen years to cover the entire surface of land on the Earth. Show your calculations clearly.

The area of the Earth's land mass is 150 000 000 km². 1 km² = 247.1 acres

Rule of twelfths

Tides do not rise or fall at a constant rate as you can see by looking at the graph below. This shows the height of the tide over a 24-hour period for Newlyn in Cornwall. The data in the table gives the height, h metres, of the tide for $7 \leqslant t \leqslant 13$ where t is the time in hours after midnight. This is the period for which the height of the tide varies from low to high tide.

Yacht and dinghy sailors and windsurfers sometimes refer to the 'Rule of twelfths'. This approximate rule is to give them some idea about how the height of the tide varies between low and high tide.

Time after midnight (hours)	Height (metres)
7	1.7
8	1.8
9	2.3
10	3.1
11	3.8
12	4.3
13	4.4

The 'Rule of twelfths' assumes

- that the tide will rise or fall over 6 hours.
- in the 1st hour the tide will rise or fall by $\frac{1}{12}$ of the range
- in the 2nd hour the tide will rise or fall by $\frac{2}{12}$ of the range
- in the 3rd hour the tide will rise or fall by $\frac{3}{12}$ of the range
- in the 4th hour the tide will rise or fall by $\frac{3}{12}$ of the range
- in the 5th hour the tide will rise or fall by $\frac{2}{12}$ of the range
- in the 6th hour the tide will rise or fall by $\frac{1}{12}$ of the range.

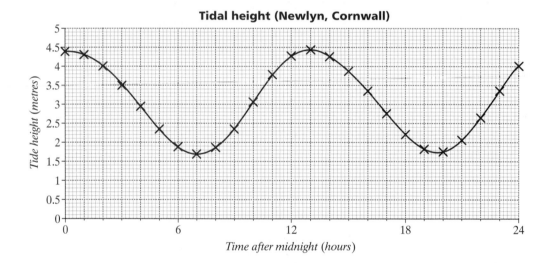

Tidal height (Newlyn, Cornwall)

Time after midnight (hours)

Tide height (metres)

Activity 1.5B

Resource Sheet 1.5B

1. Use the 'Rule of twelfths' to find the height it predicts for the tide for $7 \leqslant t \leqslant 13$.

2. Complete a copy of the table by finding:
   - the difference between the data value for h and the value for h given by the rule
   - this difference expressed as a percentage of the actual (data) value.

t	h (data)	h (rule)	difference	% difference
7	1.7			
8	1.8			
9	2.3			
10	3.1			
11	3.8			
12	4.3			
13	4.4			

3   Use your results to comment on the accuracy of the 'Rule of twelfths'.

The fastest men in the world

The graph below shows the fastest time that the men's 100 metres was run in each year from 1975–2001. A straight line has been drawn on the graph to model the data. The equation of this straight line is

$$T = 28.00729 - 0.00909Y$$

where T seconds is the time and Y is the year.

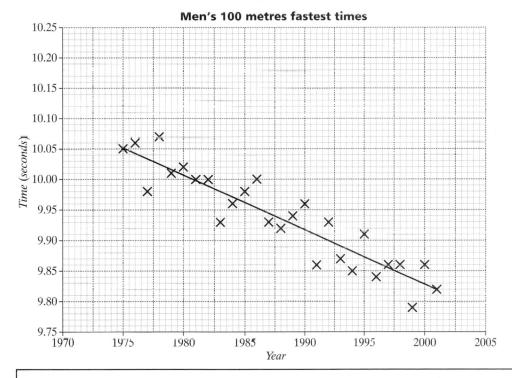

Men's 100 metres fastest times

Activity 1.5C

1   Check the suitability of the equation $T = 28.00729 - 0.00909Y$ by confirming that the line passes through the points for 1975, 1981 and 2001. Show your calculations clearly.

2   State T when $Y = 0$. Interpret what this means.

3   Find Y when $T = 0$. Interpret what this means.

4   Comment on the formula in light of your answers to **questions 2** and **3**.

1.6 Revision Summary

Models may be described using words, diagrams, algebra or graphs. Some models are given by exact rules, others are simplified models of complex situations.

Models of direct proportion

Variables x and y are in direct proportion if $y = kx$, where k is the constant of proportionality.
The graph of y against x is a straight line, with gradient k, which passes through the origin.

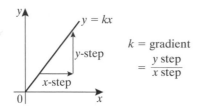

$$k = \text{gradient} = \frac{y \text{ step}}{x \text{ step}}$$

k often gives a significant measure, e.g. for a currency conversion graph k gives the rate of exchange.

Linear models

Linear models have straight line graphs with functions of the form $y = mx + c$, where m and c are constants.
The graph has gradient m and intercept on the vertical axis c.

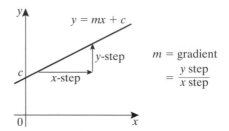

$$m = \text{gradient} = \frac{y \text{ step}}{x \text{ step}}$$

Both m and c usually give significant measures.

1.7 Preparing for assessment

Your coursework portfolio

After studying this first chapter, you could start to develop your coursework portfolio using the suggestions below.

Find data that interests you.

This can have any underlying pattern – this is best observed when you plot a graph of the data. You might like to try this at first using your graphic calculator but when you have decided which data to work with you may like to use a spreadsheet or other graph plotting software on a computer.

Consider whether you can use a linear function to model the whole or parts of your data set.

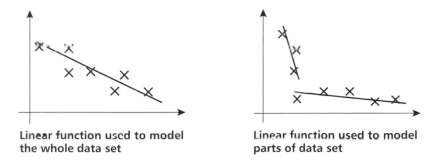

Linear function used to model the whole data set

Linear function used to model parts of data set

Find the linear rule(s):
- Show the working you use to find the gradient and intercept with the vertical axis – you may find these directly from the graph or use algebra (substituting values into the general form $y = mx + c$).
- Explain your method.

Consider how effective the linear function is.

You could think about:
- The point where the line intersects the vertical axis – this is often a significant point.
- What happens to the model in the long term – what does it predict?

Make sure you interpret the features of the linear functions clearly in terms of the situation you are investigating:
- What does the gradient tell you?
- What does the intercept with the vertical axis tell you?

Practice exam questions

1 Lorry Journey
Data

UoM1 A lorry makes a 1200 km journey across Europe.

Readings of the number of litres of diesel in the fuel tank at various distances along the route are shown plotted below. The straight line shown is a good model of this data.

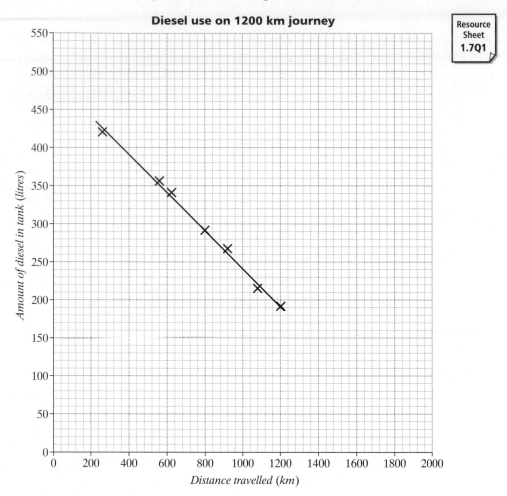

Resource Sheet **1.7Q1**

Question

a Use the straight line model to estimate:
  i how much fuel is left in the tank when the lorry has travelled half of its journey
  ii how far the lorry could go before running out of fuel.
b **i** The gradient of the line is negative. Explain why.
  ii Calculate the gradient of the line.
  iii What information does the value of the gradient give?
c **i** Find the equation of the straight line in the form $y = mx + c$, where y litres is the amount of diesel in the fuel tank when the lorry has travelled x kilometres.
  ii What information does the value of c give?

2 The graph shows average house prices in the United Kingdom for the years from 1996 to 2002.

UoM1

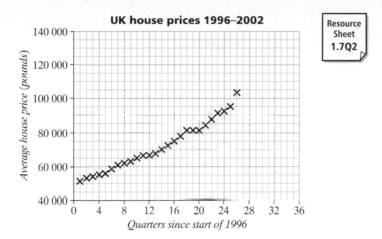

Resource Sheet 1.7Q2

The linear model $P = 4700 + 185q$ gives the average house price £P, q quarters after the start of 1996.

a **i** Draw the straight line model on a copy of the graph of the data.

    ii Use the linear model to calculate an estimate for the average house price at the end of 2004.

    iii Comment on the likely accuracy of your estimate.

b What assumption is made in using a single straight line to model the data?

The graph below shows a linear model for the first part of the data.

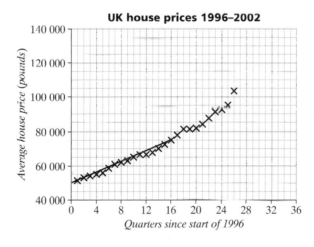

c **i** Find the equation of this straight line model.

    ii What information does the gradient of the line give?

d **i** On a copy of the graph draw a straight line to model the second part of the data.

    ii Use your straight line to estimate the average house price at the end of 2004.

    iii Compare your estimate with that obtained in part **a ii** and comment.

e Give an advantage of each of these ways of modelling the data.

2 Quadratic and other models

Contents

Consider a skydiver in freefall from an aircraft. The data and its graph show how the skydiver's distance fallen varies with time over the first twelve seconds of his fall. You can see that using a linear model of this will not be particularly effective for the first few seconds of the skydiver's motion.

As Galileo discovered in the sixteenth century, such motion is better modelled by a quadratic function. In this case the model $d = 0.46t^2$ is a good fit to the data for the first five seconds.

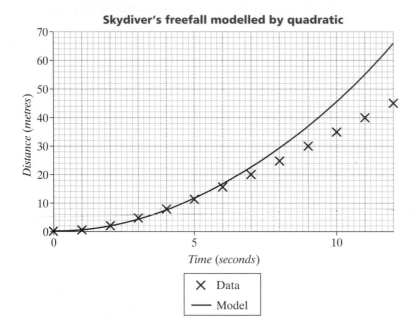

Skydiver's freefall modelled by quadratic

× Data

— Model

t seconds	d metres
0	0.00
1	0.49
2	1.89
3	4.21
4	7.38
5	11.16
6	15.36
7	19.87
8	24.63
9	29.60
10	34.69
11	39.90
12	45.20

You can see from the graph of the data that in the early part of the skydiver's motion during each successive second the distance that he falls increases. His speed is increasing – he is accelerating. After that it appears that during each successive second he falls about the same distance – his speed is constant, and you could now successfully model the data using a linear function.

In this chapter you will consider how you can use quadratic and other functions to model data, and look carefully at what the gradients of graphs of data and such models can tell you. In addition you will develop some algebraic techniques to solve problems involving quadratics, e.g. to find after how long the skydiver has fallen 5 metres or 15 metres. You will also look at the algebra involved in solving simultaneous equations and linear inequalities.

2.1 Quadratic models

Key web search terms

quadratic functions
completing the square
maximum and minimum points
factorising quadratics
quadratic solutions roots
quadratic formula

cold virus
influenza
highway code
car stopping distances
sunrise times
sunset times

Exploring quadratics

In this activity you will explore the graphs of **quadratic functions** so that you will have a good understanding of these when you use quadratics to model real data in later activities.

Activity 2.1A

Explore graphs of quadratics using a graphic calculator or a spreadsheet (or other graph plotting software).
Do this systematically as set out below.

1 **Functions of the form $y = ax^2$ ($b = 0, c = 0$)**

   a Keeping b and c at zero, experiment with different values of a.

   b Sketch a graph of $y = ax^2$ when a is positive.

   c Describe what happens as a increases from 0 to 5.

   d Sketch a graph of $y = ax^2$ when a is negative.

   e Describe what happens as a decreases from 0 to -5.

2 **Functions of the form $y = ax^2 + c$ ($b = 0$)**

   a Keeping $a = 1$ and $b = 0$, change c.

   b What happens to the curve as c changes?

   c Now keeping $a = -1$ and $b = 0$, change c.

   d What happens to the curve as c changes?

   e Try other values of a and c, keeping $b = 0$.

3 What can you say about the effect the values of a and c have on the curve?

4 **Functions of the form $y = ax^2 + bx$ ($c = 0$)**
   Note: This can be written as $y = x(ax + b)$.

   a Keeping $a = 1$ and $c = 0$ change b.

   b Describe what happens to the curve as b increases from 0 to 4. Write down anything you notice.

   c What happens to the curve as b decreases from 0 to -4?

Excel Activity

Exploring quadratics
0–60 mph
Seedlings 1   A-choo!
Stopping distance
Completing the square
Seedlings 2
Sunrise–sunset
Solving quadratic equations

Nuffield resource
UoM1 Starter Interactive Graphs

The general quadratic has the form
$y = ax^2 + bx + c$.

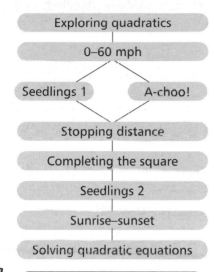

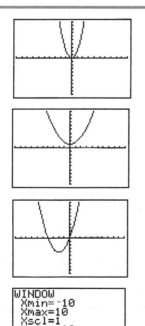

```
WINDOW
Xmin=-10
Xmax=10
Xscl=1
Ymin=-10
Ymax=10
Yscl=1
Xres=■
```

Discussion point
Can you determine the graphic calculator window settings for each of the above graphs?

d Now keep $a = -1$ and $c = 0$ and change b.

e Again describe what happens to the curve as b increases from 0 to 4, then describe what happens as b decreases from 0 to -4.

5 **The general function $y = ax^2 + bx + c$**
Experiment with different values of a, b and c.
Check what effect changing each constant has on the curve.

6 Write a summary of your findings in this activity. Illustrate your work with sketch graphs.

Activity 2.1B

Excel Activity

Quadratic functions can also be written in other forms.
For example, $y = (rx - s)(x - t)$ is a quadratic function.
Explore graphs of $y = (rx - s)(x - t)$ for different values of r, s and t.
Do this systematically by following the steps given below.

1 **Functions of the form $y = x(x - t)$**

a Keeping $r = 1$ and $s = 0$, look at the curves given for different values of t between 0 and 5.

b What do you notice about the points where the curve crosses the x axis?

c Does the same thing happen when t is negative?

2 **Functions of the form $y = rx(x - t)$**

a Change r from 1 to -1, leaving $s = 0$ and using any value of t between 1 and 5. What happens to the curve?

b Keeping $r = -1$ and $s = 0$, try different values of t.

c Use other values of r, with $s = 0$ and different values of t.

d Does the relationship between the value of t and the position of the curve still hold, whatever the value of r?

e What happens to the curve as r changes from 1 to 5?

f What happens to the curve as r changes from -1 to -5?

3 **Functions of the form $y = (x - s)(x - t)$**

a With $r = 1$, try different pairs of values for s and t.

b What is the relationship between the position of the curve and the values of s and t?

4 **Functions of the form $y = (rx - s)(x - t)$**

a Change the value of r from 1 to 2, and experiment with different values of s and t between -5 and 5.

b What is the relationship now between the points where the curve cuts the x axis and the values of s and t?

Checkpoint
Check that $y = (rx - s)(x - t)$ is a quadratic function by expanding the brackets to rearrange into a more familiar form.

Discussion point
When s and t are both zero, the general form $y = (rx - s)(x - t)$ reduces to $y = rx^2$.
What do you know about the graphs of functions of this type?

Discussion point
Why do curves with equations of the form $y = rx(x - t)$ *always* pass through the origin?

c Try other values of r.

d In general, what is the relationship between r, s and t and the points of intersection of the curve with the x axis?

5 Write a summary of what you have learnt about curves given by equations of the form $y = (rx - s)(x - t)$.

6 Use what you have learnt to find the values of x where

a $(x - 3)(x - 5) = 0$ **b** $(x - 4)(x + 4) = 0$

c $(2x - 5)(x - 7) = 0$ **d** $(x + 3)(2x - 4) = 0$

Activity 2.1C

Excel Activity

It is sometimes useful to write quadratic functions in the form $y = m(x + n)^2 + p$. This is the '**completed square**' form which you will meet again later in this section.

Explore the graphs of quadratic functions in this form.

Do this systematically by following the steps given below.

1 Functions of the form $y = m(x + n)^2$ ($p = 0$)

a Using any positive value of m between 0 and 5 and keeping $p = 0$, look at the curves given for different values of n between -5 and 5.

b What would you expect to happen to the curve if you used a negative value of m instead of a positive value? Use any value of m between 0 and -5 to test your prediction. (Keep $p = 0$ and try different values of n.)

c What can you say is always true for curves with equations of the form $y = m(x + n)^2$?

2 Functions of the form $y = m(x + n)^2 + p$

a Start with $m = 1$, $n = 2$ and $p = 0$. Now look at what happens to the curve as p increases from 0 to 4.

b What would you expect to happen for negative values of p? Try different negative values to see if you are correct.

c Now keep $n = 2$ and $p = 1$ and change m. What happens to the curve?

d Try this for other values of n and p.

Each quadratic curve has a line of symmetry.

e Try different values of m, n and p. What do you notice about the line of symmetry?

f Using a positive value of m, find a connection between n and p and the co-ordinates of the lowest point on the curve. Does this apply when m takes other positive values? What happens when m is negative?

3 Write a summary of your findings for curves of the form $y = m(x + n)^2 + p$.

Checkpoint

Check that $y = m(x + n)^2 + p$ is a quadratic function by expanding the bracket to rearrange into a more familiar form.

Discussion point

When n is zero, the general form $y = m(x + n)^2 + p$ reduces to $y = mx^2 + p$.

What do you know about the graphs of functions of this type?

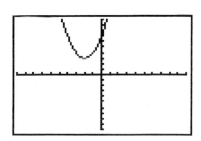

Discussion point

Can you determine the graphic calculator window settings for the above graph?

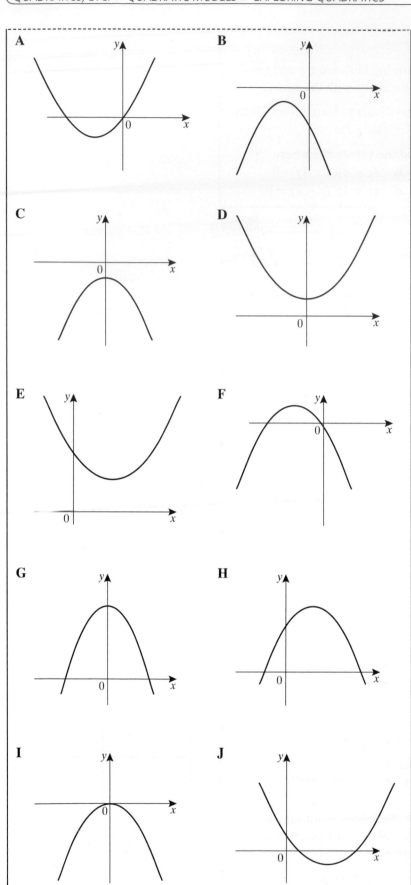

K

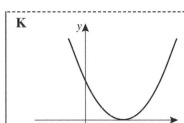

L

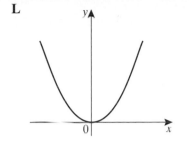

M

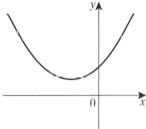

N

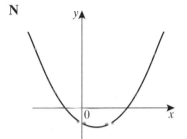

O

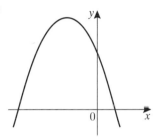

Activity 2.1D

On the page opposite and above there are sketch graphs of quadratic functions. Match each of the functions below to a graph. Write a few notes to justify your choices.

For example,

$y = -0.2x^2$ matches Graph I.

The graph of the function passes through the origin and is negative for all other values of x.

$y = (x + 2)(x - 5)$
$y = 3x^2$
$y = 4 - x^2$
$y = (x - 2)^2$
$y = 2x(x + 3)$
$y = -(x + 1)^2 + 3$
$y = (x - 1)^2 + 2$
$y = \frac{1}{2}x^2 + 4$
$y = (x + 4)^2 + 3$
$y = (x - 2)(x - 4)$
$y = -(x + 2)^2 - 1$
$y = -3 - 2x^2$

0–60 mph

The graph below shows the distance travelled, d metres, plotted against time, t seconds, for the car accelerating from 0 to 60 mph that you met in Chapter 1. The data for this is given in the table every 0.1 seconds for the interval $0 \leqslant t \leqslant 1$.

Time (seconds)	Distance (metres)
0.0	0.00
0.1	0.04
0.2	0.23
0.3	0.69
0.4	1.45
0.5	2.57
0.6	4.00
0.7	5.60
0.8	7.62
0.9	10.12
1.0	12.77

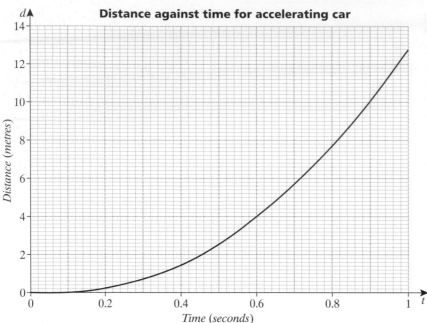

Distance against time for accelerating car

It is clear from the graph that for this car it is not appropriate to model how the distance changes with time using a linear model. It looks as though a quadratic function of the form $d = kt^2$ may give you a suitable model.

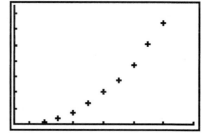

Activity 2.1E

1   **a** Use a graphic calculator to plot a graph of the data of d against t shown in the table.

   b Experiment with values of k to find a function $d = kt^2$ that is a good fit to the data.

   c Use your algebraic statement $d = kt^2$ to calculate estimates of the distance travelled by the car when $t = 0$, $t = 0.5$ and $t = 1$.

   d Find the percentage error in the distances predicted by your model at $t = 0$, $t = 0.5$, $t = 1$ and $t = 5$ (after 5 seconds the car has actually travelled 35 metres).

   e What do your percentage errors suggest about your mathematical model?

   f Use your mathematical model to find how far it predicts the car has travelled when it reaches 60 mph i.e. when $t = 10.75$

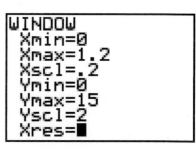

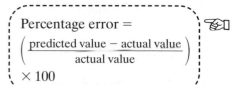

Percentage error =
$$\left(\frac{\text{predicted value} - \text{actual value}}{\text{actual value}} \right) \times 100$$

2 **a** Rearrange your model, $d = kt^2$, to give t as a function of d.

   b Use this model to predict how long the car takes to travel 100 metres.
   (Note that what you have just done is to solve the quadratic equation $100 = kt^2$.)

Seedlings 1

After it is planted, the height of a seedling is measured at 5-day intervals. The results are given in the table.

Day	Height (mm)
5	18
10	28
15	38
20	43
25	45

Activity 2.1F

1 Use a graphic calculator, spreadsheet or other graph plotting software on a computer to plot a graph of the data of height, h mm, against the day number, n.

2 On your graph plot the function $h = -0.04n^2 + 2.8n + 2.5$ to confirm that this can be used to model the data.

You will return to this model later in **Activity 2.1M**.

Discussion point

A quadratic curve can be shaped like this: ∨
or this: ∨
Which sections of such curves might provide a reasonable model for the growth of a plant?
Which sections are unlikely to provide a good model?

A-choo!

A cold spreads from one person to another in a group of people such as students in a college. There are no people with the cold at first, then the number of infected people increases as more catch the cold. Not everyone will catch the cold, and those who do will recover after a few days, so the number infected will decrease, tailing off to zero again.

This table shows the number of students in a college infected by a cold for the 22 days of an outbreak.

No. of days since outbreak	No. of cases
0	0
1	22
2	34
3	54
4	67
5	69
6	86
7	88
8	95
9	102
10	105
11	103
12	100
13	89
14	86
15	78
16	55
17	49
18	39
19	15
20	8
21	3
22	0

Activity 2.1G

1 Use your graphic calculator to plot a graph of this data.

2 Find a quadratic function to model this data as closely as possible.

Stopping distance

The *Highway Code* advises drivers to 'leave enough space between you and the vehicle in front so that you can pull up safely if it suddenly slows down or stops'.

The safe distance depends on the speed at which the car is travelling. Recommended distances are given in the chart. For each speed the chart shows that the total stopping distance consists of two parts:

* the thinking distance, i.e. the distance travelled in the time it takes the driver to respond to the emergency and apply the brakes
* the braking distance, i.e. the distance the car travels after the driver applies the brakes.

Discussion point

What factors do you think will affect how quickly a car can stop in an emergency?

Speed (mph)	Thinking distance (m)	Braking distance (m)	Stopping distance (m)
V	T	B	D
20	6	6	12
30	9	14	23
40	12	24	36
50	15	38	53
60	18	55	73
70	21	75	96

Typical stopping distances

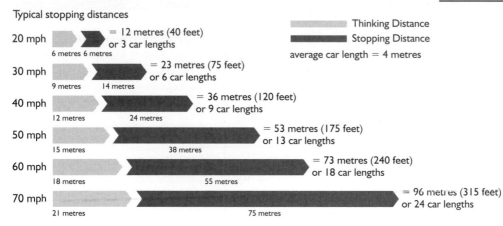

Activity 2.1H

1. Use the first two columns in the table to write down a relationship between the thinking distance, T metres, and the speed, V miles per hour.
   What type of relationship is this? What would you expect a graph of T against V to look like?

2. Plot on one set of axes graphs of
   * thinking distance (T m),
   * braking distance (B m) and
   * stopping distance (D m)
     against speed (V mph).

3. Compare your graph of T against V with the predictions you made in **question 1**.

4. Find a function of the form $B = kV^2$ to fit the braking distance data.

5. **a** Use 'stopping distance = thinking distance + braking distance' to write down an equation for D in terms of V.

Discussion points

Does the *Highway Code* allow the same 'thinking time' at each speed for the driver to react to the emergency and apply the brakes?

The *Highway Code* says 'allow at least a two-second gap between you and the vehicle in front on roads carrying fast traffic'.

How does this advice relate to the data given in the table?

b Use your answer to part **a** to estimate the total stopping distance travelled by a car from an initial speed of 45 mph. Check your answer using your graph.

Conversion factor
1 mph = 0.447 ms^{-1}

(UoM4)

6 In what way would you expect the equation for stopping distance to change if it was developed for use
- at night rather than during the day
- in wet conditions rather than dry
- with older drivers?

◎ Activity 2.1l

Researchers at a university have suggested a model that can be used to estimate stopping distances for night time driving. Estimated values taken from their website are given below:

Speed (mph)	Thinking distance (m)	Stopping distance (m)
30	14.3	27.9
40	19.1	43.1
50	23.9	61.8
60	28.7	83.4
70	33.4	107.8

a Find models relating thinking distance and stopping distance to speed.

b Compare these with those you found earlier from Highway Code data for driving in daylight.

Completing the square

Look at the quadratic models you have used so far and their graphs. The graphs of all quadratics have either a **minimum** point or a **maximum** point. Check that you agree with this. You may have to extend the range of values displayed so that the graph shows a maximum or minimum.

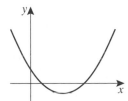

Quadratic with a minimum

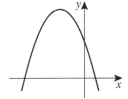

Quadratic with a maximum

How can you find the exact co-ordinates of maximum or minimum points?

For some quadratics this is easy. For example, $y = x^2$ has a minimum value of zero because something squared can never be negative. So this graph has a minimum point at $(0, 0)$.

What about $y = (x + 2)^2$?

Discussion point
Which quadratics have maximum points? Which quadratics have minimum points?

37

Activity 2.1J

The smallest possible value of $y = (x - 2)^2$ is again zero since $(x - 2)^2$ can never be negative.

1 What value of x will give this minimum value of y? In other words, what is the value of x when $x - 2 = 0$?
   Use a graphic calculator to plot the graph of $y = (x - 2)^2$ to check your answer.

2 Explain why the graph of $y = (x - 2)^2 + 4$ has a minimum point at $(2, 4)$. Use a graphic calculator to check that this is true.

3 Explain why the graph of $y = 5 - (x + 8)^2$ has a maximum point at $(-8, 5)$.

Having a quadratic in the form $y = (x - a)^2 + c$ is useful if you want to know the exact co-ordinates of the minimum point. The maximum or minimum is at the point (a, c).

The process of rearranging the equation of a quadratic function into the form $y = (x - a)^2 + c$ is called **completing the square**. It takes a bit of practice to do.

Activity 2.1K

Follow the process of 'completing the square' for $y = x^2 + 2x + 3$.

1 $x^2 + 2x = (x + 1)^2 - 1$
   Check that this is true by expanding the bracket.
   Note that in this case $a = -1$ so that you get the term in x as $2x$.

2 So adding 3 to each side:
   $y = x^2 + 2x + 3 = (x + 1)^2 - 1 + 3 = (x + 1)^2 + 2$
   Again check that this is true.

3 $y = x^2 + 2x + 3 = (x + 1)^2 + 2$ has a *minimum* point at $(-1, 2)$. Check that this is true using your graphic calculator.

Activity 2.1L

1 Use a graphic calculator to plot a graph of $y = x^2 + 5x + 6$.
   Use the **trace** function to find the coordinates of its minimum point.

2 Now complete the square for $y = x^2 + 5x + 6$.
   a $x^2 + 5x = (x + \frac{5}{2})^2 - \frac{25}{4}$
   Check that this is true by expanding the bracket.
   b So:
   $y = x^2 + 5x + 6 = (x + \frac{5}{2})^2 - \frac{25}{4} + 6 = (x + \frac{5}{2})^2 - \frac{1}{4}$
   Again check that this is true.

For the general quadratic $y = x^2 + bx + c$. The completed square form is given by:
$$y = \left(x + \frac{b}{2}\right)^2 - \left(\frac{b}{2}\right)^2 + c$$

3 Use this form to find the maximum or minimum point of $y = x^2 + 5x + 6$ and check that your answer agrees with what you found earlier from your graph.

4 Use this method to find the maximum or minimum points of

a $y = x^2 + 6x + 8$

b $y = x^2 - 4x - 10$.

c Use your graphic calculator to plot graphs to check your answers.

Seedlings 2

Earlier you plotted a graph of the data for the growth of a seedling together with the model $h = -0.04n^2 + 2.8n + 2.5$.

Activity 2.1M

1 Check that the model $h = -0.04n^2 + 2.8n + 2.5$ can be expressed in the 'completed square' form, $h = -0.04(n - 35)^2 + 51.5$, by expanding the bracket and simplifying.

2 Use this form to predict the maximum height of the plant and when it will occur. Does this prediction agree with what your graph suggests?

3 Give reasons why the quadratic function you have found will not provide a good model of the height of the seedling in the long run.

Day n	Height (mm) h
5	18
10	28
15	38
20	43
25	45

Sunrise–sunset

The table gives the sunrise and sunset times in London between 30 April and 8 August. The times are given in hours and minutes, Greenwich Mean Time.

Day n 0 = 30 April	Sunrise time t_r (GMT)	Sunset time t_s (GMT)
0	05:33	20:23
10	05:15	20:39
20	05:01	20:54
30	04:50	21:07
40	04:44	21:16
50	04:43	21:21
60	04:47	21:21
70	04:55	21:16
80	05:07	21:06
90	05:20	20:52
100	05:36	20:35

Discussion points

Which set of data will give a ∨-shaped curve and which will give an ∧-shaped curve?

What does this tell you about any quadratic functions that are used to model the data?

Activity 2.1N

1   Use a graphic calculator, spreadsheet or graph plotting software to plot a graph of sunrise time, t_r, against the day number, n.
    Before you plot your graph, convert each time to hours as a decimal value (e.g. 06 : 30 is 6.5 hours) rather than hours and minutes.

2   You can use the function $t_r = 0.0003n^2 - 0.03n + 5.4$ to model the data approximately. Draw a graph of the model and compare it with the graph of the data.

3   a   Use the model to calculate the time predicted by the model for sunrise on Midsummer's Day (21 June).
        The actual time of sunrise on Midsummer's Day in London is 04:43. Compare this with the value predicted by the model.

    b   What does the model predict will happen for large values of n? How does this compare with reality?

4   Confirm that the model can be written in the 'completed square' form $t_r = 0.0003[(n - 50)^2 + 15\,500]$.

Discussion points
If you drew graphs showing sunrise times and sunset times for the whole year, what shapes would you expect?
For what parts of these curves would you expect quadratic and linear functions to provide reasonable models of the data?

Discussion point
What maximum point is predicted by the model? Interpret this in terms of the real situation.

Activity 2.1P

1   Use your graphic calculator, spreadsheet or graph plotting software on a computer to plot a graph of sunset time, t_s, against the day number, n. Again use each time as a decimal number of hours, rather than in hours and minutes.

2   You can use the function $t_s = -0.000\,35n^2 + 0.035n + 20.3$ to model the data approximately. Draw a graph of the model and compare it with the graph of the data.

3   a   Use the model to calculate the time it predicts for sunset on Midsummer's Day.

    b   The actual time of sunset on Midsummer's Day in London is 21:22. Compare this with the value predicted by the model.

4   How accurately do you think your sunset model could predict sunset times on the following days?
    May Day, Valentine's Day, Christmas Day, your birthday. Give reasons for your answers.

5   Confirm that the model can be written in the 'completed square' form $t_s = -0.000\,35[(n - 50)^2 - 60\,500]$.

Discussion point
What minimum point is predicted by the model? Interpret this in terms of the real situation.

Solving quadratic equations

If you have a quadratic function as a model of real data you may want to find out where the function is zero (i.e. where the graph intersects the horizontal axis), or where it is another value, i.e. where $f(x) = a$.

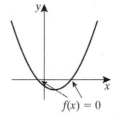

You could plot a graph of the function on a graphic calculator and use the trace function to find the solutions. Try this to find the solutions to $x^2 + 5x + 6 = 0$.

There are also three algebraic methods you can use to solve quadratic equations.

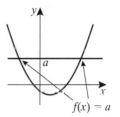

☞ 1 Factorising

Note that you can only use this method in very straightforward cases.
$x^2 + 5x + 6 = 0$ can be factorised to give $(x + 3)(x + 2) = 0$
which has the solutions $x = -3$ and $x = -2$.

2 The quadratic formula

You can use the formula $x = \dfrac{-b \pm \sqrt{b^2 - 4ac}}{2a}$ to give the two

solutions of the quadratic equation $ax^2 + bx + c = 0$.

In the case of $x^2 + 5x + 6 = 0$ the quadratic formula gives
$$x = \frac{-5 \pm \sqrt{5^2 - 4 \times 1 \times 6}}{2} = \frac{-5 \pm 1}{2} = -3 \text{ or } -2.$$

3 The 'completed square' method

To solve the equation $x^2 + 5x + 6 = 0$, write
$x^2 + 5x + 6$ as $(x + 2.5)^2 - 0.25$
so the equation becomes
$(x + 2.5)^2 - 0.25 = 0$
$\therefore (x + 2.5)^2 = 0.25$
$\therefore x + 2.5 = \pm\sqrt{0.25} = \pm 0.5$
$\therefore x = \pm 0.5 - 2.5$
So there are two answers,
$x = +0.5 - 2.5 = -2$
and $x = -0.5 - 2.5 = -3$

Checkpoint
You can always check your answers by plotting a graph on your graphic calculator and using the trace facility.

Activity 2.1Q

1 Solve the following quadratic equations using the factorising method. (In parts **f** to **j** you will need to factorise the equation first.)

a $(x + 4)(x - 1) = 0$ **b** $(2x - 3)(x + 1) = 0$

c $2(x - 3)(x + 1) = 0$ **d** $5x(10 - 2x) = 0$

e $3(2x - 1)(4 + x) = 0$ **f** $x^2 - 3x - 10 = 0$

g $x^2 - 4x - 21 = 0$ **h** $-x^2 + x + 12 = 0$

i $2x^2 + 7x - 4 = 0$ **j** $6x^2 + 27x - 15 = 0$

2 Solve the following equations using the quadratic formula.

a $x^2 + 12x + 3 = 0$ **b** $x^2 - 5x + 2 = 0$

c $x^2 - x - 2 = 0$ **d** $2x^2 - 0.5x - 3 = 0$

e $0.1x^2 + x + 0.01 = 0$ **f** $0.25x^2 + x - 0.5 = 0$

3 Solve the following quadratic equations using the 'completed square' form. (In parts **f** to **j** you will need to put the equation into the 'completed square form' first.)

a $(x - 2)^2 - 81 = 0$ **b** $(x + 4)^2 - 20 = 0$

c $2[(x - 1)^2 - 25] = 0$ **d** $4(x + 0.5)^2 - 64 = 0$

e $\frac{1}{2}(x - \frac{1}{2})^2 - \frac{1}{4} = 0$ **f** $x^2 + 4x - 5 = 0$

g $x^2 - 6x - 16 = 0$ **h** $x^2 - 6x - 91 = 0$

i $2x^2 + 2x - 24 = 0$ **j** $5x^2 + 10x - 105 = 0$

In the next two activities, you will use the methods you have practised above to solve quadratic equations to find solutions to real problems.

Activity 2.1R

1 You have used the function $h = -0.04(n - 35)^2 + 51.5$ to model the height, h mm, of a seedling after n days.

a Find n when $h = 0$, and interpret your answers.

b Find n when $h = 30$. What does this tell you.

2 You have used the function $t_r = 0.0003[(n - 50)^2 + 15\,500]$ to model t_r, the sunrise time, n days after April 30th. Use this model to calculate the dates on which the sun will rise at 05:00 (GMT).

3 You have used the function $t_s = -0.000\,35[(n - 50)^2 - 60\,500]$ to model t_s, the sunset time, n days after April 30th. Use this model to calculate the dates on which the sun will set at 21:00 (GMT).

Checkpoint

Check your answers by using a graph.

Activity 2.1S

A music shop sells all CDs at the same price. The music shop owner experiments with the price that she charges and finds that the income, £I, each week from CD sales can be modelled by the quadratic function
$I = 100x(21 - x)$ $0 \leq x \leq 21$, where £x is the price of one CD. The music shop owner wants the income from CDs to be at least £8000 a week, i.e. $100x(21 - x) \geq 8000$.

1 Show that $100x(21 - x) \geq 8000$ can be rearranged and simplified to give $21x - x^2 - 80 \geq 0$
This can be further rearranged to give $x^2 - 21x + 80 \leq 0$.
To find the values of x that will give the shop owner the income she wants, you have to solve the associated equation $x^2 - 21x + 80 = 0$.

2 **a** Show that $x^2 - 21x + 80 = 0$ can be rearranged into the 'completed square' form $(x - 10.5)^2 - 30.25 = 0$.

    b Solve $(x - 10.5)^2 - 30.25 = 0$ to show that the graph $y = x^2 - 21x + 80$ cuts the x-axis at $x = 5$ and $x = 16$.
This graph of $y = x^2 - 21x + 80$ is a $\cup$-shaped one, which is below the x-axis for values of x between $x = 5$ and $x = 16$.
This means that for the inequality $x^2 - 21x + 80 \leq 0$ to be true, $5 \leq x \leq 16$.
So, according to her model, the shop owner must price her CDs at between £5 and £16 to take at least £8000 in sales each week.

UoM4 **3** Try this process again, this time assuming the shop owner wants her income to be at least £9000 a week. Use a graph to check your answers. Experiment with different weekly takings.

UoM4 **4** What is the largest possible amount the shop owner can make each week from CD sales, according to this model?

Practice sheets:
Sketching quadratics
Solving quadratics

Nuffield Resource
UoM1 Skills activity 'Test Run'

2.2 Basic curves

Key web search terms

asymptotes
pendulum periods
Galileo

Graph shapes

Leaking container 1

Solving equations of
the form $ax^n = b$

Graph shapes

You have already met the graphs of some basic functions.
For example, the curve $y = x^2$ is shown below.

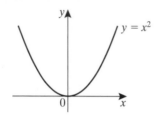

Discussion points
There are no points below the x axis
on this curve. Can you explain why?
Why is the y axis a line of
symmetry?
What happens to y as x takes very
large positive or negative values?

This graph shows both positive and negative values of x. In real
contexts x might take only positive values, e.g. if x is the length of
the sides of a square tile and y its area.

Can you think of examples of real contexts in which x may take:
• only positive values
• both positive and negative values?

Activity 2.2A

Set the axes on your graphic calculator to show values
of x from -6 to $+6$ and y from -4 to $+4$.
This will give you roughly the same scale on each axis and
graphs you draw will not be distorted by the use of very
different scales.

1 **a** Use your graphic calculator to draw $y = \sqrt{x}$.
     Draw a sketch of this on paper and label it.
   b Compare the shape of the curve $y = \sqrt{x}$ with the shape of
     $y = x^2$ for positive values of x.
     What is the relationship between $y = x^2$ and $y = \sqrt{x}$ for
     positive values of x?

2 **a** Use your graphic calculator to draw $y = x^3$.
     Draw a sketch of this on paper and label it.
   b Describe the similarities and differences between the
     curves $y = x^2$ and $y = x^3$. Can you explain these?

$y = \sqrt{x}$ can be written as
$y = x^{\frac{1}{2}}$.
This is because $x^{(\frac{1}{2} + \frac{1}{2})}$
$y = x^{\frac{1}{2}} \times x^{\frac{1}{2}} = x^{(\frac{1}{2} + \frac{1}{2})} = x^1$

Discussion point
Why do all points on the curve
$y = \sqrt{x}$ have only positive
co-ordinates?

3 a Copy and complete this table of values for $y = \dfrac{1}{x}$:

x	0.001	0.01	0.1	1	5
y					

b What would happen to the values of y if the values of x were changed from positive to negative?

c Sketch and label a graph of $y = \dfrac{1}{x}$.
Use a graphic calculator to check your sketch.

4 a If $y = \dfrac{1}{x^2}$ what happens to y when:

   i x is large and positive
   ii x is large and negative
   iii x is small and positive
   iv x is small and negative?

b Sketch and label a graph of $y = \dfrac{1}{x^2}$.
Use a graphic calculator to check your sketch.

c Describe the similarities and differences between the curves $y = \dfrac{1}{x}$ and $y = \dfrac{1}{x^2}$.
Explain why these similarities and differences occur.

5 a Use a graphic calculator to explore graphs of functions $y = x^n$ where $n = 1, 2, 3, 4, 5…$ etc.
Draw sketches of your graphs.
What conclusions can you draw about the symmetries of the different graphs?

b Extend your explorations to consider negative values of n, i.e. $n = -1, -2, -3, -4, -5…$ etc.

Write a brief summary of what you have discovered in this activity.

Discussion points

For the function $y = \dfrac{1}{x}$, the line $x = 0$ is an asymptote. This means that the graph of the function $y = \dfrac{1}{x}$ approaches $x = 0$ as x gets very small (either positive or negative) but never touches or crosses the line.
How could you convince someone of this?

The line $y = 0$ is also an asymptote of the function $y = \dfrac{1}{x}$.
Can you explain why?

Discussion point

Can you give the equations of the two asymptotes of the function $y = \dfrac{1}{x^2}$?

> **Nuffield resource**
> **UoM1 Starter 'Interactive Graphs'**

Activity 2.2B

In this activity **do not** use a graphic calculator.
In the margin are graphs of the following functions:

1 $y = x^2$ **2** $y = \sqrt{x}$

3 $y = x^3$ **4** $y = \dfrac{1}{x}$

5 $y = \dfrac{1}{x^2}$

Identify clearly which is which.

A

B

C

D

E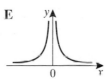

Leaking container 1

Water is leaking through a hole in a container. Measurements are taken of the depth of the water above the hole and the rate at which water leaks from the hole at intervals of 20 seconds. The data collected is given in the table where t seconds is the time, d centimetres is the depth of water above the hole and R millilitres per second is the rate at which water is leaking.

Graphs of d against t and R against d are shown below.

t	d	R
0	21.90	12.2
20	18.70	11.5
40	15.70	10.7
60	12.90	9.2
80	10.40	8.8
100	8.15	8.0
120	6.15	6.5
140	4.50	5.7
160	3.05	4.2
180	1.95	3.4
200	1.05	2.3
220	0.60	0.8
240	0.45	0.3
260	0.38	0.0

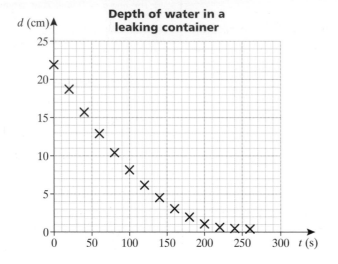

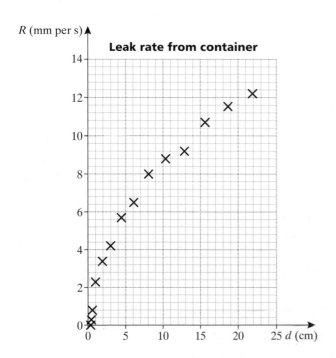

Discussion points

Look at the shape of each graph. In each case which of the following functions has a graph that is similar in shape (either in whole or part) to the shape given by the data?

$y = mx + c$, $y = x^2$, $y = x^3$,

$y = \sqrt{x}$, $y = \dfrac{1}{x}$, $y = \dfrac{1}{x^2}$,

$y = ax^2 + bx + c$.

Activity 2.2C

1 You can use the function $d = (0.017t - 4.6)^2$ can be used to model the depth of water against time.

   a Calculate the values of d given by this function when
      i $t = 0$ ii $t = 100$ iii $t = 200$
      and compare your answers with the values of d given in the table.

   b The function $d = (0.017t - 4.6)^2$ has a minimum value. Write down this minimum value and calculate the value of t when this occurs.

   c i Use your graphic calculator to draw a graph of $d = (0.017t - 4.6)^2$ and make a sketch of this on paper. (**Note:** You will need to enter the function as $y = (0.017x - 4.6)^2$ when using your graphic calculator.)
      Label your sketch graph and give the co-ordinates of the minimum point and the point where the curve crosses the vertical axis.
      ii Explain briefly why the function $d = (0.017t - 4.6)^2$ is not a good model of the real situation for values of t greater than the value of t at the minimum point.

2 The leak rate against depth of water can be modelled by the function $R = 2.7\sqrt{d}$.

   a Find the value of R given by this model when
      i $d = 15.7$ ii $d = 4.5$
      and compare your answers with the values of R given in the table.

   b i Use the model $R = 2.7\sqrt{d}$ to predict the leak rate when the depth of water above the hole is 20 centimetres.
      ii Does your answer to part b i seem reasonable in view of the data given in the table and graph?

   c The depth that would give a leak rate of 10 millilitres per second can be predicted by solving the equation $2.7\sqrt{d} = 10$.
      i Show that this equation can be written as $\sqrt{d} = 3.703$ and hence find the value of d.
      ii Does this prediction seem reasonable when compared with the data given in the table and graph?

   d Use a graphic calculator to draw a graph of $R = 2.7\sqrt{d}$ and compare the graph of the model with the graph of the data.

UoM4
3 Explain carefully how the shapes of the two graphs (i.e. for rate of leakage of water and depth of water) are interrelated. Use your explanation to interpret how the depth of water and rate at which water leaks vary with time.

Discussion point
What type of function is $d = (0.017t - 4.6)^2$?

Discussion point
Look carefully at the value of R given in the last row of the table. What does this suggest happens when $t = 260$ and $d = 0.38$? Compare this to what the model predicts will happen.

Discussion point
The graph of the model $R = 2.7\sqrt{d}$ passes through the origin. How does this compare with the graph of the real data?

Solving equations of the form $ax^n = b$

In **Activity 2.2C** you solved the equation $2.7\sqrt{d} = 10$ to find the depth that would give a leak rate of 10 millilitres per second.

This equation can also be written as $2.7d^{\frac{1}{2}} = 10$.

This is now in the form $ax^n = b$, where a, b and n are constants and x (d in the example) is an unknown value to be found.

The solution of the equation $2.7d^{\frac{1}{2}} = 10$ is given below:

$$2.7d^{\frac{1}{2}} = 10$$

$$d^{\frac{1}{2}} = \frac{10}{2.7} = 3.\dot{7}0\dot{3}$$

Squaring this gives:

$$d = (3.\dot{7}0\dot{3})^2 \simeq 13.7$$

Roots can be written as powers:

$\sqrt{x} = x^{\frac{1}{2}}$ or $x^{0.5}$,

$\sqrt[3]{x} = x^{\frac{1}{3}}$, $\sqrt[4]{x} = x^{\frac{1}{4}}$ or $x^{0.25}$

$\sqrt{x^3} = x^{\frac{3}{2}}$, $\sqrt[3]{x^2} = x^{\frac{2}{3}}$

$\dfrac{1}{\sqrt{x}} = x^{-\frac{1}{2}}$ and so on.

In general $x^{\frac{m}{n}} = \sqrt[n]{x^m}$

and $x^{-\frac{m}{n}} = \dfrac{1}{\sqrt[n]{x^m}}$.

Equations of the form $ax^n = b$ are solved in the same way using the steps given below:

$$ax^n = b$$

$$x^n = \frac{b}{a}$$

$$x = \left(\frac{b}{a}\right)^{\frac{1}{n}}$$

Squaring is the **inverse** (opposite) of taking the square root.

Activity 2.2D

1   The time taken for the pendulum in a clock to swing from one side to the other, t seconds, is related to its length, l millimetres, by $t = 0.03172\sqrt{l}$.
Calculate to the nearest millimetre the length of the pendulum that will swing from one side to the other in one second.

2   A manager models the output of his factory using the function $N = 400x^{\frac{2}{3}}$ where N is the number of items produced per day when x workers are employed.

   a How many workers does the model predict will be needed to achieve an output of 1000 items per day?

   b Use a graphic calculator to draw a graph of N against x and use the trace function to check your answer to part **a**.

   c How well do you think this model would reflect the real situation? (Consider what happens when $x = 0$ and what happens as x increases to large values in terms of the number of workers and the output of the factory)

Discussion point
Compare the shape of this graph with those of other powers of x.

3   On 7 September 1991 the town of Edmonton in Canada
    suffered a hailstorm in which inhabitants claimed to have
    seen hailstones the size of golf and tennis balls. Some people
    kept hailstones in their freezers as evidence in their insurance
    claims for damage done to their houses during the storm.
    Meteorologists model hailstones as spheres with volumes
    given by $V = \frac{4}{3}\pi r^3$ where r is the radius.

    a   Use this model to find the radius of a hailstone whose
        volume is
        i 1 cm³   **ii** 5 cm³   **iii** 10 cm³.

    b   Draw a graph of V against r on your graphic calculator and
        use the trace function to check your answers to **a**.

4   A supermarket models the demand for plums with the
    function $D = 500p^{-2}$ where D is the number of tonnes that
    they could sell at a price of £p per kilogram.

    a   Use the model to find out how much the supermarket
        should charge per kilogram if they wish to sell 100 tonnes
        of plums.

    b   Draw a graph of D against p on a graphic calculator and
        use the trace function to check your answer to part **a**.

    c   Does the shape of the graph suggest that this may be a
        reasonable model of the real situation? Explain your
        answer.

5   In tall building spaces, smoke from a fire at floor level
    can form a stagnant layer before it reaches the ceiling. For
    a particular fire the height of the smoke layer can be
    modelled by $h = 30T^{-0.6}$ where h is the height in metres
    of the smoke layer above the fire and T is the temperature
    difference between the bottom and top of the building
    space.

    a   Use the model to find:
        i the value of h when $T = 10$
        ii the value of T when $h = 10$.

    b   Use your graphic calculator to draw a graph of h against
        T and check your answers to part **a**.

    c   Do you think this model would be suitable for:
        i very small values of T
        ii very large values of T?

    Explain your answers.

Some of the hailstones that fell
on Edmonton, Canada on
7 September 1991

Discussion point
Which of the graphs that you met at
the start of this section is similar in
shape to this one?

Discussion point
Compare the shape of this graph
with those of other basic curves.

Practice sheets:
Solving $ax^n = b$

2.3 Gradients

In **Chapter 1** you studied gradients of straight lines and the way in which they can give information about real situations. You will now begin to investigate the gradients of curves and how these also give rates of change.

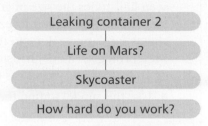

Leaking container 2

Life on Mars?

Skycoaster

How hard do you work?

Leaking container 2

Water is leaking through a hole in a container. The graph below shows how the volume of water in the container decreases with time. At any particular time the **rate** at which the water is leaking from the container can be found by finding the gradient of the curve. The gradient of a curve can be estimated by drawing a **tangent** to the curve at the point under consideration.

Note: This is the same leaking container as in **Section 2.2**.

A tangent to a curve just touches the curve at a single point. It does not cut the curve.

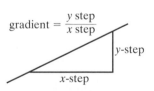

If the tangent is rotated in any direction about the point where it touches the curve it will cut the curve and is no longer a tangent.

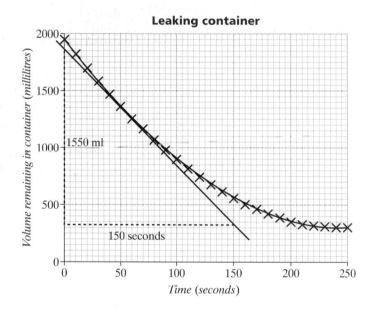

Leaking container

For example, to find the rate at which water is leaking from the container after 50 seconds, a tangent has been drawn at the point on the curve where $t = 50$. The gradient of the curve at $t = 50$ is equal to the gradient of this tangent.

Gradient at $t = 50 = -\dfrac{1550}{150} = -10.\dot{3} \approx -10$.

In this case, the negative sign indicates that the volume is decreasing.

This gives an estimate of 10 millilitres per second for the rate at which water is leaking from the container after 50 seconds.

Reminder

$$\text{gradient} = \frac{y \text{ step}}{x \text{ step}}$$

y-step

x-step

When the tangent goes down from left to right, the gradient is negative. The gradient is the rate of change of y with respect to x.

It is difficult to draw a tangent accurately. Always round the value you calculate for the gradient sensibly.

Activity 2.3A

Resource
Sheet
2.3A

1   Copy and complete this table by drawing tangents to the
    curve at intervals of 50 seconds and calculate their gradients.
    Notice that the leak rate has been given here as positive as
    though the rate of increase of volume that you find is positive.

Time (t s)	0	50	100	150	200	250
Leak rate (m/ s^{-1})						

2   Compare the values in your table with the data given for the
    leaking container in **Section 2.2**.

Discussion point
What happens to the leak rate as
time passes? How is this shown by
the shape of the graph of volume
against time?

Life on Mars?

As part of the Pathfinder mission NASA collected measurements to
investigate the atmosphere, meteorology and surface geology of
Mars.

The graph shows how temperature on Mars varied over a period of
50 hours.

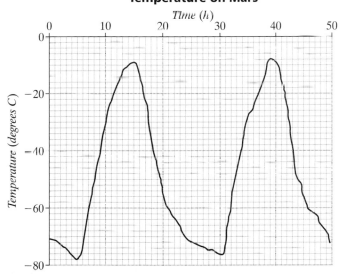

Temperature on Mars

Discussion point
In what ways do you think that a
graph of temperature against time
for a place on Earth would be
similar to this graph?
In what ways do you think it would
be different?

Activity 2.3B

Resource
Sheet
2.3B

1   Find the rate at which the temperature is rising after
    a   7 hours   b   12 hours.

2   Find the rate at which the temperature is falling after
    a   18 hours   b   22 hours   c   26 hours.

3   At what times is the gradient of the graph zero?

Discussion point
In what way is the gradient different
when the temperature is falling to
when it is rising?

The points where the graph has a gradient of zero are called maximum and minimum points. These occur when the temperature reaches its highest and lowest values during each Martian day.

There are two minimum points: (5, −78) and (30, −77)

After 5 hours the temperature falls to a minimum of −78°C before rising again and after 30 hours it falls to a minimum of −77°C before rising again.

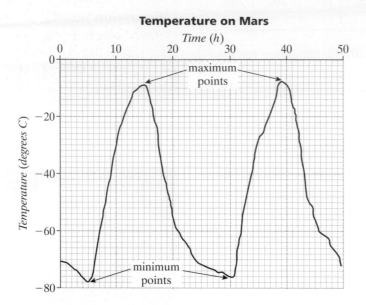

Temperature on Mars

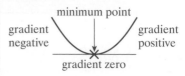

A Martian day is called a **sol**.

Note (30, −77) is a minimum point even though the temperature falls to the lower value of −78°C later.

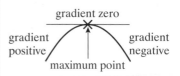

A **minimum point** is any point where the gradient becomes zero when changing from negative to positive.

A **maximum point** is any point where the gradient becomes zero when changing from positive to negative.

Maximum and minimum points are sometimes referred to as *local* maximum and minimum points.

Activity 2.3C

1 Write down the co-ordinates of the maximum points on this graph.

2 **a** What is the time difference between the minimum points?

 b What is the time difference between the maximum points?

 c How long is a Martian day?

Discussion point

If the graph were drawn for a longer period it might be possible to see other points where the temperature falls and then rises (or vice versa). This means that there may be other maximum and minimum points.

Skycoaster

A Skycoaster is a theme park ride that combines the thrills of bungee jumping and hang-gliding. You can fly with one or two friends or solo. After pulling a ripcord you free-fall for about a second before the steel cables holding you tighten. Then you swing backwards and forwards over the theme park at speeds of up to 60 mph.

The graph below shows a model of how the height of a flyer above the ground, h metres, varies with time, t seconds, during the first part of a flight.

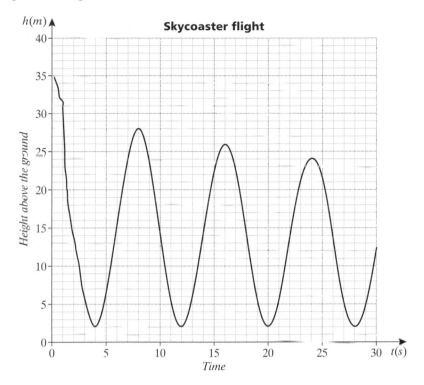

SKYCOASTER

Resource Sheet 2.3D

Activity 2.3D

1 What is the height of the flyer above the ground when the flight begins?

2 **a** Write down the co-ordinates of the first minimum point.

  b What information do these co-ordinates give?

3 **a** Write down the values of h at the maximum points where
    i $t = 8$ **ii** $t = 16$ **iii** $t = 24$.

  b Explain what these values tell you about the real situation.

4 **a** Find the gradient of the graph when
    i $t = 2$ **ii** $t = 5$ **iii** $t = 9$.

  b Explain what these gradients tell you about the real situation.

5 Use the graph between $t = 20$ and $t = 28$ to describe in general terms what is happening in the real situation between these times.

Discussion point

In which section of the curve does the gradient give the velocity of the flyer? Why is the gradient not equal to the velocity in other sections of the curve?

How hard do you work?

A production manager has carried out a survey to find out how the productivity of his workers varies during eight hours of shift work.

The results suggest that a worker's productivity rate can be modelled by the function

$$n = 0.06t^4 - t^3 + 4t^2 - t + 49$$

where n represents the number of items produced per hour and t represents the time in hours since the beginning of the shift.

> Functions like this one that consist of a sum of integer power terms (with or without a constant term) are called **polynomial** functions.

Activity 2.3E

1   Use your graphic calculator to draw a graph of
    $n = 0.06t^4 - t^3 + 4t^2 - t + 49$ for $0 \leqslant t \leqslant 8$.

2   What is the productivity rate of the worker at the beginning of the shift?

3   **a** Find the time for which the worker has been working when the productivity rate reaches its maximum value. Give your answer in hours and minutes.

    b What is the productivity rate at this time?

4   Describe the way in which the worker's productivity rate changes over the course of the eight hours.

5   **a** Alter the display on your graphic calculator so that you can see the graph of $n = 0.06t^4 - t^3 + 4t^2 - t + 49$ for $0 \leqslant t \leqslant 12$.

    b How well do you think this function would model the production rate of a worker during the last four hours of a twelve hour shift?

> When using your graphic calculator you need to use x and y rather than t and n.
>
> Use the **trace** function on your graphic calculator for **questions 2** and **3**.

Discussion point
The model does not take any account of lunch or tea breaks. How do you think the graph would change if such breaks were included?

Nuffield resource
UoM1 Skills activity
'Tin Can'

2.4 Simultaneous equations

Graphs of simultaneous equations

'**Simultaneous**' means 'at the same time' so the solution of a **pair of simultaneous equations** fits both equations at once. For example, if you know that a girl is twice as old as her sister and that their ages add up to 12, you can probably quite quickly work out that the girl must be eight and her sister four. You have solved a pair of simultaneous equations, finding a pair of numbers (8, 4) that add up to 12 and in which the first number is twice the second.

Each of the two conditions, one age twice as great as the other, and the total being 12, can be satisfied by many different pairs of numbers, but there is only one pair that fits both the conditions at once.

This is a very simple example that can be solved using common sense; not all situations are as simple as this so you may have to use algebraic and graphical methods to work out the solutions.

Activity 2.4A

1   Write two equations about the ages of the girl and her sister, using *g* years as the age of the girl and *s* years as the age of her sister.

2   Use any method you know to solve the equations algebraically.

3   Draw, on one diagram, graphs of the two equations and find the simultaneous solution, the point that is on both graphs. (You may use your graphic calculator to do this if you wish)

Supply and demand

As you saw in **Section 2** of Chapter 1, a supplier determines the quantity of goods available for sale; he or she wants to make a profit, and is likely to supply more goods if the selling price gets higher. The buyer determines the quantity of goods sold; he or she is likely to buy more goods if the price gets lower. The interaction between these two situations determines the price and quantity of goods sold.

A small company sells computer games. The production manager says that the connection between selling price and the number of games that can be produced each week is as shown in the table.

Graphs of simultaneous equations

Supply and demand

Solving simultaneous equations

Non-linear simultaneous equations

Discussion point
How many different solutions are there to each of the two conditions? Does it make a difference if you are considering numbers instead of ages?

Discussion point
This is a very simple description of the way a market operates. What other factors are likely to affect the situation?

Selling price of games	Number that can be produced per week (supply)
£15	500
£20	700
£25	900
£30	1100

Market research provides the following information.

Selling price of games	Number that will be sold per week (demand)
£15	1050
£20	900
£25	750
£30	600

Activity 2.4B

1 Draw a graph to show this data. Use axes to show selling price and number of games supplied/demanded. Plot the two sets of data as points using these axes. Comment on what is shown by the graph.

2 Join each set of points with a straight line and find the equilibrium position, i.e. find the values of the selling price and the number of games sold when the supply and the demand are equal.

3 How much money does the games company make per week from the sales of computer games when the supply and the demand are equal?

Note: Use the horizontal axis for selling price.

Discussion point
How could you have found the equilibrium point by using the two tables rather than drawing a graph?

Drawing graphs of the data is an easy and powerful way of determining a pair of values that satisfy the relationship between price and supply and that between price and demand.

The answer can also be found algebraically.

Activity 2.4C

1 Show that the equation connecting price and supply is $N = 40P - 100$, where N is the number of games produced each week when the price is £P.

2 Show that the equation connecting demand and price is $N = 1500 - 30P$, where N is the number of games sold each week when the price is £P.

At the equilibrium position, the same values of N and P fit both of the equations, so to find these values you need to solve the equations simultaneously.

There several different ways of doing this; you may be familiar with one or more of them already.

Solving simultaneous equations

Solving simultaneous equations by elimination

In this method, the two linear simultaneous equations are manipulated so that one of the variables can be eliminated, leaving one equation from which the other variable can be obtained. The eliminated variable can then be determined by substitution.

Here are the two equations from **Activity 2.4C**.

$$N = 40P - 100 \text{ and}$$
$$N = 1500 - 30P$$

It is usual to rearrange the equations so that the variables are on the left-hand side of the equals sign, so this gives

$$N - 40P = -100 \text{ and}$$
$$N + 30P = 1500$$

Now make the coefficient of one of the variables the same in both equations, if necessary, by multiplying. In this case, there is just one N in both equations, so we can eliminate N by subtracting one equation from the other. This can be done either way round, either subtracting the second equation from the first or subtracting the first equation from the second. In this case subtracting the first equation from the second gives

$$30P - (-40P) = 1500 - (-100),$$
so
$$70P = 1600$$
so
$$P = \frac{1600}{70} \approx 22.9$$

Your equations contain multiples of the variables (in this case N and P). The multiplying value is known as the **coefficient**.

You can find N by putting this value of P back into one of the original equations. Using the second one gives

$$N + 30 \times \frac{1600}{70} = 1500$$
so
$$N \approx 1500 - 686 = 814$$

(Note: use the more accurate value of P here, i.e. $\frac{1600}{70}$

Compare these values with the ones you found earlier using your graph.

Checkpoint
Substitute the values you have found back into the original equations to check that they work – and are therefore correct.

Solving simultaneous equations by substitution

You can also solve simultaneous equations algebraically by the method of substitution. This has the advantage that it can be applied to a range of simultaneous equations, rather than just linear ones.

Here are the two equations about the ages of a girl and her sister that you found in **Activity 2.4A**.

$$g = 2s$$
$$s + g = 12$$

Discussion point
Which of these methods for solving simultaneous equations (graphical, elimination, substitution) do you prefer? What are the advantages and disadvantages of each?

The first equation gives g in terms of s, $g = 2s$, so we can substitute this for g in the second equation. This gives

$$s + 2s = 12$$

so

$$3s = 12$$

$$s = 4 \text{ and so } g = 8$$

The supply and demand equations in their original form,

$$N = 40P - 100 \text{ and}$$

$$N = 1500 - 30P$$

Both give N in terms of P, so you can simply equate the two right-hand sides to give a single equation in P.

$$40P - 100 = 1500 - 30P$$

Discussion points

When you have a single unknown variable, you can solve a single linear equation to find its value. Can you explain why? When you have two unknown variables you need two equations connecting them if you wish to find their values. Can you see why?

Activity 2.4D

1 Solve $40P - 100 = 1500 - 30P$ to find P and substitute this value into one of the original equations to find N.

2 It would not be very sensible in this case, but it is possible to find P in terms of N from either of the two equations and substitute this into the other. Show that the first equation, $N = 40P - 100$, can be rearranged to give $P = \dfrac{N}{40} + \dfrac{10}{4}$ then substitute this into the second equation to find N.

Non-linear simultaneous equations

The supply and demand models used above, where the supply and demand functions are both represented by straight lines, is a very simplified version of reality. A more realistic model for demand could use a quadratic function to represent the demand at different selling prices.

For example, the selling price and the demand for computer games could be as shown in this table

Selling price of games	Number that will be sold per week (demand)
£15	1025
£20	900
£25	825
£30	800

The demand is no longer a linear function of the selling price, but instead the figures fit the quadratic model

$$N = P^2 - 60P + 1700.$$

The supply model remains the same, $N = 40P - 100$.

Discussion point

How does this model differ from the linear one? Is it more realistic?

So, to find the equilibrium position, we need to find the values of P and N that satisfy simultaneously the linear equation

$N = 40P - 100$

and the quadratic equation

$N = P^2 - 60P + 1700.$

As these are both equations giving N in terms of P we can equate the right-hand sides of the two equations, giving

$40P - 100 = P^2 - 60P + 1700.$

Activity 2.4E

1 Show that $40P - 100 = P^2 - 60P + 1700$ can be simplified to give $P^2 - 100P + 1800 = 0$.

2 Show that the values of P that satisfy this equation are $P = 23.54$ and $P = 76.46$ and find the corresponding values of N.

3 Sketch a graph of the two equations and check that these solutions are consistent with the graph. Explain why there are two pairs of solutions whilst there was only one pair when you used two linear models.

Practice sheets:
Solving simultaneous equations

2.5 Linear inequalities

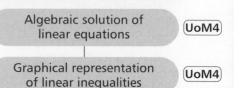

Algebraic solution of linear inequalities

In **Section 2.4** you used the equation $N = 40P - 100$ to model the number, N, of computer games supplied with the price, £P.

You can use this to find, for example, the price at which the company will supply 1000 games a week by solving the equation

$$1000 = 40P - 100.$$

This gives:

$$1100 = 40P$$

$$\therefore \quad P = \frac{1100}{40} = 27.5.$$

So the company will supply 1000 games a week if the price is £27.50.

Suppose you want the supply to be *at least* 1000 games a week? This means you need to solve the linear inequality $N \geqslant 1000$, i.e. $40P - 100 \geqslant 1000$.

In many ways, this is very similar to solving the equation above:

$$40P - 100 \geqslant 1000$$

$$\therefore \quad 40P \geqslant 1100$$

$$\therefore \quad P \geqslant \frac{1100}{40}$$

$$\therefore \quad P \geqslant 27.5$$

So, if the company is to supply at least 1000 games a week, it requires a price that is greater than or equal to £27.50.

The equation

$$N = 1500 - 30P$$

connects the price, £P, with the number, N, of games sold each week.

If the sales are to be 1000 games per week, the price can be found by solving the equation

$$1000 = 1500 - 30P.$$

This gives:

$$30P + 1000 = 1500$$

$$\therefore \quad 30P = 500$$

$$\therefore \quad P = \frac{500}{30}$$

$$\therefore \quad P \approx 16.6$$

So if the sales are 1000 per week the price should be £16.67.
If the sales are to be *at least* 1000 games a week, you have to solve the inequality $N \geqslant 1000$

$$\Rightarrow 1500 - 30P \geqslant 1000.$$

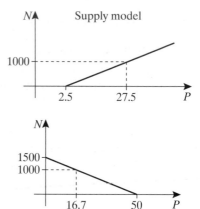

Discussion point

The graphic calculator screen-shot below shows graphs of both models together. Can you determine the window settings used?

This gives:

$$1500 \geqslant 1000 + 30P$$
$$\therefore \quad 500 \geqslant 30P$$
$$\therefore \quad \frac{500}{30} \geqslant P$$
$$\therefore \quad 16.67 \geqslant P$$

Reading this inequality from right to left, $P \leqslant 16.7$.

For sales of at least 1000 games per week, the price should be less than or equal to £16.67.

The solutions of the two inequalities show that the two conditions are incompatible; the price cannot be less than or equal to £16.67 *and* greater than or equal to £27.50.

Activity 2.5A

1   Is it possible to find a price at which at least 500 games a week are supplied and sold? Work through the solution of the linear inequalities above, but putting $N \geqslant 500$, to see if compatible results to the two inequalities can be obtained. Interpret what you find. You may find plotting graphs of the two linear functions on the same diagram useful.

2   In **Chapter 1**, you used the mobile phone charges shown in the table. Show that the call times for which the Just Chat tariff costs less than the Talk Time tariff fit the inequality

$$12 + 0.08t < 16 + 0.06t.$$

Solve this inequality. Plotting graphs of the two linear functions on the same diagram may be useful.

Tariff name	Line rental (£/month)	Call time (pence/min)
Just Chat	12	8
Talk Time	16	6

Graphical representation of linear inequalities

The graph of any straight line $y = mx + c$ forms the boundary between two regions.

On one side of the line,

  y is **less than** $mx + c$ ($y < mx + c$)

and on the other side of the line

  y is **greater than** $mx + c$ ($y > mx + c$).

On the line itself, of course, y is **equal to** $mx + c$ ($y = mx + c$).

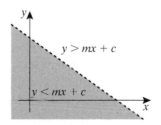

If the line $y = mx + c$ is shown dashed, it indicates that the line is not included with the region. A solid line indicates that the boundary is included.

For example, to illustrate the region $y + 2x \leqslant 5$ first draw the graph of $y + 2x = 5$, drawing it with a solid line. (The boundary is included in the region in this case because the inequality is 'less than or equal to'.)

Then shade the region where the inequality is not satisfied leaving the region that does satisfy clear. If it is not obvious to you which region satisfies the inequality, choose a point in one of the regions and calculate the value of $y + 2x$ to see if it is greater than or less than 5 to find which side of the line is which. For example, choose the point $(2, 3)$. At this point, $y + 2x$ is equal to 7, which is more than 5, so the correct region is on the other side of the line.

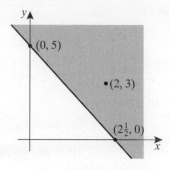

Activity 2.5B

1 Draw a diagram to show the region $y > 3x$.

2 Write down the algebraic description of the region between the two lines $x = 5$ and $x = 10$, including $x = 5$ but not $x = 10$.

3 The graph below shows two different rules for converting between Celsius and Fahrenheit temperatures for a range of cooking temperatures.

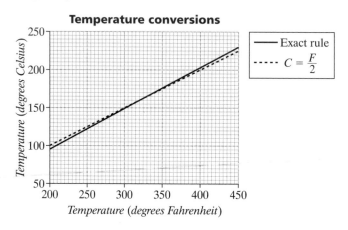

Note: the exact rule for converting from a temperature in Fahrenheit to Celsius is $C = \frac{5}{9}(F - 32)$

a Shade the region on the diagram where the 'halving' rule gives a lower Fahrenheit temperature than the exact rule.

b Write down the algebraic description of that region.

c Solve the algebraic inequality to find the Fahrenheit temperatures for which the halving rule gives a lower Celsius temperature than the exact rule.

4 The distance–time sketch graph shows the distance, d miles, travelled by two drivers on a motorway in time t hours, one travelling at 70 mph and one travelling at 60 mph.

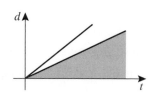

a Copy the sketch and label each line with its equation.

b Write down the inequality that describes the shaded region.

c Make another sketch of the graph. On this shade the region in which a straight line could be drawn for a driver travelling between 60 mph and 70 mph.

d Write down the two inequalities that must be satisfied by lines in this region.

5   A lorry driver starts a journey with a full 500-litre fuel tank and uses one litre of diesel every two miles.

   a Write a linear function expressing the number of litres of diesel in the tank, L, in terms of m, the number of miles driven.

   b Sketch a graph of your function, plotting L on the vertical axis and m on the horizontal axis.

   c The driver wants the amount of diesel in the tank to be no less than 50 litres. Express this as an algebraic inequality.

   d Solve your inequality to show that the driver should travel no more than 900 miles without refuelling.

2.6 Revision summary

Quadratic functions

Quadratic functions can be written as
$y = ax^2 + bx + c$ where a, b and c are constants.
You can generate every possible quadratic
function by changing the values of a, b and c.
Quadratic functions can also be written in other
forms. Completing the square gives the form
$y = m(x + n)^2 + p$.
If m is **positive**, this function has a **minimum**
value of p, when $x = -n$.
If m is **negative**, this function has a **maximum**
value of p, when $x = -n$.

Quadratic equations

Quadratic equations can be solved by:
- using a graph
- completing the square
- factorising
- using the formula $x = \dfrac{-b \pm \sqrt{b^2 - 4ac}}{2a}$

Quadratic models can be used to model all or
part of a set of data.

Quadratic graphs

Quadratic graphs have either a single
minimum point or a single **maximum**
point.

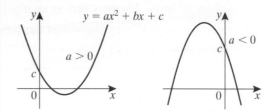

Graphs can be used to solve equations
by finding the x co-ordinates of the points
of intersection with the x axis or other
lines.

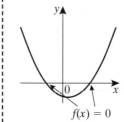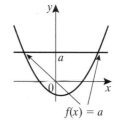

Models of the form $y = kx^n$

$n = 1$ gives straight lines.
$n = 2$ gives quadratic curves.
$n = 3$ produces cubic graphs like this:

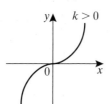

$n = \frac{1}{2}$ gives a curve that
exists only for positive
values of x.

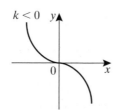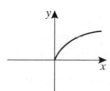

If n is a negative integer the graphs of the
functions are discontinuous.

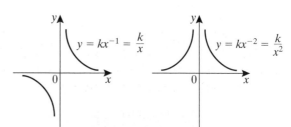

$k > 0$
The x and y axes are asymptotes

Gradients

You can find the gradient of a curve (which is fitted to data or is of a function) at a point by drawing a tangent to the curve at the point.

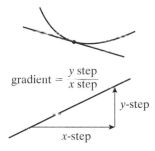

$$\text{gradient} = \frac{y \text{ step}}{x \text{ step}}$$

When the tangent goes down from left to right, the gradient is negative.

The gradient is the rate of change of y with respect to x.

The gradient – rate of change – often tells you a significant measure, e.g. on a distance–time graph it tells you speed.

A local **minimum point** is any point where the gradient becomes zero when changing from negative to positive.

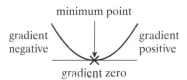

A local **maximum point** is any point where the gradient becomes zero when changing from positive to negative.

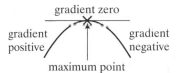

Simultaneous equations

Simultaneous equations have solutions where their graphs intersect.

When you have a pack of linear simultaneous equations you can find their solution algebraically by eliminating one of the variables.

One method of doing this to equate the two equations

i.e. $y_1 = y_2$

so $m_1 x + c_1 = m_2 x + c_2$.

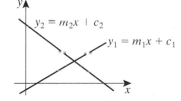

This equation in one variable allows you to find x. You can then find y by substituting this value of x into one of the original equations.

Linear inequalities

The graph of any straight line forms the boundary between two regions. On one side of the line $y < mx + c$, on the other side $y > mx + c$.

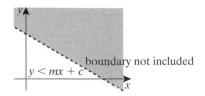

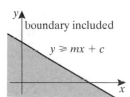

Linear inequalities can be solved algebraically in the same manner as solving linear equations – a graph may help you make sense of your solution.

2.7 Preparing for assessment

Your coursework portfolio

After studying this chapter, you could start to develop your coursework portfolio using the suggestions below.

Find data that can be modelled by a quadratic function. Some ideas are given in the chapter. Sometimes you can use a quadratic function to model part of a data set although it may not be suitable for the whole data set.

Find the parameters of the quadratic function (e.g. if using $y = kt^2$, find k).
Show clearly how you find the parameter(s).

Consider how effective the quadratic function is as a model for the data. Questions you could ask:
- What happens to the model in the long term?
- What happens when the value of y is equal to zero?
- What happens at the turning point (maximum or minimum)?

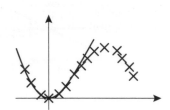

Tide or sunrise/sunset data with function $y = kt^2$ used to model subset near origin

If possible, use the quadratic function $f(x) = ax^2 + bx + c$ to solve an equation, e.g. $ax^2 + bx + c = 0$ or $ax^2 + bx + c = d$. Don't forget to check your solutions by substituting them back into the original equation.

Solve the equation in different ways and comment on the methods. You could consider how useful/accurate a graphical solution to the same equation is.

Make sure that you explain key features of your model in terms of what they tell you about the real situation – for example, where the model crosses the axes and the maximum or minimum point. Describe what the changing gradient of the model tells you about the situation.

Practice exam questions

Emergency Stop data

1 A car accelerates to a speed of 30 miles per hour before doing an emergency stop. The graph shows the
UoM1 distance travelled by the car, d feet, plotted against the time, t seconds, after the car started to move.

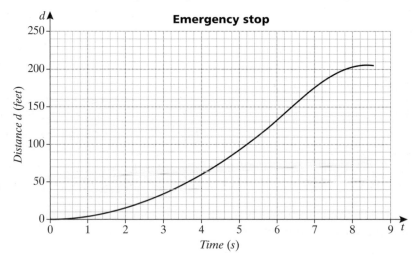

The car begins to move when $t = 0$, accelerates to a speed of 30 miles per hour and then comes to rest at $t = 8.5$ after performing an emergency stop.

a Approximately how far does the car travel altogether?

b Estimate the car's average speed in miles per hour. (1 mile = 5280 feet)

c Write down two values of t where the gradient of the curve is zero.

Resource Sheet 2.7Q1

d Find the gradient of the graph when
  i $t = 2$
  ii $t = 5$
  iii $t = 8$.

e Estimate the value of t when the gradient of the curve is greatest.

f Describe what your answers to parts **d** and **e** tell you about the real situation.

2 The graph below shows the speed of the car, v miles per hour, plotted against time t, seconds.

UoM1

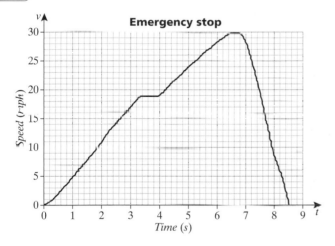

a i Without carrying out any calculations, compare the gradient of the graph at the points where $t = 2$ and $t = 5$. At which of these points is the gradient greater?
  ii What does this tell you about the real situation?

b i Identify two time intervals when the gradient of the graph is zero.
  ii Describe what you think is happening in the real situation during each of these time intervals.

Resource Sheet 2.72

c The data for the period during the emergency stop from $t = 7$ to $t = 8.5$ can be modelled by a linear function.
  i Find the gradient of the straight line joining the points on the curve where $t = 7$ and $t = 8.5$.
  ii Hence find the equation of the straight line joining these points.
  iii What would you expect to happen to the gradient of this model if the test was carried out with a car that has more powerful brakes?

UoM4

3 A company that produces confectionery products is introducing a new type of chocolate bar.
It models the profit that it expects to make on these chocolate bars with the function $P = 12\,000x - 2000x^2 - 5500$, where £$P$ represents the expected profit per month and x years is the time after the new bar is launched onto the market.

a Use the model to calculate how much profit the company expects to make per month one year after the launch of the new chocolate bar.

b Find the two values of x for which $12\,000x - 2000x^2 - 5500 = 0$.

c i Show that P can be written as $P = -2000[(x - 3)^2 - 6.25]$.
  ii Hence find the maximum expected profit per month.
  iii How long after the launch is the profit per month expected to reach this value?

d i Sketch the graph of P against x. Show the co-ordinates of the maximum point and the points where the curve meets the axes.
  ii Interpret the sections of the curve that lie below the x axis in terms of the real situation.

e The company decides to stop producing these chocolate bars when profits fall to £1000 per month. Estimate how long the chocolate bars will have been on the market when this occurs. Give your answer to the nearest month.

3 Modelling Growth

▶ Contents

The graph shows the growth in the number of mobile phone subscribers in the UK over the 1990s. You can imagine that data of this type is very useful to mobile phone companies as they plan ahead hoping to sell more mobiles in the future. The table shows one set of predictions for the growth of mobile phone use throughout the world.

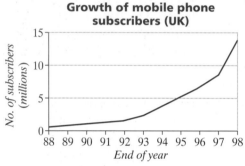

Growth of mobile phone subscribers (UK)

Forecasted world totals

Region	2001	2002	2003	2004	2005
Africa	29.0	48.2	67.4	84.5	101.6
Americas	98.7	140.6	181.3	214.7	240.5
Asia–Pacific	330.9	444.5	564.2	678.2	780.2
Eastern Europe	44.5	60.3	75.8	89.9	102.3
Western Europe	367.2	494.1	607.5	694.4	754.5
Middle East	14.9	20.9	29.0	38.6	48.5
USA/Canada	139.9	165.2	191.6	216.7	239.7
World	**1025.3**	**1373.8**	**1716.8**	**2016.9**	**2268.0**

Discussion point

How good were these predictions? Compare them with some current data.

In this chapter you will use mathematics to model situations where there is growth and/or decay. This will involve you in using **exponential functions**. You will also learn about associated **logarithmic functions**.

3.1 Examples of growth and decay

Key web search terms

savings interest rates
chain letters
carbon dating

compound interest
pyramid schemes
radioactive isotopes

Who wants to be a millionaire?

The TV quiz show *Who wants to be a millionaire?* has been very popular in countries around the world. Its obvious appeal is the possibility of winning a million – but equally appealing for the viewer is the fact that contestants can also lose large amounts of money. The table shows the prize money at each of the fifteen steps to one million. In most cases the jump is such that you double your money – for example from £100 to £200.

Activity 3.1A

Resource Sheet 3.1A

The graph below shows how the prize money increases in the *Who wants to be a millionaire?* TV quiz.

1 In a new version of the game:
   • a correct answer to the first question earns £100
   • you double your money for each successive correct answer.

   Make a table to show how the prize money increases in this case. Plot points on a copy of the graph below to show what you would win in this version of the game.

2 How much would you win in this new version of the game if you answer 15 questions correctly?

3 In the new version of the game the prize money £P, for n questions correct is given by $P = 100 \times 2^{n-1}$ ($n = 1, 2, 3 \ldots$)

   Check that the formula $P = 100 \times 2^{n-1}$ is correct by using it to calculate values of P and checking these against the values you found by doubling.

1 MILLION
500,000
250,000
125,000
64,000
32,000
16,000
8,000
4,000
2,000
1,000
500
300
200
100

Checkpoint

When $n = 1$,
$P = 100 \times 2^{1-1} = 100 \times 2^0$
$= 100 \times 1 = 100$
Use your calculator to check that $2^0 = 1$.

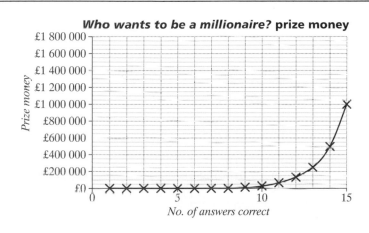

Who wants to be a millionaire? prize money

No. of answers correct

Discussion point

Should you join points on this graph with a continuous line? What meaning do points on the line have?

69

In your interest

If you put money into a savings account, it will gain interest and so your savings will increase as time goes on. Imagine you put £1000 into a savings account at 4% interest per year. Usually the interest for each year is added to the amount already in the account. This means that the interest for each successive year is calculated using a larger amount than the year before (assuming you don't withdraw any money). This interest is then added onto what is already in the account. This is called **compound interest**.

Discussion point
Of course in real life things are not so simple. What factors make actual interest calculations more complicated?

Activity 3.1B

For the example of £1000 savings invested at 4% per year:

1   a   What is the amount of interest for the first year?

     b   Show that the amount of interest for the second year is £41.60.

     c   Find the total amount in the savings account at the end of the 10th year.

2   Use your graphic calculator or a spreadsheet to draw a graph of the amount in the account at the end of each year for the first 10 years.

Note: You can increase an amount by 4% by multiplying by 1.04. This is the same as multiplying by $\frac{104}{100}$, i.e. the same as finding 104%.

In reality the interest may be calculated and added on twice a year instead of once. So instead of 4% interest being added once a year, 2% may be added every six months – usually December and June.

Activity 3.1C

1   Compare adding 2% every half-year with that of adding 4% once a year. Do this by finding the interest after

     a   1 year   b   2 years   c   10 years

     and comparing with your answers to **Activity 3.1B**.

UoM4   2   Explain why the money grows more quickly when 2% is paid every half-year than when 4% is added every year.

Hint: At the end of the first half-year the amount in the account will be
$1.02 \times £1000 = £1020$.
At the end of the second half-year it will be
$1.02 \times £1020$ and so on.

The amount of money in an account on which a **fixed rate** of compound interest is paid grows by more and more each year. The interest is proportional to what is in the account, so the more there is in the account, the more interest is paid.

Activity 3.1D

1   Explain why the formula for the amount of money, £A, in an account in which £2500 is invested at 2.5% per year, compounded annually, after t years is $A = 2500(1 + 0.025)^t$.

2   After how many years will the amount in the account be double the original amount? Answer this question by drawing up a table or plotting a graph.

UoM4

3 In general, for compound interest of $r\%$ added once a year, the amount £A in an account after t years is given by

$$A = A_0\left(1 + \frac{100 + r}{100}\right)^t$$

where £A_0 is the initial amount in the account.

a Show that the above formula is true by using it to calculate the amount in an account after 10 years for which the compound interest rate is 4% per year and the initial investment is £1000. Compare your answer with what you got for **question 2** in **Activity 3.1B**.

b How does the starting amount affect the time taken for the amount in the account to double?

c Explain how you could double your money in a shorter time.

Chain letters 1

Unscrupulous people may attempt to use a chain letter to make money.

> Dear ....,
>
> Here is your chance to make £30 000+!!
> Enclosed is a list of the names and
> addresses of just 6 people – this is what
> you have to do:
> Send £2 to the person at the top of the
> list. Delete this person from the list, move
> everyone else up one place and add your
> own name and address at the bottom.
> Send a copy of this letter and the list to
> five friends.
>
> Sit back and in just a few days you will find
> your post will be arriving with cheques that
> will total over £30 000!
>
> Good luck!

Discussion points

Can you explain why such schemes are called 'pyramid' schemes? Why is the chain letter unlikely to give you the amount promised? What is likely to happen? Who will make money and who won't? Why are such schemes fraudulent?

When you send out your letter you will be in sixth place on the list of people it contains. If each of your friends carries on the chain by sending the letter to five other friends, you will then be in fifth place on the list of people going out in 25 chain letters.

Activity 3.1E

Investigate the claims in the letter by drawing up a table and a graph to show the potential growth in money due to the scheme. List the assumptions that you have made.

A Persian mummy?

At the end of the year 2000 it was claimed that the mummy of a Persian princess wearing a gold crown and mask had been found inside a stone coffin which was itself inside a wooden sarcophagus. Never before had a Persian mummy been found – in fact mummification was thought to have been unique to the ancient Egyptians. Scientists became suspicious and investigated using CT scans, X-rays and carbon dating. The carbon dating led them to conclude that the mat that the mummy was lying on was, at the most, 50 years old. Further investigations found that bone and tissue samples suggested that the woman died in 1996.

The mummy was a fake.

Carbon dating relies on the decay (measured in disintegrations per minute) of a radioactive isotope of carbon (known as carbon-14). Carbon-14 is produced in the atmosphere at a more or less constant rate and is spread evenly throughout the world. All living organisms absorb this carbon-14, so that each has the same concentration of carbon-14 in it. When an organism dies it no longer picks up carbon-14 and the carbon-14 in the organism at death decays. But this means that as the amount of carbon-14 gets less there will be a lower rate of decay. After 5730 years, half of the carbon-14 will have gone. After another 5730 years, another half will have gone, and so on. In living organisms there is an average of 15.3 disintegrations per minute per gram of carbon.

'CT' stands for 'computed tomograph', where scans of sections of the body are taken and reconstructed by computer.

The time taken for half of a radioactive substance to have decayed is called the **half-life**. For carbon-14 it is 5730 years.

Activity 3.1F

Resource Sheet 3.1F

1 Use the information above to complete the table below to show how the radioactive decay of carbon-14 reduces with time.

No. of half-lives	Time (years)	Amount of carbon-14 (grams)	Radioactivity (disintegrations/minute/ gram of total carbon)
0	0	1	15.3
1	5730	0.5	7.65
2	11460	0.25	3.825
3			
4			
5			
6			

2 Use your graphic calculator to draw a graph of the radioactivity against time to show how carbon-14 decays.

3.2 Exponential growth and decay

Key web search terms

exponential growth
exponential decay
E. coli
half-life

rate of increase

radioactive waste
plutonium

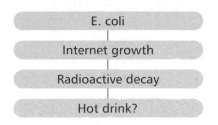

E. coli

Internet growth

Radioactive decay

Hot drink?

E. Coli

E. coli bacteria can cause diarrhoea, dehydration and even death. The source is usually contaminated and under-cooked foods. Experiments have shown that, in favourable conditions, a colony of E. coli doubles in size every 20 minutes. The graph below shows the number of bacteria plotted against time in this case.

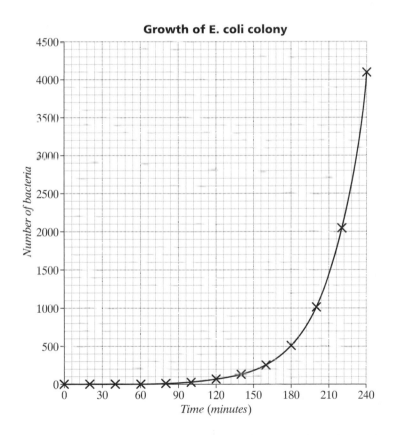

Growth of E. coli colony

Number of bacteria (y-axis: 0, 500, 1000, 1500, 2000, 2500, 3000, 3500, 4000, 4500)

Time (minutes) (x-axis: 0, 30, 60, 90, 120, 150, 180, 210, 240)

In his book, *The Andromeda Strain*, the author Michael Crichton wrote:

'The mathematics of uncontrolled growth are frightening. A single cell of the bacterium E. coli would, under ideal circumstances, divide every twenty minutes. That is not particularly disturbing until you think about it, but the fact is that bacteria multiply geometrically: one becomes two, two become four, four become eight and so on. In this way it can be shown that in a single day, one cell of E. coli could produce a super-colony equal in size and weight to the entire planet Earth.'

Doubling time is the time taken for a quantity to double in size. For E. coli the doubling time is 20 minutes.

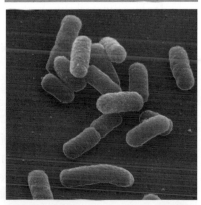

E. coli bacteria

The graph shows that the rate of growth of the E. coli colony will be relatively slow at the start when the colony is small, but that the rate of growth will increase as the size of the colony increases. You may have heard situations like this described as 'exponential growth'. You will learn the maths behind such growth in this section.

Such growth, where the *rate of increase of the population is proportional to the size of the population, is called exponential growth*. Growth of this type may be modelled by a function of the form $y = ka^{mx}$ where k, m and a are positive constants (or parameters) with $a > 1$.

The number of bacteria, N, after t minutes can be modelled using $N = 2^{0.05t}$.

Discussion point

How does the theory that the E. coli colony doubles in size every 20 minutes lead to the function $N = 2^{0.05t}$?

Resource Sheet 3.2A

Activity 3.2A

1   Use the fact that the number of E. coli bacteria doubles every 20 minutes to complete a copy of the table.

2   Check that the function $N = 2^{0.05t}$ can be used to model the growth of E. coli by using a graphic calculator to plot, on one set of axes, graphs showing

   • the data for the E. coli colony (from the table)
   • the function $N = 2^{0.05t}$

3   The general model for exponential growth is $y = ka^{mx}$. What are the values of the parameters k, a and m in the model for the growth of E. coli?

4   Use the model $N = 2^{0.05t}$ to calculate the number of bacteria when

   a $t = 40$ **b** $t = 120$ **c** $t = 240$.

   Compare these with the values you got in your table when answering **question 1**.

5   Predict the number of bacteria in the colony after

   a six hours   **b** twelve hours.

UoM4   6   Michael Crichton says that '*in a single day, one cell of E. coli could produce a super-colony equal in size and weight to the entire planet Earth.*'

   a Predict the number of bactera in the colony after one day.

   b The mass of one E. coli bacterium has been estimated to be 10^{-12} grams and the mass of the earth is approximately 5.98×10^{24} kilograms.
   Use these values to check whether the answer to part a supports Michael Crichton's statement.

UoM4   7   Sketch, on one set of axes, graphs of the growth models $N = 2^{kt}$, where

   a $k < 0$ **b** $0 < k < 1$ **c** $k > 1$.

   Indicate clearly which graph is which.
   Write a sentence or two to explain the effect of different values of k in the growth model $N = 2^{kt}$.

Time (minutes)	No. of bacteria
0	1
20	2
40	4
60	
80	
100	
120	
140	
160	
180	
200	
220	
240	

Discussion points

What factors affecting the growth of bacteria have not been taken into account by the theory?
In what way would the graph change due to these factors?

This activity involved growth in a population of bacteria. Experimental data suggests that the colony takes a while to get established, but then the population does grow in line with the model's predictions, until lack of nutrients or too much toxic waste start to inhibit growth. You will look at ways to model growth so that such factors are taken into account in **Chapter 7**.

Internet growth

The Internet began as a US military network, ARPANET, which was gradually linked to educational and research organisations within the USA and then to other networks across the world. In recent years growth in the Internet has been rapid. An organisation called Internet Software Consortium has attempted to measure this growth since 1987.

Some of their data are given in the table.

No. of years (after Jan 1990)	No. of Internet hosts (millions)
1	0.38
2	0.73
3	1.31
4	2.22
5	4.85
6	9.47
7	16.15
8	29.67
9	43.23
10	72.40

An **Internet host** is a computer to which other computers have access via the Internet.

Activity 3.2B

Resource Sheet 3.2B

1 Plot a graph to show how the number of Internet hosts has grown during the decade 1990–2000.

The data can be modelled by $N = 0.21 \times 1.84^t$ where N is the number of Internet hosts and t is the number of years after January 1990.

2 In this case, what are the values of the parameters k, a and m in the general model $y = ka^{mx}$?

3 **a** Plot the graph of $N = 0.21 \times 1.84^t$ on the axes used for **question 1**. (Add a column to your table for values predicted by the model.)

   b For which years in this decade does the model
     i over-estimate   **ii** under-estimate
   the number of Internet hosts?

   c **i** For which year is the model least accurate?
     ii Find the percentage error in the predicted value compared with the real value.

4 Use the model $N = 0.21 \times 1.84^t$ to calculate the predicted value of N when t is:

   a 0   **b** 15   **c** 30

   d −10   **e** −20

   In each case interpret your answer and say, with reasons, whether or not the value you found is likely to be realistic.

5 Do you think $N = 0.21 \times 1.84^t$ provides a good model in this situation? Explain your answer.

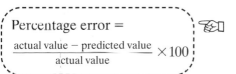

Percentage error =

$$\frac{\text{actual value} - \text{predicted value}}{\text{actual value}} \times 100$$

Discussion point

Is it wise to use a model outside the range of values for which you have real data?

Radioactive decay 1

A major concern of the opponents of nuclear power is the problem of nuclear waste. Nuclear power stations produce a number of radioactive waste products. One of these is plutonium-239 which has a half-life of about 24 000 years.

Half-life is the time taken for the quantity of a radioactive isotope to reduce to half of the initial quantity.

Number of half-lives	Time (thousands of years)	Amount of plutonium (grams)
0	0	1000
1	24	500
2	48	
3	72	
4		
5		
6		
7		
8		

Activity 3.2C

Resource Sheet 3.2C

1. The amount of plutonium halves every 24 000 years. Complete a table to show how one kilogram of plutonium will decay over time.

2. Draw a graph of amount of plutonium, y grams, against time, t thousand years.

UoM4 3. Use your graph to estimate after how long 100 grams of the original kilogram of plutonium would be left. How can you do this when you have data points plotted on your graphic calculator?

UoM4 4. A quick rule of thumb is that for any radioactive material the amount present will reduce to roughly 0.1% of the original amount in 10 half-lives. Show clearly how this follows from the definition of half-life.

The graph you have drawn shows the typical shape for **exponential decay**. The rate of decay is rapid at first but becomes slower as the amount of material decreases.

☞ For exponential decay, as in the case of exponential growth, the rate of change is proportional to the amount present. In the case above the rate of decay is proportional to the amount of radioactive plutonium present.

Both exponential growth and exponential decay can be modelled by functions of the form $y = ka^{mx}$ where k and a are positive constants. When a is greater than 1, the constant m in the index is *positive* for *exponential growth* and *negative* for *exponential decay*.

The graphs of all such functions cross the y axis at $(0, k)$.

The x axis is an asymptote to the curve.

An **asymptote** is a line which the curve approaches more and more closely but which the curve never touches or crosses.

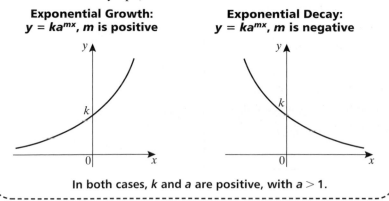

Exponential Growth:
$y = ka^{mx}$, *m* is positive

Exponential Decay:
$y = ka^{mx}$, *m* is negative

In both cases, *k* and *a* are positive, with *a* > 1.

Discussion point

In what ways does the gradient of a growth curve differ from the gradient of a decay curve? What does this tell you about the rate of change?

Activity 3.2D

1 The function $y = 1000 \times 1.029^{-t}$ can be used to model the radioactive decay of one kilogram of plutonium, where y is the number of grams of plutonium remaining after t **thousand** years. Compare this with the general form $y = ka^{mx}$. What are the values of the parameters k, a and m in this case?

2 **a** Use the model $y = 1000 \times 1.029^{-t}$ to calculate how much plutonium will remain after 10 thousand years.

    b Draw the function $y = 1000 \times 1.029^{-t}$ on your graphic calculator so that you can compare it with the graph you have drawn of the data for **question 2** of **Activity 3.2C**.

3 **a** During a year's operation a typical 1000 Megawatt nuclear reactor produces about 230 kilograms of plutonium. Use the model to predict, to the nearest gram, the amount that would remain if this were left in the power station's cooling pond for 40 years.

    b If 2 tonnes of plutonium were buried, use the model to predict, to the nearest kilogram, how much would remain after 5 centuries.

UoM4

4 Nature has in the past produced its own nuclear reactors. Almost 2 billion years ago six spontaneous nuclear reactions occurred within a rich vein of uranium ore at Oklo in Africa. These natural reactors continued for about 500 000 years, producing about 1.5 tonnes of plutonium before dying away. Use the model to predict how much of that plutonium is still in existence.

UoM4

5 **a** Krypton-85 is another isotope produced in a nuclear reactor. It has a half-life of 10 years. What percentage of the krypton produced will remain at the end of a century?

    b Cobalt-60, with a half-life of 5 years, is produced in the cooling system of a nuclear power station. What percentage of cobalt-60 will remain at the end of a century?

UoM4

6 Sketch on one set of axes graphs of the model $y = 1000 \times a^{-t}$, where

    a $a > 1$ **b** $0 < a < 1$ **c** $a < 0$.

    Label each graph. Write a sentence or two to explain the effect of using different values of a in the model of exponential decay $y = 1000 \times a^{-t}$.

UoM4

7 Sketch a graph to show how one kilogram of plutonium will decay over 96 000 years (i.e. four half-lives). On your graph sketch curves to show how this decay would be affected if the half-life were

    a greater   **b** less.

    Label each graph.

The High Level Waste Storage Plant at Sellafield

An alternative model for the decay of a kilogram plutonium is given by the function:

$$y = 1000 \times 0.972^t$$

Use your graphic calculator to compare this function with $y = 1000 \times 1.029^{-t}$; you should see that they are identical.

This follows since

$$y = 1000 \times 1.029^{-t}$$

$$= 1000 \times \frac{1}{1.029^t}$$

$$= 1000 \times \left(\frac{1}{1.029}\right)^t$$

$$= 1000 \times 0.972^t$$

Hot drink?

The temperature of a cup of coffee was measured every 10 minutes as it cooled. The results are given in the table.

Experimental data such as this is subject to human error. The accuracy with which the measurements are made also depends on the sensitivity of the instruments used.

Suppose that the times in the table are correct to the nearest 10 seconds (i.e. they could be up to 5 seconds more or less), and that the temperatures are correct to the nearest 2 degrees (i.e. they could be up to 1 degree more or less).

When a graph is drawn of temperature against time, you can use error bars to show the range of possible values for each temperature taken. The diagram shows how you would do this for the temperature after ten minutes. The value given in the table is 75°C. To allow for an error of ±1°C, you would draw a vertical bar stretching from 74°C to 76°C. In this case because the possible time error of ±5 seconds is small compared with the times measured in minutes, you would not draw an error bar to show this.

However, if you read the time less accurately, you could use a horizontal error bar. This second diagram shows how you would show an error of ±1 minute. In this case, the true data point could lie anywhere within the rectangle defined by the error bars. When you draw a curve to represent the way in which the temperature changes with time, it does not need to pass through the point where the error bars meet, but should pass through the rectangle defined by the error bars.

Time (minutes)	Temperature (°C)
0	86
10	75
20	66
30	58
40	51
50	46
60	41
70	37
80	34
90	31
100	29
110	28
120	27
130	26
140	25
150	24

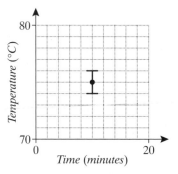

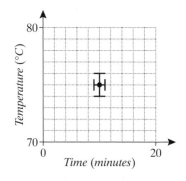

Activity 3.2E

Resource Sheet 3.2E

1   Plot a graph of temperature against time for the cooling cup of coffee. Draw error bars to show the possible error of ±1°C in each temperature. Draw a smooth curve, ensuring that it passes through the rectangle defined by the error bars.

2   a   How low do you think that the temperature of the coffee will eventually fall?

    b   Why is the fall in temperature limited?

3   On the same set of axes, draw a graph of the model $y = 67 \times 1.018^{-t} + 19$ where y is the temperature in degrees Celsius after t minutes have passed.
    Identify sections where the graph of the model fits the data closely and sections where the fit is not quite so good.

Discussion point

In what way does this function differ from the standard function in the form $y = ka^{mx}$?

4 **a** Use the model $y = 67 \times 1.018^{-t} + 19$ to predict the temperature of the coffee when t is

    i 0   **ii** 100   **iii** 200

    iv 300   **v** 400.

  b What does the model predict will happen in the long run?

UoM4 **5** You could argue that errors in the temperatures might be larger than $\pm 1°C$ because of variation in the temperature of the coffee in different parts of the cup. The larger the assumed error, the greater the number of functions that you can find to model the data. The graph shows the data with error bars of $\pm 2°C$ and also three possible models:

  Model A $y = 67 \times 1.018^{-t} + 19$ (as before)
  Model B $y = 68 \times 1.017^{-t} + 18$
  Model C $y = 65 \times 1.019^{-t} + 20$

  Describe the differences between the models in terms of the parameters a, b and c of the models expressed in the form $y = ab^{-t} + c$. Explain the values of the parameters in terms of the real situation.

Discussion point

What is the significance of the answers to **4a i** and **4b**? What happens to the term 1.018^{-t} as $t \to \infty$?

Discussion point

The following functions are alternative forms for Models **A**, **B** and **C**.

A $y = 67 \times 0.982^{t} + 19$
B $y = 68 \times 0.983^{t} + 18$
C $y = 65 \times 0.981^{t} + 20$

Can you explain why?

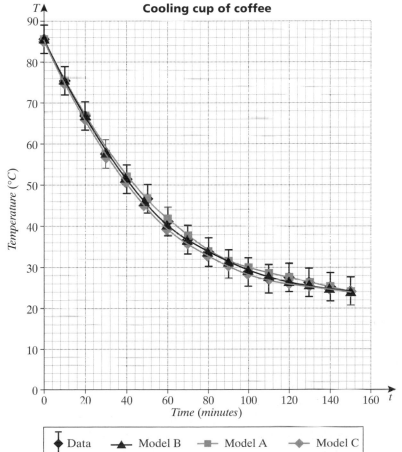

Cooling cup of coffee

Temperature (°C) vs *Time (minutes)*

Legend: Data Model B Model A Model C

Practice sheets:
Error bars

3.3 Exponential and logarithmic functions

Key web search terms

exponential functions
logarithmic functions

the number e
inverse functions

Exponential functions

The number e

Graphs of exponential functions

Logarithmic functions

☞ **Note:** A **function** is a rule or formula that gives just one **output** for every **input**. For example, $y = x^2$ is a function because for every value of x there is just one value of y. $y = \pm\sqrt{x}$ is not a function because there are two values of y for every positive value of x. However $y = +\sqrt{x}$ is a function because for every value of x there is just one value of y.

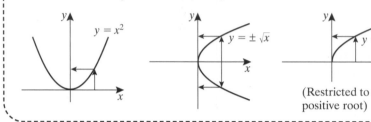

(Restricted to positive root)

Exponential functions

In the last section you modelled growth and decay using exponential functions in the form $y = ka^{mx}$, where k, a and m are parameters that depend on the situation. For example, in **Activity 3.2B** you used the function $N = 0.21 \times 1.84^t$ to model the number of Internet hosts for the years since 1990. In this example, $k = 0.21$, $a = 1.84$ and $m = 1$.

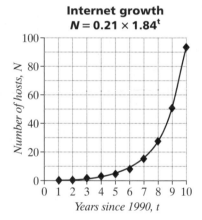

Internet growth
$N = 0.21 \times 1.84^t$

Number of hosts, N

Years since 1990, t

Activity 3.3A

Excel Activity

Use a graphic calculator throughout this activity.

You can draw the same exponential graph from apparently different versions of $y = ka^{mx}$.

1 As an illustration of this, draw graphs of $y = 0.5 \times 8^x$ and $y = 0.5 \times 2^{3x}$. They should be the same.

2 Explain why the two functions produce the same graph.

3 Explain why $y = 0.5 \times 8^x$ is NOT the same as $y = 4^x$. Draw graphs to check.

4 Express $y = 3 \times 9^x$ as a different version of $y = ka^{mx}$ that still has the same graph. Draw graphs to check that you are correct.

The number e

Every exponential function $y = ka^{mx}$ can be expressed using the same value of a by changing the value of m. It is sometimes convenient to use 10 as the value of a; every exponential function can then be written in the form $y = k \times 10^{mx}$.

For example, the function $y = 0.5 \times 8^x$ can be written as $y = 0.5 \times 10^{0.9031x}$.

You are not expected to be able to work out the value of m for yourself in all cases, but you could find some easy equivalent expressions, such as expressing $y = 4 \times 100^x$ in the form $y = k \times 10^{mx}$.

Activity 3.3B

Excel Activity

Use a graphic calculator throughout this activity.

1 Draw graphs to test that $y = 0.5 \times 8^x$ and $y = 0.5 \times 10^{0.9031x}$ are equivalent.

2 Try these, and draw graphs to check that you are correct:
  a Express $y = 1000^x$ in the form $y = 10^{mx}$.
  b Express $y = 100^x$ in the form $y = 10^{mx}$.
  c Express $y = 10^x$ in the form $y = 1000^{mx}$.

Any positive value of a can be used as the base for exponential functions of the forms $y = ka^{mx}$. A standard method is to express exponential functions in terms of the number e, which is a mathematical constant.

The following activity demonstrates one of the interesting properties of the number e.

Activity 3.3C

Excel Activity

If you invest £1 at 100% per annum interest (most unlikely!) at the end of a year you will have £2, if the interest is compounded just once at the end of the year.

1 If, instead, the interest is compounded half-yearly, so 50% interest is added twice during the year, show that at the end of the year you will have £2.25.

2 If the interest is compounded every month, explain why the amount at the end of the year is $£(1 + \frac{1}{12})^{12}$ and calculate this amount.

3 What happens if the interest is compounded every week? Or every day? Or every hour? Or every minute?
Investigate using a spreadsheet.

Discussion point
What is a likely interest rate when you invest money in a bank or building society?

The amounts you have calculated get closer and closer to the value of the number e. The value of e correct to 5 decimal places is 2.718 28. Did you get close to it?

You can get the number on your calculator using the key labelled e^x and using $x = 1$.

$e = 2.718\ 281\ 828\ 459\ 045\ 235\ 36$ (to 20 decimal places)

Like π, e is an irrational number. If you express e as a decimal, it has no pattern – it is non-recurring and infinite, and so it is more conveniently denoted by a letter.

Graphs of exponential functions

Activity 3.3D

Resource Sheet 3.3D

Investigate graphs of $y = ke^{mx}$.

Do this systematically by:

a keeping $m = 1$ and varying k, so you investigate graphs of $y = ke^x$ for $-5 \leqslant k \leqslant 5$

b keeping $k = 2$ and varying m, so you investigate graphs of $y = 2e^{mx}$ for $-5 \leqslant m \leqslant 5$.

Make some notes and sketches of your main findings.

Logarithmic functions

If you know x you can find $y = e^x$ using a graph or a calculator. Of course a calculator will give you a more accurate result than a graph.

If you know $y = e^x$ how can you find x?

You could use a graph but this will not give a very accurate answer. For a more accurate answer, you need to use the **inverse function** of e^x, which is the **natural logarithm** 'ln' on your calculator.

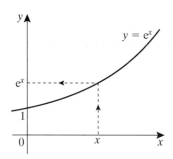

If $y = e^x$ then $x = \ln y$. Sometimes the notation $\log_e x$ is used instead of $\ln x$. This is because **natural logarithms** are **logarithms in base e**.

In general, if $y = a^x$, then $x = \log_a y$ (or $\log_a y = x$).

That is, if $y = a^x$, the exponent x is defined as the **logarithm to the base a of y**.

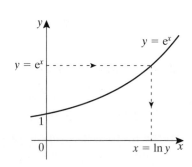

This is an important definition that you should learn and understand.

Activity 3.3E

Excel
Activity

1   Choose any positive number, p.
    Use your calculator to find $\ln p$, then use e^x to find $e^{\ln p}$. What
    do you notice? Try again with some other positive numbers.

2   Now use the two functions in the reverse order, finding first
    e^p then $\ln(e^p)$.

3   Try **questions 1** and **2** with negative numbers.

4   What does this indicate about the functions $\ln x$ and e^x?

5   Use your graphic calculator to draw the graph of $y = \ln x$.
    Sketch and describe the main features of the graph.

6   What feature of the graph indicates that you can find $\ln x$
    only for $x > 0$?

7   Using a graphic calculator with the same scale on each axis
    draw graphs of
    • $y = e^x$
    • $y = \ln x$
    • $y = x$
    on one diagram.
    What do you notice?

You should see that the graphs of $y = e^x$ and $y = \ln x$ are
reflections of each other in the line $y = x$, indicating that the
functions are the inverses of each other.

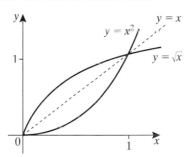

The diagram shows the graphs of $y = x^2$ and $y = \sqrt{x}$, which
are inverses of each other and reflections of each other in the
line $y = x$.

The general form of natural logarithmic functions, where the base
of the logarithms is the number e, is $y = m\ln x + k$.

Changing the values of m and k produces different members of the
family of graphs.

It is also possible to have logarithms to other bases but e and 10 are
the most commonly used: the **log** key on your calculator gives you
logarithms to the base 10.

Discussion point
Can you think of any other pairs of
inverse functions?
Are their graphs reflections of each
other in the line $y = x$?

Discussion point
What is the effect on the graph of
changing the parameters m and k?
Investigate using your graphic
calculator or a spreadsheet.

Activity 3.3F

1 Compare the graph of $y = \log_{10} x$ with that of $y = \ln x$.
What are the similarities and differences?

2 Draw the graphs of
- $y = 10^x$
- $y = \log_{10} x$
- $y = x$

on the same diagram and with the same scales on the x axis
and y axis. Comment on the result.

Activity 3.3G

Below are a number of graphs of functions based on the
exponential function $y = e^x$.

Identify which of the following functions matches which graph –
give a reason for your answer. Try to match each function with its
graph before you use your graphic calculator.

For example, $y = 0.5e^x$ and graph D match, because the intercept
of the graph with the y-axis is at the point $(0, 0.5)$.

1 $y = e^x$ **2** $y = e^x + 2$ **3** $y = e^{-x}$
4 $y = 2 - e^x$ **5** $y = 2e^x$ **6** $y = 4 - e^x$

A
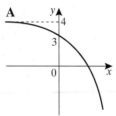

B
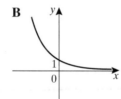

C
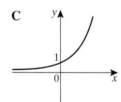

D
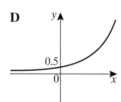

E
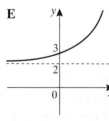

F
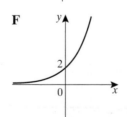

G
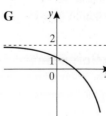

Practice sheets:
**Sketching exponential and
logarithmic graphs**

3.4 Growth models in practice

Key web search terms

crude oil production data
population growth models
cane toads
radioactive decay
chain letters
pyramid schemes

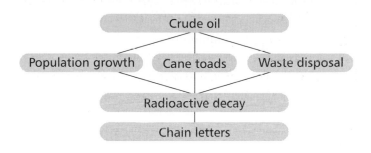

Crude Oil

The table and graph below show how world production of crude oil increased between 1900 and 1970.

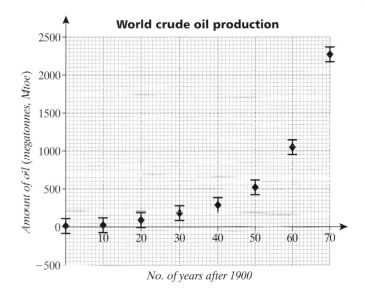

No. of years after 1900, t	Oil production (megatonnes)
0	20.2
10	44.1
20	99.3
30	195.3
40	293.1
50	519.2
60	1050.3
70	2271.8

The error bars indicate that other sources of global estimates suggest different totals.

Activity 3.4A

1 Estimate the size of the error shown by the error bars.

2 It is suggested that $y = 23.3e^{0.0646t}$ might provide a good model for the data, where y megatonnes is the annual amount of oil produced t years after 1900.

   a Draw a graph showing the original data and this exponential model.

   b How well do you think the model fits the data?

Discussion point

Does a graphic calculator, a spreadsheet or a hand-drawn graph on graph paper provide the most efficient method of comparing the data and model?

3 Use the model to predict the amount of oil produced in the world in

    a 1980   **b** 1990.

4 In fact the total amount of oil produced in 1980 was 2976 megatonnes and in 1990 the total was 3219 megatonnes. Find the percentage error in the values predicted by the model for total world oil production in

    a 1980   **b** 1990.

5 **a** What does the model predict will happen as $t \to \infty$?

    b What do you think will happen in practice?

6 Use the model $y = 23.3e^{0.0646t}$ to calculate world oil production when

    a $t = -10$ **b** $t = -50$.

    What information should these values predict? How realistic do you think these values are?

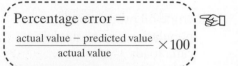

Percentage error =

$$\frac{\text{actual value} - \text{predicted value}}{\text{actual value}} \times 100$$

Discussion points

What happened in the 1970s that affected the production of crude oil?

What do experts predict will happen in the future? What are Hubbert's Peak and the Olduvai Theory?

Population growth

The table shows world population in the 20th century.

This data can be modelled by the exponential function $P = 8.7 \times 10^{-12}e^{0.0136t}$ where P billion is the population in the year t.

The graph below shows this model plotted with the original data.

Year t	Population, P (billions)
1900	1.65
1910	1.75
1920	1.86
1930	2.07
1940	2.30
1950	2.56
1960	3.04
1970	3.71
1980	4.46
1990	5.28
2000	6.08

Discussion point

How can you tell at a glance which curve is the model and which is the data?

World population 1900–2000

◆ Data
■ Model

Population (billions) vs *Year*

Activity 3.4B

1   For which years in the 20th century does the model

   a over-estimate   **b** under-estimate
   world population?

2   **a** Use your calculator to find the population predicted by the model for the year 2000.

   b The actual population in 2000 was 6.08 billion.
   What is the percentage error in the predicted value?

Percentage error =

$$\frac{\text{actual value} - \text{predicted value}}{\text{actual value}} \times 100$$

3   The population of the world in 1800 was about 900 million. Compare this with the value predicted by the model.

4   What is the value of P given by the model when $t = 0$? What information should this value predict? Comment.

5   **a** What does the model predict will happen to the world population as $t \to \omega$?

   b Describe what you think will actually happen to world population in the long run. What types of functions do you think could be used to represent world population in future years?

6   Using the model, in what year

   a will the world population be 10 billion

   b was the population 1 million

   c was the population 2 people?

7   The surface area of the land masses of the earth is approximately $1.5 \times 10^8 \text{ km}^2$. Ignoring factors such as changes in water level and the possibility of land sinking into the sea, find the year in which the model predicts that population density will be

   a 100 people per km²   **b** 1 person per m².

Note the units.

Cane toads

Cane toads are large (up to 15 cm long), poisonous and covered with warts. In June 1935 they were introduced into Queensland, Australia, to control beetles that were decimating the sugar cane crop. The project backfired. Not only did the cane toad fail to control the cane beetle, but it spread rapidly and became a major threat to native wildlife.

The table shows how the area of land occupied by cane toads increased during a thirty-five year period after their introduction.

Year	Area (km²)
1939	32 800
1944	55 800
1949	73 600
1954	138 000
1959	202 000
1964	257 000
1969	301 000
1974	584 000

Activity 3.4C

1   Use a graphic calculator or a spreadsheet to draw a graph of the area occupied by the cane toads against time in years. Use A to represent the area in thousands of square kilometres and t to represent the number of years after 1939, i.e. representing the year 1939 by zero, the year 1940 by 1 etc.

2   a   On the same diagram, draw a graph of the function $A = 36.45 \times 1.081^t$.

   b   For which year in the table is the prediction given by this model least accurate?

   c   Calculate the percentage error for that year.

3   a   Use the data values for the years 1939, 1959 and 1974 to find a quadratic function $y = at^2 + bt + c$ to model the data. Give values of a, b and c to 3 significant figures.

   b   Draw a graph of the quadratic model and compare it with that of the original data. For which year in the table is the prediction given by this model least accurate?

   c   Find the percentage error for that year.

UoM4   4   a   Draw up a table showing the prediction given by each model for the area occupied by cane toads in each year from 1935 to 1938 inclusive.

   b   Which of the models do you think gives more realistic predictions? Explain why.

UoM4   5   a   The area of Australia is 7 619 000 square kilometres. Use each model to estimate the year in which cane toads are predicted to reach every part of Australia.

   b   Do you think either of these predictions is reasonable? Explain your answer.

UoM4   6   a   What does each model predict will happen to the area occupied by the cane toads as $t \to \infty$?

   b   What do you think will actually happen?

Discussion point

Why do you think the area is given rather than the number of toads? Do you think this is a good measure?

Percentage error =
$$\frac{\text{actual value} - \text{predicted value}}{\text{actual value}} \times 100$$

Discussion point

What factors will affect how rapidly cane toads spread across Australia?

What would you expect the graph of area occupied by cane toads against time to look like in the long run?

Waste disposal

The East London Waste Authority is responsible for disposing of the waste generated in the London boroughs of Barking and Dagenham, Havering, Redbridge and Newham. The table shows the quantity of waste that they have dealt with since 1992.

Year	Waste (thousands of tonnes)	Annual increase
1992	403	0.8%
1993	408	1.2%
1994	412	1.0%
1995	416	1.0%
1996	420	1.0%
1997	440	4.8%
1998	465	5.7%
1999	475	2.2%
2000	505	6.3%
2001	530	5.0%

Activity 3.4D

1   The table additionally gives the percentage increase in the amount of waste each year. Show calculations to check the percentage increase for 2001.

2   By considering the figures in the table, state whether or not you think this situation is one of exponential growth. Explain your reasoning.

3   Use a graphic calculator or a spreadsheet to draw a graph of the amount of waste, y thousands of tonnes, against time, t years, where t is the number of years after 1992, i.e. plot 403 tonnes against 0 years (1992), 408 tonnes against 1 year (1993) etc.

4   Here are two possible models of the waste data.

   Model A $y = 1.7t^2 - 1.5t + 405$
   Model B $y = 2.6e^{0.40t} + 400$

   Show each of these models on your graph.

5   a   Which of the two functions do you think is a better model for the period from 2001 to 2005? Explain your reasoning.

   b   Which of the two functions do you think gives better values for the amount of waste prior to the year 1992? Explain your reasoning.

6   A third possible model uses linear functions.

   a   Use the real data for the years 1992 and 1996 to find a linear model for $0 \leqslant t \leqslant 4$.

   b   Use the real data for the years 1996 and 2001 to find a linear model for $4 \leqslant t \leqslant 9$.

   c   Compare this model with those given in **question 4**.

Radioactive decay 2

In **Section 3.1** you saw that every 5730 years, the amount of carbon-14 in a dead organism will have halved. You drew up a table like that shown alongside.

Time (years)	Mass of carbon-14 (grams)
0	1
5730	0.5
11460	0.25
17190	0.125
22920	0.0625

Activity 3.4E

You can use a function $m = e^{kt}$ to model the mass, m grams, of carbon-14 in a dead organism t years after the organism died.

1   a   Show that this function is a good model if $k = -0.000121$ by using a graphic calculator to plot on one graph:
      i   the data from the table
      ii the function $m = e^{kt}$.

   b   Explain what will happen to the carbon-14 in the long term. Does the model reflect this? Can you explain why?

2 It takes 5730 years for the amount of carbon-14 to halve, i.e.
○ $m = 0.5$ when $t = 5730$, so $0.5 = e^{5730k}$.
Solve $0.5 = e^{5730k}$ using logarithms to find k (you will see how to do this in detail in the next section).

Chain letters 2

In **Section 3.1** there was an investigation of a certain chain letter. In this particular case you:

- receive a list of 6 names and addresses;
- send £2 to the person at the top of the list, cross them off, move everyone else up one place and add your name and address at the bottom;
- send a copy of the letter and list to five friends.

The table shows what is supposed to happen after you post your letter.

If every person follows the rules, then 15 625 people will each send you £2 when you reach the top of the list. In return for your £2 'investment' you will receive £31 250.

No. of copies of letter	Your position in list
5	6
25	5
125	4
625	3
3125	2
15 625	1

Activity 3.4F

In each question assume every participant follows the rules of the scheme.

1 Show the calculations, based on the number of people each copy of the list is sent to (5) and the number of positions in the list (6), for

   a the number of people who will send you money

   b the amount you will receive for an investment of £2.

2 A chain letter contains a list of n people and you are asked to send it out to x people.
Write a formula for:

   a the number of people who will send you money;

   b the amount you will receive for an investment of £P.

For the rest of this activity you may like to use a spreadsheet.

3 Details of two pyramid schemes are given below. Which scheme would give participants the most money?

Make Money
Send £2 to each of 3 names on a list. Remove the person at the top of the list, move up the other two names and add your name to the bottom. Send out 12 copies of the letter, including the new list of names. Wait for the money to roll in.

The Dave Rhodes chain letter is an electronic version of this scheme that has appeared on the Internet. It contains a list of 10 people but participants are asked to forward the letter to bulletin boards rather than people.

Women only

Send £1 to each of 4 women on a list. Remove the woman at the top of the list, move up the other three names and add your name to the bottom. Send out 10 copies of the letter, including the new list. Sit back and wait for the money to arrive.

4 Suppose copies of a chain letter are sent out by each participant to 10 new recruits. The table below shows, in theory, the total number of people who will have participated in the scheme at each stage.

Stage	New recruits	Total participants
1	1	1
2	10	11
3		
4		
5		
6		
7		
8		
9		
10		

a Copy and complete the table.

b In view of the fact that the world's population is less than 7 billion, how likely is it that the scheme will continue to the next stage?

5 An all-female pyramid scheme called 'Women Empowering Women' was introduced in the Isle of Wight. Women were invited to 'gift-parties' in homes or pubs. On payment of a 'gift' of £3000 a participant joins a pyramid chart. The participant must then recruit two new members before moving up to the next level of the pyramid. After moving up two more levels the woman theoretically receives £24 000 and leaves the scheme.

a Show a calculation to explain why the promised return on a 'gift' of £3000 is £24 000.

b Draw up a table to show the total number of women that would participate in the scheme if it continued to the 25th level.

c The adult female population of the Isle of Wight is approximately 52 000 and the adult female population of England is about 19 million.
Comment on how long you think the scheme is likely to continue.

In some countries (Albania 1997, Romania 1993) hundreds of thousands of people have lost money in pyramid schemes.

Even police officers have been prosecuted for their involvement.
(Sacramento 1995/6)

Information about these and other pyramid schemes in Britain (such as The Titan Business Club) can be found on the Internet.

3.5 Solving exponential and logarithmic equations

Key web search terms

laws of logarithms
earthquake magnitudes
decibel scale

logarithmic bases
pH scale

Solving exponential equations

Earthquakes

Laws of logarithms

Using different bases

Solving exponential equations

The model $P = 8.7 \times 10^{-12}e^{0.0136t}$ can be used for the world's population, where the population is P billion people in year t. (You may have met this in **Activity 3.4B**)

You can use this model to give an estimate of the population for any year by substituting the relevant value of t into the equation.

For example, to find a value for the world's population in the year 2005:

$$P = 8.7 \times 10^{-12}e^{(0.0136 \times 2005)}$$
$$P = 8.7 \times 10^{-12}e^{27.268}$$
$$P = 6.05 \qquad \text{(to 3 significant figures)}$$

The model predicts that the population in 2005 is 6.05 billion people.

It is also possible to use the model 'backwards' to predict when the population will be, for example, 10 billion people, i.e. to find t when $P = 10 = 8.7 \times 10^{-12}e^{0.0136t}$.

The following example using easier numbers illustrates the method you need to use.

Assume that the number, y million, of bacteria in a colony after x days can be modelled by:

$$y = 5e^{\frac{x}{2}}$$

To predict when the number of bacteria will be 20 million, you need to find the value of x for which y is 20, i.e. to solve the equation:

$$20 = 5e^{\frac{x}{2}}$$

First divide each side of the equation by 5, to give:

$$4 = e^{\frac{x}{2}}$$

This means that:

$$\ln 4 = \frac{x}{2}$$
$$\therefore \quad x = 2\ln 4 \approx 2.77$$

So there are 20 million bacteria after about 2.8 days, or about 66 hours.

Now go back to using the world population model $(P = 8.7 \times 10^{-12}e^{0.0136t})$ to predict the year in which the world population will become 10 billion.

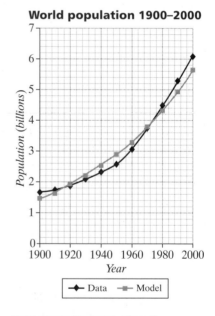

World population 1900–2000

Population (billions) vs *Year*

Legend: Data, Model

If $4 = e^{\frac{x}{2}}$ then $\ln 4 = \frac{x}{2}$.

(This follows from the definition of what a logarithm is, see **Section 3.3**.)

Checkpoint

You can check your answer by substituting back into the original model, i.e.

$$y = 5e^{\frac{2.77}{2}} = 20$$

To do this, you have to solve the equation $10 = 8.7 \times 10^{-12}e^{0.0136x}$.

Start by dividing each side of the equation by 8.7×10^{-12} giving

$$\frac{10}{8.7 \times 10^{-12}} = e^{0.0136t}.$$

So, using the definition of logarithms:

$$\ln\left(\frac{10}{8.7 \times 10^{-12}}\right) = 0.0136t$$

$$\therefore \qquad 27.77 = 0.0136t$$

Dividing both sides by 0.0136 gives:

$$\frac{27.77}{0.0136} = t$$

$$\therefore \qquad t = 2042$$

So the population will be 10 billion in about 2040 according to this model.

Work through the solution of the equation a few times until you feel confident with the process.

Activity 3.5A

1 The number of bacteria, N million, in a colony after t days can be modelled by $N = 7.5e^{0.1t}$.
   Find how long it takes for the number of bacteria to reach 15 million, using the method shown above.

2 Use the model $P = 8.7 \times 10^{-12}e^{0.0136t}$, which gives the world population, P billion in year t, to find the year in which the population was 5 billion. Check whether your answer is approximately correct using the graph on page 92.

3 The function $y = 23.3e^{0.0646t}$ can be used to model world crude oil production (between 1900 and 1970) giving y megatonnes of oil produced t years after 1900.
   Use the model to find the year it predicts that production was 500 megatonnes and compare this with the given data.

4 The mass, m grams, of carbon-14, in a body t years after it dies is given by the function $m = e^{-0.000121t}$ when the original amount of carbon-14 was 1 gram.
   Use this function to find how long it takes for the mass of carbon-14 to halve, i.e. when $0.5 = e^{-0.000121t}$.

In some cases it may be worthwhile to rearrange a model $y = Ae^{kx}$ into the form $x = \ldots$

For example, when using the world population model, $P = 8.7 \times 10^{-12}e^{0.0136t}$, if you have several different years to find for different populations, it is worth rearranging the model to give the year in terms of the population.

The steps are the same as for solving the numerical equation.

$$P = 8.7 \times 10^{-12} e^{0.0136t}$$

$$\therefore \quad \frac{P}{8.7 \times 10^{-12}} = e^{0.0136t}$$

$$\therefore \quad \ln\left(\frac{P}{8.7 \times 10^{-12}}\right) = 0.0136t$$

$$\therefore \quad t = \frac{1}{0.0136}\ln\left(\frac{P}{8.7 \times 10^{-12}}\right)$$

Activity 3.5B

1 The decay of 1 kilogram of carbon-14 can be modelled by the function $m = 1000e^{-0.000121t}$ where m is the mass in grams of carbon-14 remaining after t years. Rearrange the function $m = 1000e^{-0.000121t}$ to give '$t = \dots$' using the method above.

2 How many years does it take 1 kilogram of carbon-14 to decay to

   a 500 grams

   b 250 grams

   c 125 grams

   d 62.5 grams?

   e What is the half-life of carbon-14?

Earthquakes

The magnitude, M, of an earthquake measured on the Richter scale is given by

$$M = \log_{10} A$$

where A millimetres is the amplitude of the oscillations caused by the earthquake as recorded on a suitably calibrated seismograph.

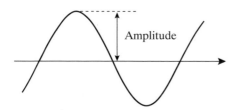

Amplitude

(*Note: This is a simplified model which makes no allowance for the distance of the seismograph from the earthquake.*)

This model is presented in this way because you can measure A and use it to give a value of M.

You can use the equation to find A if you know M, because if $M = \log_{10} A$, then $A = 10^M$.
(This follows from the definition of a logarithm. See **Section 3.3**.)

Earthquake frequency (world)

Descriptor	Magnitude	Annual average no. of occurences
Great	8+	1
Major	7–7.9	18
Strong	6–6.9	120
Moderate	5–5.9	800
Light	4–4.9	6,200*
Minor	3–3.9	49,000*
Very minor	2–2.9	1000/day*
	1–2	8000/day*

*estimates

The Richter scale was developed by Charles Richter working in California in the 1930s. This scale has no upper and lower limits – it is logarithmic (in base 10) so each one-point increase on the scale represents a ten-fold increase in amplitude of the earthquake. An earthquake of magnitude between 2 and 3 is the lowest that we can

Activity 3.5C

Resource
Sheet
3.5C

Use the rearranged form of the model that gives the amplitude,
A millimetres, of an earthquake of magnitude M on the Richter
scale, i.e. $A = 10^M$, to complete a copy of the table below.

Richter magnitude	Amplitude, A (millimetres)
0	
1	
2	
3	
4	
5	
6	
7	
8	
9	

normally feel. A magnitude of
about 5 is considered
moderate whereas a
magnitude of 6 or more is
considered major. The very
largest earthquakes have had
a magnitude of about 9. The
famous earthquake of San
Francisco in 1906 had a
magnitude of 8.3.

The most violent earthquake
recorded in Britain was in
1931. It measured 5.5 on the
Richter scale and had its
epicentre at the Dogger Bank
in the North Sea.

Discussion point

What do you notice about how the
amplitude of the oscillations
increases as the Richter magnitude
increases?
Does this help you appreciate the
value of using a logarithmic scale?

Laws of logarithms

In this sub-section you will learn some ways to manipulate
logarithms. These **'laws of logarithms'** are derived below.

1   Remember that: $2^3 \times 2^4 = 2^7$
    $(2 \times 2 \times 2) \times (2 \times 2 \times 2 \times 2) = 2 \times 2 \times 2 \times 2 \times 2 \times 2 \times 2$

    In general, $a^m \times a^n = a^{(m+n)}$
    If $x = a^m$ and $y = a^n$ then $xy = a^m a^n = a^{(m+n)}$
    $\therefore \log_a xy = m + n$
    But $x = a^m$, so $m = \log_a x$
    and $y = a^n$, so $n = \log_a y$

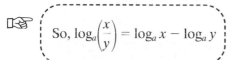

So, $\log_a xy = \log_a x + \log_a y$

2   Also remember that:
    $$\frac{5^6}{5^2} = \frac{5 \times 5 \times 5 \times 5 \times 5 \times 5}{5 \times 5} = 5^4$$

    In general, $a^m \div a^n = a^{(m-n)}$
    Using $x = a^m$ and $y = a^n$ as above,
    $$\frac{x}{y} = a^{m-n} \Rightarrow \log_a\left(\frac{x}{y}\right) = m - n$$

So, $\log_a\left(\frac{x}{y}\right) = \log_a x - \log_a y$

3   And finally remember that: $(3^2)^3 = 3^2 \times 3^2 \times 3^2 = 3^6$
    In general, $(a^m)^k = a^{m \times k}$
    Using $x = a^m$ as above, $x^k = a^{m \times k}$
    So $\log_a x^k = m \times k = (\log_a x) \times k$

☞ $\log_a x^k = k \log_a x$

☞ So the three laws of logarithms are
    $\log_a x + \log_a y = \log_a xy$

    $\log_a x - \log_a y = \log_a \left(\dfrac{x}{y}\right)$

    $k \log_a x = \log_a x^k$

Activity 3.5D

$\ln 2 = 0.6931$ $\ln 11 = 2.3979$
$\ln 3 = 1.0986$ $\ln 13 = 2.5649$
$\ln 5 = 1.6094$ $\ln 17 = 2.8332$
$\ln 7 = 1.9459$ $\ln 19 = 2.9444$

You can use these values together with the laws of logarithms to find the natural logarithms of other numbers.

For example:

$\ln 15 = \ln(3 \times 5) = \ln 3 + \ln 5 = 1.0986 + 1.6094 = 2.7080$

$\ln 16 = \ln 2^4 = 4\ln 2 = 4 \times 0.6931 = 2.7724$

1   Find the natural logarithms of the first 20 integers using the logarithms of the prime numbers given above. Show all your working.
    Check your answers using your calculator.

2   $\log 2 = 0.3010$
    $\log 3 = 0.4771$
    Use the laws of logarithms to find:

    a $\log 4$ b $\log 6$
    c $\log 8$ d $\log 9$
    e $\log 12$ f $\log 16$
    g $\log 24$ h $\log 144$

Using different bases

The general form of an exponential function is $y = ka^{mx}$. You have used different values of the base a, in particular e and 10. You also used 2 as the base in the model for the growth of E. coli in **Section 3.2**.

You can rearrange the model $y = ka^{mx}$ using inverse operations to find x in terms of y:

$$y = ka^{mx}$$

$$\therefore \quad \frac{y}{k} = a^{mx}$$

Since both sides of the equation are equal, their logs are also equal.

$$\therefore \ln\left(\frac{y}{k}\right) = \ln(a^{mx})$$

Use the logarithm law $\boxed{\log_a x^k \log_a x}$ to give:

$$\ln\left(\frac{y}{k}\right) = mx \ln a$$

Use the logarithm law $\boxed{\log_a\left(\frac{x}{y}\right) = \log_a x - \log_a y}$ to give:

$$\ln y \quad \ln k - mx \ln a$$

$$\therefore \quad \frac{\ln y - \ln k}{m \ln a} = x$$

> **Note:** The x in the logarithmic law box is **not** the same x as in the general model.

Activity 3.5E

1 a Rearrange the model for the growth of E. coli, $N = 2^{0.05t}$, to express t in terms of N, where N is the number of cells and t is the time elapsed in minutes.

   b Use your rearranged model to predict after how many minutes the number of E. coli bacteria will be 1000.

   c Use your graphic calculator to draw a graph of the model and use the trace function to check that your prediction is (approximately) correct.

2 a In **Activity 3.4C** you used the function $A = 36.45 \times 1.081^t$ to model the area, A thousand square kilometres, occupied by cane toads in Australia, t years after 1939.
      Show that this can be rearranged to give:

$$t = \frac{\log_{10} A - \log_{10} 36.45}{\log_{10} 1.081}$$

   b Use the rearranged model to find in what year it predicts cane toads will occupy approximately half of the area of Australia, i.e. $A = 3800$. Check that your answer is correct using your graph.

3 a In **Activity 3.2D**, you used the function $y = 1000 \times 1.029^{-t}$ to model the radioactive decay of 1 kilogram of plutonium, where y gives the number of grams of plutonium remaining after t thousand years.
      Use natural logarithms to rearrange the function into the form '$t = ...$'.

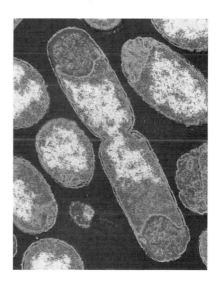

b Use your rearranged function to find the half-life of plutonium, i.e. how long it takes for y to equal 500. Check that your answer is correct using your graph.

4 The temperature above room temperature, $\theta°C$, of a cooling cup of coffee after t minutes can be modelled using $\theta = 75 \times 1.02^{-t}$.

   a Find the temperature of the coffee above room temperature when $t = 0$

   b Rearrange the function so that it is in the form '$t = \ldots$'.

5 The pH value of an aqueous solution is defined as $pH = -\log_{10}[H_3O^+]$, where H_3O^+ is the molar hydronium-ion concentration.

Solutions with a pH value of less than 7 are acidic, whilst those with a pH value above 7 are alkaline. Solutions with a pH of 7 are neutral.

   a Find the pH value of milk with $[H_3O^+] = 4 \times 10^{-7}$.

   b Find the molar hydronium-ion concentration of neutral solutions.

   c Explain how the equation $pH = -\log_{10}[H_3O^+]$ can be rearranged to give $H_3O^+ = 10^{-pH}$.

   d The pH scale runs from 0 to 14. Use a graphic calculator to draw a graph showing how the molar hydronium-ion concentration varies over the full range of this pH scale. Use this to confirm that the pH function maps small positive values that are relatively close together on the hydronium-ion concentration into numbers that are further apart on the pH axis.

6 The decibel scale was first used to compare different sound intensities. The intensity level, N decibels, of sound is given by $N = 10\log_{10}\left(\dfrac{I}{10^{-16}}\right)$, where I watts per cm^2 is the power of the sound.

   a Find the intensity level in decibels of normal conversation with a power of 10^{-10} watts per cm^2.

   b A whisper has an intensity level of 20 dB. What is its power in watts per cm^2?

   c A jet aircraft taking off has an intensity of 140 dB. What is its power in watts per cm^2?

   d Use your graphic calculator to plot a graph of N against I. Make a sketch of your graph giving some indication of scale on each axis.

> **Practice Sheets:**
> **Solving exponential equations**
> **Laws of logarithms**

3.6 Revision summary

Functions

A function is a rule or formula that gives just one output for every input.

Examples:
$y = x^2$ is a function.
(Every value of x gives just one value of y.)

$y = \pm\sqrt{x}$ is not a function.
(There are two values of y for every value of x.)
Restricting this to just the positive root:

$y = \sqrt{x}$ is a function.
(Each value of x now gives just one value of y.)

Inverse functions

The graphs of inverse functions are reflections of each other in the line $y = x$.
$y = x^2$ and $y = \sqrt{x}$ are inverses of each other.

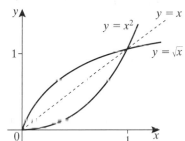

Exponential growth and decay

Exponential growth and decay can be modelled by $y = ka^{mx}$ where k is a positive constant.
When $a > 1$, a positive value of m gives growth and a negative value of m gives decay.
In both growth and decay:

* the rate of change of y with respect to x is proportional to the magnitude of y
* the graph crosses the y axis at $(0, k)$ and the x axis is an asymptote.

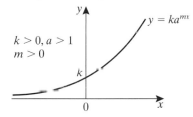

Exponential growth curve

Exponential decay curve

Logarithms

If, $y = a^x$ the exponent x is defined as the logarithm (base a) of y.
i.e. If $y = a^x$, $\log_a y = x$.

The most frequently used bases are 10 and e.

For base e $y = e^x$ gives $\ln y = x$.

For base 10 $y = 10^x$ gives $\log_{10} y = x$.

Laws of logarithms

For any base a:

$\log_a xy = \log_a x + \log_a y$

$\log_a \left(\dfrac{x}{y}\right) = \log_a x - \log_a y$

$\log_a x^k = k \log_a x$

Graphs of $y = \ln x$ and $y = e^x$

$y = e^x$ and $y = \ln x$ are inverse functions.
Their graphs are reflections of each other in the line $y = x$.

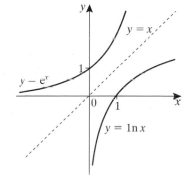

3.7 Preparing for assessment

Your coursework portfolio

There are many situations in which growth or decay occurs and you may be able to use an exponential function to model these – examples you have met in this chapter include:

- savings
- radioactive decay
- bacteria growth
- cooling liquid
- population growth.

You could investigate such a situation as part of the work you do towards your coursework portfolio.

Collect some data for a situation in which growth or decay occurs. You could either:

- carry out an experiment of your own, e.g. measure the temperature of a cooling liquid, or
- find some data from a source such as the Internet.

Plot a graph of the data. You may like to do this using a spreadsheet or other graph plotting software on a computer.

Find an exponential function that models the data.

Show your mathematical working to find the parameters of the model, e.g. if using $P = P_0 e^{kt}$, show how you find P_0 and k. Explain your methods clearly.

Consider how effective your exponential function is as a model. You could think about:

- the point where the line intersects the vertical axis – this is often a significant point
- what happens in the long term – what does the model predict? Is this likely?

You could now:

- Consider using a linear function for part(s) of the data. If you are only interested in part(s) of the data set would a linear model(s) be useful? If so, find the linear function. Look back at **Section 1.7** for some advice.
  Remember to make clear why you are justified in using a linear model for part of the data and why it cannot be used to model the whole data set.
- Consider how errors in your data (perhaps due to rounding) may affect the function you found, e.g. could you find different values of the parameters P_0 and k in your model $P = P_0 e^{kt}$, or different values of the parameters m and c in your model $P = mt + c$?

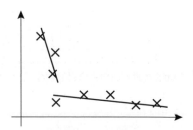

Linear function used to model parts of data set

Use your exponential model to solve a problem, e.g. find when a population reaches a certain value, i.e. find t_1 when $P = P_1$ ($P_1 = P_0e^{kt}$). Solve this algebraically showing your working clearly and using correct notation. Compare this with the solution you can find using your graph. Comment on the accuracy of the two methods.

Practice exam questions

Data

(UoM1) **Fruit flies**

Fruit flies are often found in homes, restaurants and supermarkets when fruit is allowed to rot and ferment. They are quick to breed, the entire life cycle from egg to adult being completed in about a week. This short life cycle and the fact that fruit flies have large chromosomes make them ideal subjects for genetic studies.

In an experiment to find out how quickly a colony of fruit flies will grow, twenty fruit flies were put into a container with food. The number of flies in the container were counted on the ninth day and then after every three days. The results are given in the table below.

Day, t	Number of flies, N
0	20
9	35
12	95
15	138
18	205
21	355
24	429

Resource Sheet 3.7

Question

1 An exponential function of the form $N = N_0e^{kt}$ is used to model the fruit fly data, where N represents the number of fruit flies in the container after t days. The constants N_0 and k are chosen so that the model gives the same number of flies as the original data for $t = 0$ and $t = 12$.

   a   i Explain why $N_0 = 20$.

     ii Show that $k = 0.13$ gives $N = 95$ correct to the nearest whole number when $t = 12$.

b Use the model $N = 20e^{0.13t}$ to complete a copy of the table below. Give values of N correct to the nearest whole number.

Day t	Number of flies, N	
	Data	**Model**
0	20	20
9	35	64
12	95	95
15	138	
18	205	
21	355	
24	429	

c The graph below shows the actual number of fruit flies plotted against time. On a copy of this graph, plot the points in the table you completed in part **b** to show the model $N = 20e^{0.13t}$.

Resource Sheet 3.7Q1

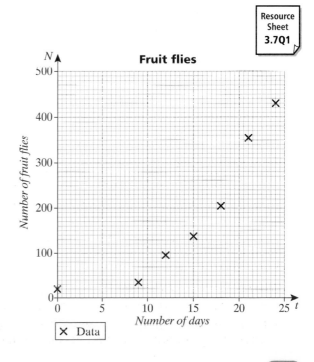

d Find the error in the number of fruit flies predicted by the model after 9 days expressed as a percentage of the actual number of fruit flies.

e **i** Calculate the number of fruit flies predicted by the model after twelve weeks.

    ii Give a reason why the number of fruit flies is unlikely to reach this value.

f An alternative form for the model is $N = 20a^t$.
Find the value of a that gives the same value of N as the original data when $t = 12$.

(UoM4) **Time of death**

2 When a corpse is found in a hotel room at 8 am its temperature is 28°C. Two hours later its temperature has fallen to 26°C.

The pathologist knows that normal body temperature for a living person is approximately 37°C. She also knows that the central heating in the hotel room maintains a constant room temperature of 20°C.

The pathologist can use a function of the form $\theta = 8e^{-kt} + 20$ to model the temperature of the corpse, $\theta°C$, at time t hours after the body was discovered.

a Show that the model $\theta = 8e^{-kt} + 20$ gives a temperature of 28°C for the body when it is first discovered.

b **i** Show that the function $\theta = 8e^{-kt} + 20$ can be rearranged to give $t = -\dfrac{1}{k}\ln\left(\dfrac{\theta - 20}{8}\right)$.

    ii Use the temperature after 2 hours to calculate a value for k.

    iii By calculating the value of t when $\theta = 37$, estimate the time of death. Give your answer to the nearest hour.

c **i** What does the model $\theta = 8e^{-kt} + 20$ suggest will happen to θ as $t \to \infty$?

    ii Explain briefly how this relates to the real situation.

    iii Sketch a graph of the model $\theta = 8e^{-kt} + 20$.

d Compare the accuracy of this method of estimating the time of death when a corpse is discovered soon after death with the case when the time of discovery is much later.

4 Simulations

Have you ever been on a motorway journey when the traffic has come to a halt (or almost) before picking up speed after some time with no apparent reason. It may have been that earlier there was an accident. Although the vehicles involved may have been cleared by the time you get to the scene a bunching effect still occurs in the traffic flow.

On some stretches of motorway, such as on the M25 as it passes Heathrow Airport, there are variable speed limits. This is in an attempt to ensure that as many vehicles as possible can travel past any particular point. How do traffic engineers investigate such situations?

In supermarkets, shops, banks, building societies and post offices, managers must decide how many counters to open at different times of the day. How are decisions like these made?

The answers to questions like these may be found by developing a **mathematical model** that involves **simulating** the situation.

In this chapter you will learn how to do this for relatively simple situations in which you use **random numbers** to **simulate events** such as the behaviour of people coming to join a queue.

☞ As with other models a simulation involves a number of stages that are highlighted by this diagram.

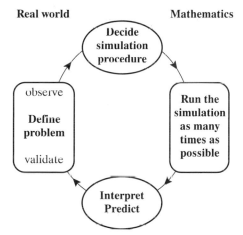

You might like to consider the stages of mathematical modelling as you work through problems.

4.1 Random events

Key web search terms

random events

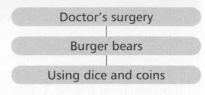

Doctor's surgery

Burger bears

Using dice and coins

Doctor's surgery

Why is it that, although you have an appointment to see your doctor, you always seem to end up sitting in the waiting room for a long time before you are seen?

The simple answer is that when the receptionist makes appointments for patients no one knows how long each will need with the doctor. Each patient is therefore allocated the same amount of consultation time. How long, then, should the receptionist allocate?

Developing a simple model

Assume that each patient is allocated a 10 minute appointment, and spends 5, 10 or 15 minutes with the doctor with equal likelihood. The table shows what might happen at the start of a typical morning.

You could set up a **simulation** of what might happen.

What you don't know is whether each patient will spend 5, 10 or 15 minutes with the doctor – you can use random events to help you decide this.

When a coin is tossed, you know you will get a head or tail, but not which. This is a **random** event – you cannot predict the outcome with certainty.

Similarly, when you throw a dice you know that the result will be 1, 2, 3, 4, 5 or 6, but you don't know for any particular throw what value you will get, or what sequence of values will occur if you throw the dice a number of times.

Random events such as throwing a coin or a dice can be used to simulate unpredictability in situations involving random behaviour, such as the length of time each patient spends with the doctor.

In the simple model of the doctor's waiting room, assume that it is equally likely that a patient will spend 5, 10 or 15 minutes with the doctor. You can therefore use a dice to decide how long each patient takes. Assume that if you throw a

- 1 or 2 the patient takes 5 minutes
- 3 or 4 the patient takes 10 minutes
- 5 or 6 the patient takes 15 minutes.

	Patient 1	Patient 2	Patient 3
Appointment time	9:00	9:10	9:20
Time starts consultation	9:00	9:10	9:25
Length of time with doctor	5	15	10
Time ends consultation	9:05	9:25	9:35
No. of minutes waiting	0	0	5

Discussion point

In what other ways can you assign the random numbers obtained by throwing a dice to represent waiting times of 5, 10 and 15 minutes?

Activity 4.1A

1   Simulate the doctor's waiting room. Use a dice as suggested above to decide how long each patient spends with the doctor.
    Draw up a table to record your results.
    Assume:
    • a patient is allocated 10 minutes with the doctor
    • patients always arrive at the exact time allocated for their appointments
    • the first appointment is at 09:00
    • the last appointment is at 11:00.

2   a How long does the final patient wait to see the doctor?

    b What is the average waiting time for a patient?

3   Compare results with other students in your group. Discuss your findings.

Discussion point
Why is this simulation unrealistic and how may it be improved? (You will have the opportunity to improve the simulation later in this chapter.)

Burger bears

A burger bar gives away a free teddy bear with each child's meal bought. There are three bears in the set: Daddy bear, Mummy bear and Baby bear. How many meals do you need to buy to get the full set?

Obviously, this will depend on how likely you are to get each particular bear with a meal. Assume for the moment that you are equally likely to get any of the three bears. You can simulate this situation using a dice with two numbers representing each bear. One possibility is:

Daddy: 6 and 5   Mummy: 4 and 3   Baby: 2 and 1

You can carry out the simulation by throwing the dice until you have got all three bears.

For example, a sequence of throws on the dice could give:
3 (M)   4 (M)   1 (B)   4 (M)   2 (B)   3 (M)   4 (M)   2 (B)
4 (M)   2 (B)   6 (D)

In this run it took 11 meals before the full set of bears was collected. Is this what you would have expected?

Activity 4.1Ba

Why is it better to carry out the simulation a number of times, rather than just once? Try this simulation yourself. Pool results with other students in your group. On average, how many meals does it take?

What happens if it is not equally likely that you will get each of the three bears. Suppose, for example, half of the bears given away by the burger bar are Daddy bears, one third are Mummy bears and only the remaining sixth are Baby bears. You need to change the rules for the simulation to reflect the new probability of getting each bear. One way of doing this is to assign dice numbers to each bear as follows.

Daddy: 6, 5, 4   Mummy: 3, 2   Baby: 1

Discussion point

In what other ways can you assign the random numbers obtained by throwing a dice to represent getting Daddy, Mummy and Baby bears?

Activity 4.1Bb

Resource Sheet 4.1Bb

Try this simulation a number of times and pool your results with other students. On average, how many meals does it take now to collect the set of bears?

Discussion point

If the burger bar wants to maximise their sales should the bears be distributed in meals?

Using dice and coins

Activity 4.1C

Choose to do one or two of the following questions.

1   **Babies**
    A couple plan to continue having children until they have at least one boy and at least one girl. They want to know how large their family is likely to be if they do this.
    a   **i**   Describe how you could use a coin to simulate this situation.
        ii   Run the simulation a number of times.
        iii   What do you think is the most likely number of children the couple will have?
        iv   Estimate how likely they are to have a family of 5 or more children.

    b   Repeat, using a dice instead of a coin.
        How well do your results agree?

2   **Tennis**
    Alex and Bob are well-matched tennis players who are equally likely to win any game of tennis they play against each other. During the deciding set in a match, Alex and Bob play until one player has won at least six games and has at least two games more than the other player.

    a   Describe how you could use a coin to simulate the results in the deciding set.

    b   Run the simulation a number of times.

    c   What do you think is the most likely number of games played during the deciding set?

3 Collecting the set

a A confectioner produces chocolate eggs for Easter. Each egg contains one of six different, but equally likely, toy chicks.

   i Design a simulation of this situation using a dice.

   ii Run the simulation a number of times to find out how many eggs you are likely to need to buy to collect the full set of chicks.

b The confectioner also sells a different type of egg, each containing a toy rabbit. There are four different rabbits: Flopsy, Mopsy, Cotton-tail and Peter.

The confectioner has put equal numbers of Flopsy and Mopsy rabbits into eggs and equal numbers of Cotton-tail and Peter rabbits, but there are twice as many Flopsy and Mopsy rabbits as Cotton-tail and Peter rabbits.

   i Design a simulation of this situation using a dice.

   ii Run the simulation a number of times to find out how many eggs you are likely to need to buy to obtain the full set of rabbits.

4.2 Random numbers

Key web search terms

(pseudo) random numbers
random number tables
discrete probability distributions

Random numbers from
calculators and spreadsheets

Customer service

Selection of simulations

Random numbers from calculators and spreadsheets

It is often impractical to use a coin or dice to simulate random events. A more convenient and efficient way is to use **random numbers** from your graphic calculator or spreadsheet or a table of random numbers specially compiled for such use.

The **random number generator** in a graphic calculator is usually listed in the probability menu as RAN# or RAND#. Find this for your calculator and generate some random numbers. Look carefully at the numbers produced. You may be surprised to find that consecutive digits are often the same and that sometimes a particular digit does not appear for quite a while. When people try to produce a list of random digits themselves, they avoid such events and usually produce a series of digits that are not random. Many embezzlers, ballot-riggers and disreputable scientists have been caught out by doing this.

So how does a calculator or computer generate random numbers? The short answer is that they can't. They actually generate *pseudo-random numbers* rather than genuine random numbers. The sequence of digits is usually produced using a 'linear congruential' method. (You don't need to know anything about this method.) This takes an initial value, called a **seed**, and then uses a formula to generate the sequence. The formula used generates sequences of digits that mirror true random numbers in terms of frequency distribution, repeating digits and absence of patterns. Such sequences are found to work well in simulations of **random processes**.

Examples of random numbers from a graphic calculator:
0.809 498 353 8
0.566 634 137 3
0.399 888 287 6
0.019 293 493 9

The function INT( ) finds the integer part of a number.
For example: int(2.718) = 2

$0.\dot{9}$ is the mathematical notation for 0.999 999 9...

Activity 4.2A

1   a   Investigate, using your calculator, whether the commands in the table below give the indicated outcomes.

Command	Outcome
RAND	Random number between 0 and $0.\dot{9}$
10*RAND	Random number between 0 and $9.\dot{9}$
INT(10*RAND)	Random integer 0, 1, 2, 3, 4, 5, 6, 7, 8, 9
INT(10*RAND)+1	Random integer 1, 2, 3, 4, 5, 6, 7, 8, 9, 10
INT(6*RAND)+1	Random integer 1, 2, 3, 4, 5, 6
INT(2*RAND)	Random integer 0, 1

Discussion point

Using the random command on your calculator gives a random number between 0 and $0.\dot{9}$. Can you therefore explain why each of the other commands work?

b Complete a copy of the table below, filling in either the missing command or the missing outcome.

Command	Outcome
5*RAND	
	Random integer 1, 2, 3, 4, 5
	Random integer 0, 1, 2, 3
4*INT(2*RAND)	
	Random integer −1, 0, 1

2 a Investigate, using a spreadsheet, whether the commands in the table below give the indicated outcomes.

Command	Outcome
=5*RAND( )	Random number between 0 and 4.9̇
=INT(10*RAND( ))	Random integer 0, 1, 2, 3, 4, 5, 6, 7, 8, 9
=INT(5*RAND( ))+1	Random integer, 1, 2, 3, 4, 5
=INT(2*RAND( ))	Random integer 0, 1

b Complete a copy of the table below, filling in either the missing command or the missing outcome.

Command	Outcome
=10*RAND( )	
=INT(10*RAND( ))	
=INT(10*RAND( ))+1	
=INT(3*RAND( ))−1	
	Random integer 0, 1, 2, 3, 4
	Random integer 1, 2, 3, 4, 5
	Random integer 1 to 100 (inclusive)

Checkpoint

Check that you are correct by using the command in your calculator.

Discussion point

Can you explain why each of the other commands works if =RAND( ) gives a random number between 0 and 0.9̇?

Checkpoint

Check that you are correct by using the command in a spreadsheet.

As an alternative to using random numbers generated by a calculator or computer, you can use random number tables. These are basically just lists of random digits that are arranged in a convenient format and printed.

Here is a small table of random digits organised in pairs. You can read across in rows or up and down in columns.

If you wish, you can use these instead of the numbers generated by your calculator or computer when completing activities throughout this chapter. For example:

- If you want only the random digits 1 to 5 inclusive, you can use the table by ignoring the digits 0, 6, 7, 8 and 9
- If you want a random number in a different range, you can use the commands shown in the tables above.
- If you want to repeat a simulation a number of times using the random digits in this table, or any other table of random digits, don't forget that you will need to start at a different point in the table on each occasion so that you do not use the same numbers as last time.

17	25	89	40	46
43	79	71	35	33
60	17	35	49	31
19	21	93	36	25
54	13	21	11	52
38	70	33	21	27
22	81	53	79	96
49	24	09	35	42
27	37	45	11	74
04	29	52	82	87

Customer service

Incoming phone calls to a customer service desk are put into a queue until the operator is free to answer them. Suppose that on average there is one incoming call every two minutes. Obviously each customer's query will take a different length of time for the operator to deal with. You could carry out a survey to see what happens in reality. Suppose researchers have done this and summarised the results of their analysis in the table.

Query time (min)	Probability
1	0.2
2	0.4
3	0.2
4	0.1
5	0.1

You can use random numbers to simulate the situation and explore the way in which a queue forms and how the waiting times increase for customers.

You must assign random digits to each of the query times according to their probabilities. Use ten equally likely random digits (0, 1, 2, 3, 4, 5, 6, 7, 8, 9) which each occur with probability 0.1. So each query time that has a probability of 0.1 is assigned one random digit, each query time that has a probability of 0.2 is assigned two random digits and the query time that has a probability of 0.4 is assigned four random digits. One way of doing this is given in the table. You can use a calculator to generate random digits 0 to 9 inclusive.

Query time (min)	Probability	Random digits
1	0.2	0, 1
2	0.4	2, 3, 4, 5
3	0.2	6, 7
4	0.1	8
5	0.1	9

This is of course a simplification of results: the times are given to the nearest minute and the probabilities simplified, so that you end up with a **discrete probability distribution**.

A discrete probability distribution is when probabilities are assigned to discrete rather than continuous values. In this case, the values are 1, 2, 3, 4 or 5 minutes. No other values are allowed.

Activity 4.2B

1   Use the table below to simulate the 'customer calls'.
    In this simulation, it has been assumed that:
    • there is a new call every two minutes starting from 09:00
    • calls are answered in the order in which they are made
    • a query starts as soon as the operator is free to answer
    • there is only one operator answering calls.

    Random digits have been entered into the third column for you. Use the first 15 entries to make sure you understand how the table is being used.

Call number	Call time	Random number	Time taken (minutes)	Query start	Query end	Wait time	Queue length at time of call
1	09:00	8	4	09:00	09:04	0	0
2	09:02	9	5	09:04	09:09	2	1
3	09:04	6	3	09:09	09:12	5	1
4	09:06	9	5	09:12	09:17	6	2
5	09:08	4	2	09:17	09:19	9	3
6	09:10	7	3	09:19	09:22	9	3
7	09:12	0	1	09:22	09:23	10	3
8	09:14	4	2	09:23	09:25	9	4
9	09:16	7	3	09:25	09:28	9	5
10	09:18	6	3	09:28	09:31	10	5
11	09:20	4	2	09:31	09:33	11	5
12	09:22	6	3	09:33	09:36	11	5
13	09:24	9	5	09:36	09:41	12	5
14	09:26	8	4	09:41	09:45	15	5
15	09:28	3	2	09:45	09:47	17	5
16	09:30	1					
17	09:32	7					
18	09:34	6					
19	09:36	5					
20	09:38	6					
21	09:40	6					
22	09:42	0					
23	09:44	4					
24	09:46	1					
25	09:48	2					
26	09:50	3					
27	09:52	9					
28	09:54	9					
29	09:56	4					
30	09:58	8					

Note
'Queue length' is the number of people waiting to have their query answered. The person being served is not counted.

2 Write a brief description of what your simulation tells you. You should refer to:
   • the time that callers wait for their call to be answered;
   • the length of the queue.

3 Make a list of improvements that you could make to the simulation. To do this, refer carefully to the assumptions that have been made when drawing up the simulation.

4 Draw a graph to illustrate the growth of:
   • the number of calls in the queue;
   • waiting times.

5 If you have time, re-run the simulation using your own random numbers.

Nuffield resource
UoM4 Starter 'Queues'

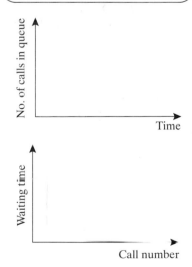

Selection of simulations

Discussion point
What would you advise the customer service desk manager as a result of carrying out this simulation?

The following activity has a number of situations which you can simulate. You should complete at least two of these.

Activity 4.2C

Excel Activity

1 **Car park**

When coming out of a multi-storey car park, cars join a queue to pay what they owe at a kiosk.

In observations taken during the busiest half-hour at the end of the working day, cars were found to join the queue at an average rate of two per minute. Assume therefore that a car joins the queue every half a minute.

The time taken at the pay kiosk varied according to the probability distribution in the table.

Pay time (min)	Probability
0.5	0.5
1	0.3
1.5	0.1
2	0.1

a Describe how you would assign randomly generated integers 0–9 inclusive to simulate this distribution.

b Use a simulation like the one in **Activity 4.2B** to show how the queue of cars and waiting times might increase over half an hour. Record your results in a table.

c Draw a graph of
  i queue length against time
  ii waiting time against time.

d Run the simulation several times (or pool your results with other students) then write a brief summary of what your simulation indicates.

e Describe briefly the ways in which the simulation may not reflect reality and suggest how it could be improved.

2 **Bulbs**

The colour of flowers grown from a type of bulb are white, blue or pink in the ratio $2 : 3 : 5$.

a Describe how you could assign randomly generated integers 0–9 inclusive to simulate the distribution of flower colours.

b Simulate the combination of colours in pots containing 5 bulbs. Run the simulation and complete tables for 20 pots.

c Pool results with other students if possible, then write a summary of what your results show.

Table for one pot:

		Pot No. 1
Bulb 1	Rnd	
	Col	
Bulb 2	Rnd	
	Col	
Bulb 3	Rnd	
	Col	
Bulb 4	Rnd	
	Col	
Bulb 5	Rnd	
	Col	

3 Doctor's surgery revisited

Appointments at a doctor's surgery are made every 5 minutes from 9 am until 10 am.

The receptionist has carried out a survey to find how long each patient spends with the doctor. He finds that patients take 5, 6, 7, 8 or 9 minutes with the probabilities shown in the table.

a Design a simulation that can be used to investigate the way a queue develops in the waiting room, explaining any assumptions you make.

b Run the simulation, recording results in a table.

c Draw a graph of
  i queue length against arrival time
  ii waiting time against arrival time.

d If possible run the simulation several times or pool your results with other students.
  Write a brief summary of what the simulation indicates.

e Describe any ways in which the simulation may not reflect reality and suggest how it could be improved.

Time (min)	Probability
5	0.1
6	0.3
7	0.3
8	0.2
9	0.1

Patient No.	1	2	3
Arrival time	9:00	9:05	9:10
Rnd No.			
Length of consultation			
Time start			
Time end			
Waiting time			
Queue length at arrival			

4 Mixed biscuits

A baker makes up packs containing 10 biscuits taken at random from a large mixed supply that consists of 40% plain biscuits, 20% chocolate biscuits and 40% creams.

a Describe how you could use random numbers to simulate the combinations of biscuits in a pack.

b Draw up a table in which results for 20 packs can be displayed.

c Run the simulation to complete the table and pool your results with other students if possible.

d Use the results to estimate the proportion of packs that contain
  i no chocolate biscuits
  ii more than 5 plain biscuits.

5 Light bulbs

In a quality control test it is found that one out of every five light bulbs produced on a production line is faulty. The light bulbs have been sent out to shops in packs of three. Before recalling consignments that have been sent out, the manufacturer wants to estimate how likely it is that customers will buy a pack containing one or more faulty bulbs.

a Design a simulation that could be used by the manufacturer.

b Run the simulation a number of times and summarise your results.

c What advice would you give to the manufacturer?

4.3 More complex simulations

Key web search terms

queue simulations
radioactive decay

Simulations may need to be more complex than those you explored in **Section 4.2** to reflect reality more closely. For example, it is sometimes necessary to use more than one set of random numbers to simulate different variables in the real situation.

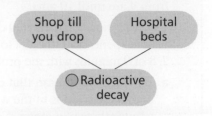

Discussion points

What simplifying assumptions have been made in setting up this model of the real situation?

How could these assumptions affect the results of the simulation?

Shop till you drop

A department store is busy over the lunchtime period between 12:30 and 1:30. Queues at tills often grow to unacceptable lengths. A survey shows the following distribution of the time between the arrivals of consecutive customers at a till.

Time between arrivals (min)	0.5	1.0	1.5	2.0
Probability	0.2	0.3	0.4	0.1

The time taken for an assistant to serve a customer varies with the probabilities given below.

Serve time (min)	0.5	1.0	1.5	2.0	2.5	3.0
Probability	0.1	0.2	0.2	0.2	0.2	0.1

You can simulate each of these events by assigning random integers to each event.

Time between arrivals (min)	0.5	1.0	1.5	2.0
Probability	0.2	0.3	0.4	0.1
Random numbers	0, 1	2, 3, 4	5, 6, 7, 8	9

Serve time (min)	0.5	1.0	1.5	2.0	2.5	3.0
Probability	0.1	0.2	0.2	0.2	0.2	0.1
Random numbers	0	1, 2	3, 4	5, 6	7, 8	9

The table on the following page shows one way of organising a simulation of this situation. Random numbers have been entered into two columns to simulate the variability in the time between the arrival of consecutive customers and the time taken to serve them.

Customer No.	Random No.	Time between arrivals (mins)	Arrival time	Time service starts	Random No.	Time to serve (mins)	Time service ends	Waiting time (mins)	Queue length at arrival
1			12:30	12:30	2	1	12:31	0	0
2	3	1	12:31	12:31	5	2	12:33	0	0
3	2	1	12:32	12:33	7	2.5	$12:35\frac{1}{2}$	1	1
4	4	1	12:33	$12:35\frac{1}{2}$	6	2	$12:37\frac{1}{2}$	2.5	1
5	7	1.5	$12:34\frac{1}{2}$	$12:37\frac{1}{2}$	6	2	$12:39\frac{1}{2}$	3	2
6	4	1	$12:35\frac{1}{2}$	$12:39\frac{1}{2}$	9	3	$12:42\frac{1}{2}$	4	2
7	1	0.5	12:36	$12:42\frac{1}{2}$	6	2	$12:44\frac{1}{2}$	6.5	3
8	5	1.5	$12:37\frac{1}{2}$	$12:44\frac{1}{2}$	6	2	$12:46\frac{1}{2}$	7	3
9	1	0.5	12:38	$12:46\frac{1}{2}$	4	1.5	12:48	8.5	4
10	9	2	12:40	12:48	4	1.5	$12:49\frac{1}{2}$	8	4
11	9	2	12:42	$12:49\frac{1}{2}$	2	1	$12:50\frac{1}{2}$	7.5	5
12	6	1.5	$12:43\frac{1}{2}$	$12:50\frac{1}{2}$	5	2	$12:52\frac{1}{2}$	7	5
13	2	1	$12:44\frac{1}{2}$	$12:52\frac{1}{2}$	9	3	$12:55\frac{1}{2}$	8	5
14	6	1.5	12:46	$12:55\frac{1}{2}$	8	2.5	12:58	9.5	6
15	5	1.5	$12:47\frac{1}{2}$	12:58	7	2.5	$13:00\frac{1}{2}$	10.5	6

Activity 4.3Aa

Excel Activity

1 Check that you understand how the table for the simulation has been used for the first 15 customers, then complete the simulation for customers arriving up to 2 o'clock.

2 How long is the queue at the end of the lunchtime period? Is the waiting time acceptable?

3 The manager of the store argues that this simulation is not realistic. Make a list of points she might make in her argument and for each give a response as to how you might improve the simulation to meet her concerns.

The manager of the department store decides that she should use an extra assistant (and till) at this service point, during the lunchtime period. She expects that at least one of the two assistants will have some free time and wants to use this time to get some paperwork done. She says that customers should always be served by assistant A if possible, with assistant B only serving a customer when A is already busy, and otherwise assistant B should get on with the paperwork.

The table below shows one way in which a simulation can be carried out to see how well this plan is likely to work in practice. An extra column shows which of the two assistants serves each customer.

Customer No.	Random No.	Time between customers (mins)	Arrival time	Served by	Time service starts	Random No.	Time to serve (mins)	Time service ends	Waiting time (mins)	Queue length at arrival
1			12:30	A	12:30	0	0.5	$12{:}30\frac{1}{2}$	0	0
2	1	0.5	$12{:}30\frac{1}{2}$	A	$12{:}30\frac{1}{2}$	7	2.5	12:33	0	0
3	9	2	$12{:}32\frac{1}{2}$	B	$12{:}32\frac{1}{2}$	8	2.5	12:35	0	0
4	3	1	$12{:}33\frac{1}{2}$	A	$12{:}33\frac{1}{2}$	6	2	$12{:}35\frac{1}{2}$	0	0
5	5	1.5	12:35	B	12:35	0	0.5	$12{:}35\frac{1}{2}$	0	0
6	4	1	12:36	A	12:36	7	2.5	$12{:}38\frac{1}{2}$	0	0
7	5	1.5	$12{:}37\frac{1}{2}$	B	$12{:}37\frac{1}{2}$	6	2	$12{:}39\frac{1}{2}$	0	0
8	8	1.5	12:39	A	12:39	6	2	12:41	0	0
9	1	0.5	$12{:}39\frac{1}{2}$	B	$12{:}39\frac{1}{2}$	0	0.5	12:40	0	0
10	7	1.5	12:41	A	12:41	3	1.5	$12{:}42\frac{1}{2}$	0	0

Activity 4.3Ab

Excel Activity

1 Continue the table to show what would happen during the lunchtime period 12 till 2 o'clock in this simulation.

2 Write a brief report for the manager of the store explaining how well her plan will work. In this you should report on
   • how long customers are likely to have to wait
   • how much time assistant B will have to carry out paperwork
   • any limitations you think the simulation has.

Discussion points

In what ways are the results of the simulation unrealistic?

Why has this occurred?

What can the manager do to improve the simulation?

Hospital beds

A hospital manager wants to identify the minimum number of beds that should be available in a children's ward.

After a paediatrician examines the children each morning, the number of children who are allowed to go home varies according to the following distribution:

Number of children leaving	0	1	2	3	4
Probability	0.12	0.30	0.34	0.19	0.05

New patients arrive during the day according to this distribution:

Number of children arriving	0	1	2	3
Probability	0.05	0.40	0.30	0.25

If a bed is not immediately available in the ward, patients are kept on beds in the corridor, but this is not felt to be acceptable.

Assigning random numbers

The manager carries out a simulation. It is assumed that the number of children in the ward at the start of the simulation is 10.

Because some of the probabilities are given to 2 decimal places it is necessary to use pairs of random digits, rather than single random digits for this simulation. Since there are 100 possible pairs (from 00 to 99), each pair has a probability of 0.01.

So, for example, the twelve pairs of random numbers from 00 to 11 have a total probability of 0.12 and can be used to represent the event that no children leave the hospital on a particular day. The probability of one child leaving is 0.3. This is represented by the next 30 pairs of random digits, i.e. from 12 to 41. Continuing to assign pairs of random digits to the number of children gives the tables alongside.

No. of children leaving	Probability	Random numbers (inclusive)
0	0.12	00–11
1	0.30	12–41
2	0.34	42–75
3	0.19	76–94
4	0.05	95–99

No. of children arriving	Probability	Random numbers (inclusive)
0	0.05	00–04
1	0.40	05–44
2	0.30	45–74
3	0.25	75–99

Activity 4.3B

Resource Sheet 4.3B

1   Check that you understand how the table below can be used to simulate the use of beds in the children's ward, then complete the table for one month of 30 days.

Excel Activity

Day No.	No. of patients at start of day	Random No.	No. arriving	Random No.	No. leaving	No. of patients at end of day
0	10	25	1	53	2	9
1	9	06	1	20	1	9
2	9	80	3	10	0	12
3	12	75	3	02	0	15
4	15	65	2	86	3	14
5	14	35	1	56	2	13
6	13	42	1	96	4	10
7	10	94	3	72	2	11
8	11	28	1	34	1	11
9	11	61	2	84	3	10
10	10	22	1	85	3	8

2   Draw a graph that shows the number of patients at the end of each day as predicted by your simulation.

3   What advice would you offer to the hospital manager about the number of beds that should be available on this children's ward?

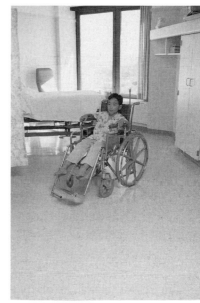

Radioactive decay

You have used exponential functions in **Chapter 3** to model the decay of radioactive substances. This physical phenomenon has many useful applications including generating electrical power, in medical treatments and in dating ancient organic materials. Here you will use simulations to see how a random event – the decay of an atomic nucleus – can be modelled by a function.

The nuclei of the atoms of most substances are stable. However, the nuclei of some atoms are unstable. When these unstable nuclei break up radiation is given out – the process is know as radioactive decay.

The probability that any one unstable atomic nucleus will decay in a given time interval is fixed. You can therefore use random numbers in a simulation to see what will happen to a 'large' number of unstable nuclei.

Activity 4.3C

Excel Activity

1 a Suppose that in each time interval each radioactive nucleus has a probability of one-sixth of decaying. Throwing a six on a dice can represent a nucleus decaying. Imagine that each person in your group is one nucleus of a radioactive substance. If each one of you throws a dice who decays in the first time interval?

Fill in a copy of this table (for up to 20 time intervals) to record who decays in each time interval – remember once you have decayed you have changed state and no longer need to throw the dice (1 indicates that the nucleus still exists, 0 that it has decayed). You may wish to consider more nuclei and perhaps do the simulation a number of times and record outcomes in one table.

Nucleus No.	Time (intervals)										
	0	1	2	3	4	5	6	7	8	9	10
1	1										
2	1										
3	1										
4	1										
5	1										

b Draw a graph showing how many nuclei still exist after each time interval.

2 Now suppose that in each time interval nuclei of a different radioactive substance have an equal chance of decaying or remaining.

a Describe how you can use a random number generated by your graphic calculator or spreadsheet (i.e. between 0 and 0.9) to determine what happens to each nucleus during each time interval.

b Fill in a table to show what will happen to 5 such nuclei over 10 time intervals.

You can use the function $N = N_0 e^{-kt}$ to simulate radioactive decay where N represents the number of radioactive atoms that remain after time t, N_0 is the original number of radioactive atoms and k is a constant.

k is related to the probability that an atom remains after each time interval. For example, in the simulation you have just investigated, theoretically after just one time interval there will be only half of the nuclei remaining.

The time taken for the mass of a radioactive substance to decay to half of its original amount is called its **half-life**.

$$\frac{N_0}{2} = N_0 e^{-k \times 1}$$

$$\tfrac{1}{2} = e^{-k}$$

$\therefore \qquad \ln \tfrac{1}{2} = -k$

$\therefore \qquad k = 0.693$

So, $\qquad N = 50 e^{-0.693t}$

In the simulation where the probability of decay is 0.1, after one time interval there will theoretically be 0.9 of the nuclei remaining; after two time intervals there will be 0.9 of 0.9 of the original nuclei remaining; after n time intervals there will be 0.9^n of the original nuclei remaining.

There will therefore be $\tfrac{1}{2}$ of the original number of nuclei remaining when $0.9^n = \tfrac{1}{2}$, so $n = \dfrac{\ln \tfrac{1}{2}}{\ln 0.9}$.

In this case,

$$\frac{N_0}{2} = N_0 e^{-k \times n}$$

$$\ln \tfrac{1}{2} = -k \times n$$

$$\ln \tfrac{1}{2} = -k \times \frac{\ln \tfrac{1}{2}}{\ln 0.9}$$

$$k = \ln 0.9$$

$$k = 0.1054$$

So N expressed in terms of t is $N = 50 e^{-0.1054t}$.

Note: There is an opportunity to work on the details of the maths on this page in the exercise at the end of the chapter. Just take it on trust for now if it seems hard.

Activity 4.3D

Resource Sheet 4.3D

The following questions provide comprehension practice based on the mathematics explained above.

1 Explain why the text says 'in the simulation you have just investigated, theoretically after just one time interval there will be only half of the nuclei remaining'.

2 It is stated that $\tfrac{1}{2} = e^{-k}$, therefore $\ln \tfrac{1}{2} = -k$.
   Explain why this is true.

3 In the simulation, where the probability of decay is 0.1, the half-life is found by solving $0.9^n = \tfrac{1}{2}$.
   Explain why this is the case.

4 Show carefully the steps taken to get from
   $$0.9^n = \tfrac{1}{2} \text{ to } n = \frac{\ln \tfrac{1}{2}}{\ln 0.9}.$$

5 In a further simulation, the probability of decay can be taken to be 0.2.
   For this case, show that $k = 0.223$, so that the decay can be modelled by the function $N = 50 e^{-kt}$, where N is the number of nuclei that remain after time t.

4.4 Revision summary

You can use mathematical simulations to model real-life situations that involve random discrete events, such as customers arriving to queue to be served in a bank, so that you can analyse what is likely to happen and perhaps suggest how to improve things.

Random events

Coins, dice or random numbers can be used to generate random data, such as how long a person waits, or what gift is in a cereal packet.

If you know, for example, that half the packets of a particular cereal will have a plastic Harry Potter, a third will have a Ron and one sixth will have a Hermione, you can simulate this by using a dice. Throwing 1, 2 or 3 can be used to represent a packet with Harry in, 4 and 5 to represent Ron and 6 to represent Hermione.

You can estimate how many packets you need to buy to get the set of three (or to get any other combination you want) by throwing the dice and noting how many throws are needed to achieve the outcome you want. You must run the simulation many times, or pool results, to get a good estimate of the number of packets needed.

Using random numbers

Coins and dice are suitable for small-scale simulations. For a bigger study, random numbers from tables, a calculator or computer can be used in a similar way.

You need to find out the probability of the events you are interested in occurring – for example, if the probability that a patient takes 5 minutes to see the doctor is one-fifth, the probability of taking 15 minutes is also one-fifth and the probability of taking 10-minute is three-fifths – you can then allocate random numbers accordingly. For simple fractions like fifths, you can allocate single-digit random numbers easily to each waiting time; for probabilities expressed in, say, percentages, you may need to use two-digit random numbers.

As before, the simulation is run to estimate what may happen in real life. It should be run many times to obtain good results.

Complex simulations

Many real-life situations involve more than one set of random events – for example, the number of customers who arrive during each 5-minute interval and the length of time it takes for them to be served.

To simulate such situations you can use two or more sets of random numbers (from simple generators such as coins and dice, or using calculators or computers). Each set of numbers will be allocated in proportion to the likely distribution of events in each aspect of the situation being considered.

4.5 Preparing for assessment

Practice exam question

(UoM4) **Enrolment**

During college enrolment, prospective students are given appointments at 10-minute intervals so that they can meet the lecturer who will teach their course.

A secretary finds that students take 9, 10, 11, 12 or 13 minutes with lecturers with the following probabilities:

Time (min)	9	10	11	12	13
Probability	0.1	0.4	0.3	0.1	0.1

a   Describe how you would use randomly generated integers to simulate the times students spend with a lecturer.

b   The table below shows the appointments made for an afternoon session with a particular lecturer. Complete a copy of the table using the random numbers given in the third column to generate times as you described in part **a**. Assume that all students arrive exactly on time for their appointments.

c   According to the simulation, what is the most common time students have to wait for their appointments?

d   According to the simulation, what is the most common time that students spend having an interview?

e   Identify two ways in which the simulation may not reflect reality and explain briefly how it could be improved.

Resource Sheet 4.5	Student number	Arrival time	Random number	Time taken (mins)	Start time	End time	Waiting time (mins)
	1	14:00	3				
	2	14:10	1				
	3	14:20	9				
	4	14:30	1				
	5	14:40	0				
	6	14:50	6				
	7	15:00	5				
	8	15:10	0				
	9	15:20	8				
	10	15:30	5				
	11	15:40	3				
	12	15:50	8				

MAKING SENSE OF PLANETARY MOTION

Have you ever looked up at the stars at night and wondered about how they appear to move? The problem of explaining the motion of the Earth and stars at night is a challenge that has exercised many of the best minds over thousands of years.

It was only after the mid-1500s that it was accepted by most people that the sun was at the centre of the Solar System. Copernicus proposed that each planet moves around the Sun on a circular path and has a different period of revolution, with this being greater the further the planet is from the Sun. This model of the Solar System seemed to allow the astronomers of the time to account for their observations and measurements. However, not all planetary motion that was observed from the Earth could be accounted for and eventually Johannes Kepler proposed a modified model.

Figure 1: The 1543 publication of Copernicus' evidence that the Earth revolves around the Sun changed Western thought

Kepler's model is described by three laws (published in *The Harmony of the World* in 1619):

Law 1   The orbit of each planet is an ellipse with the Sun located at one focus of the ellipse.

Law 2   In equal time–intervals a line from a planet to the Sun will sweep out equal areas.

Law 3   The squares of the periods of revolution of any two planets about the Sun are proportional to the cubes of their mean distances from the Sun.

This third law can be expressed as $T^2 \propto R^3$, where R is the mean distance of the planet from the Sun and T is the period of revolution (the time for one complete revolution around the Sun).

So, $R^3 = KT^2$ or $\dfrac{R^3}{T^2} = K$ where K is often known as Kepler's constant.

A planet moves on an elliptical orbit in such a way that a line from the Sun (at a focus of the ellipse) to the planet will sweep out equal areas in equal time intervals.

Planetary paths are elliptical but more nearly circular than in this exaggerated diagram.

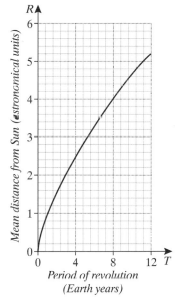

Figure 2: Graph showing $R = T^{\frac{2}{3}}$

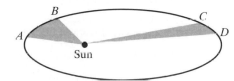

Figure 3: The planet travels from A to B in the same time as it travels from C to D. The shaded areas are equal

If R is measured in astronomical units and T is measured in Earth years, then, when $R = 1$, $T = 1$ so $K = 1$. One astronomical unit is the mean distance of the Earth from the Sun.

The table shows data for the planets of the Solar System with the final column in the table showing values of K calculated using this data.

Planet	Mean distance from the Sun, R (AU)	Orbit Period, T (Earth years)	K
Mercury	0.3871	0.2408	1.0000
Venus	0.7233	0.6152	1.0000
Earth	1.0000	1.0000	1.0000
Mars	1.5237	1.8808	0.9999
Jupiter	5.2034	11.8626	1.0011
Saturn	9.5371	29.4750	0.9985
Uranus	19.1913	84.0168	1.0013
Neptune	30.0690	164.7913	1.0011
Pluto	39.4817	247.9207	1.0013

Figure 4: Data for each of the planets of the Solar System

Moon	Orbital mean radius (km)	Period (days)
Io	422 000	1.77
Europa	671 300	3.55
Ganymede	1 071 000	7.15
Calisto	1 883 000	16.69

Figure 5: Data for Jupiter's four largest moons

The four largest of Jupiter's sixteen moons were discovered by Galileo in 1610. His discovery of these moons allowed Galileo to show, for the first time, that not everything in the sky goes around the Earth.

For these moons $\dfrac{R^3}{T^2} = K$, but the value of K

is different from that for the planets in orbit around the Sun.

Figure 6: The moons of Jupiter

Kepler's laws were based purely on investigations of observable data – it fell to Isaac Newton to answer the question 'Why?' in his famous *Principia* published in 1687.

In *Book Three* of the *Principia*, Newton showed that Kepler's laws applied to the moons of Jupiter and the five moons of Saturn. His masterstroke was to introduce the idea of Universal Gravitation that accounts for:

• the planets staying in their orbits about the Sun
• satellites (moons) of planets staying in their orbits
• the acceleration of falling objects
• objects staying on the Earth
• the ocean's tides.

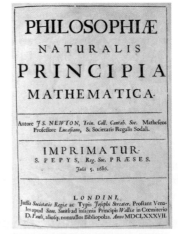

Figure 7: First edition of Sir Isaac Newton's cornerstone work in traditional physics

This fundamental Law of Universal Gravitation may be written mathematically as

$$F = G\frac{Mm}{R^2}$$

where F is the force of attraction between two objects of masses M and m, that are a distance R apart. G is a constant (the Universal Gravitation constant) the value of which depends on the units of F, M, m and R.

Newton was not the only mathematician to think that each planet had a force inversely proportional to the square of its distance from the Sun acting on it but he was the first to show, using his Law of Universal Gravitation, that Kepler's third law must be true.

His argument relies on the second of his three laws of dynamics which can be summarised as $a = \dfrac{F}{m}$. This law gives a, the acceleration of a body of mass, m, that results from an applied force, F.

Newton had also realised that when something travels at a constant speed, v, on a circular path, it is nevertheless accelerating because the direction of its travel is changing. The magnitude of this acceleration is given by $a = \dfrac{v^2}{r}$.

Assuming that the path of a planet is circular, its speed, v, is given by $v = \dfrac{2\pi R}{T}$ where T is the time taken by the planet to make one complete revolution of radius R.

Equating Newton's Law of Universal Gravitation and his second law for a satellite of mass, m, in orbit about a body of mass, M gives:

$$\frac{GMm}{R^2} = m \times \frac{4\pi^2 R}{T^2}$$

leading to $\dfrac{R^3}{T^2} = \dfrac{GM}{4\pi^2}$.

So this is consistent with Kepler's third law where $\dfrac{GM}{4\pi^2} = K$.

(If G is in units of $\text{Nm}^2\,\text{kg}^{-2}$ and M is measured in kg then K is given in units of $\text{m}^3\,\text{s}^{-2}$).

Figure 8: Newton realised that the motion of the Moon around the Earth was subject to the same type of force – gravitation – as an apple falling from a tree.

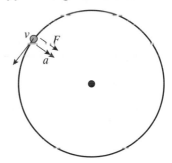

Figure 9: A body moving at constant speed, v, on a circular path (such as the Moon orbiting the Earth) has an acceleration towards the centre of the motion. This is caused by a force, F, that acts towards the centre of the motion

Average Moon to Earth distance: 384 000 km

Period of Moon in orbit about the Earth: 27.3 days

Mass of Sun: 1.989×10^{30} kg

Mass of Earth: 5.97×10^{24} kg

Universal Gravitation constant: $G = 6.67 \times 10^{-11}$ $\text{Nm}^2\,\text{kg}^{-2}$

Figure 10: Additional planetary data

Comprehension Questions

1   The graph in **Figure 2** shows $R = T^{\frac{2}{3}}$, where R can be taken to
    be the distance of a planet from the Sun measured in
    astronomical units and T can be taken to be its period of
    revolution measured in Earth years.
    a   On a copy of this graph, indicate the point representing
        the Earth.
    b   Explain clearly how you identified this point.

2   Kepler's third law can be expressed as $R^3 = KT^2$.
    For the planets in orbit around the Sun, with R measured in
    astronomical units and T measured in Earth years, $K = 1$.
    For different systems, such as moons in orbit about one of
    the planets, $K \neq 1$. On a copy of **Figure 2** sketch graphs of
    $R^3 = KT^2$ for which
    i $K < 1$ ii $K > 1$.
    Indicate clearly which graph is which.

3   Assume that the Earth orbits the Sun on a path of mean
    radius 1.50×10^{11} metres and that one Earth year is 365 days.
    a   Use data from **Figure 4** to calculate
        i the mean radius of the orbit of Mercury, giving your
           answer in kilometres
        ii the period of Mercury giving your answer in days.
    b   Find a value for Kepler's constant for planets in the Solar
        System in units of kilometre³/day².

4   a   Use the data in **Figure 5** for Jupiter's moon Io (with
        mean radius in kilometres and period in days) to
        calculate Kepler's constant, K_j (in units of
        kilometre³/day²) for the system of Jupiter's moons.
    b   Use K_j to calculate the period of another of Jupiter's
        moons, Leda which you may assume to have an orbit of
        mean radius 1.11×10^7 km.

5   Explain why the mean speed, v, of a planet with a circular
    orbit of radius R and period T is given by $v = \dfrac{2\pi R}{T}$.

6   Show clearly the working that leads to the equation
    $\dfrac{GMm}{R^2} = m \times \dfrac{4\pi^2 R}{T^2}$ by equating Newton's Law of Universal
    Gravitation and his second law.

7   The article states that for a satellite of mass m, in orbit about
    a body of mass M, $\dfrac{GM}{4\pi^2} = K$. Use this, together with data
    from the article, to find K for the Moon in orbit about the
    Earth.

COMPOUNDING YOUR INTEREST

The finances of borrowing and investing money are not new. For example, an early reference to lending money can be found on a monument (a stele) from the reign of the Babylonian king Hammurabi who reigned between 1792 and 1750 BC. This monument sets out a code of laws, one of which restricts the rate of interest that could be charged by money lenders for silver to 20% and for grain to $33\frac{1}{3}$%. This stele of Hammurabi can now be viewed in the Louvre in Paris.

A clay tablet from the time asks the question, "How long will it take a sum of money to double if invested at an annual rate of 20% compounded annually?"

Before answering this particular question you need to have a clear understanding of what is meant by 'compounding' interest. Consider the case where you invest £100 and gain 20% interest per year. At the end of the first year you will have the original £100 plus 20% of £100,

i.e. $£100\left(1 + \dfrac{20}{100}\right)$.

At the end of the second year, assuming that you leave all of your money invested, you will gain interest on this amount of money. So in total you will have

$£100\left(1 + \dfrac{20}{100}\right) \times \left(1 + \dfrac{20}{100}\right) = £100\left(1 + \dfrac{20}{100}\right)^2$.

At the end of t years your original investment of £100 will have become $£A$, where

$A = 100\left(1 + \dfrac{20}{100}\right)^t$ (Equation 1)

The table in Figure 2 shows, to the nearest pound, how an investment of £100 will grow each year; this is illustrated in the graph of Figure 3. From this you can see that an initial investment of £100 doubles in value somewhere during year 4.

The question now is, 'How far through year 4 is the investment worth twice its initial value?'

Figure 1: The stele of Hammurabi, now in the Louvre, Paris

No. of years invested	Value
0	£100
1	£120
2	£144
3	£173
4	£207
5	£249
6	£299

Figure 2: The growth of £100 invested at an interest rate of 20% paid annually

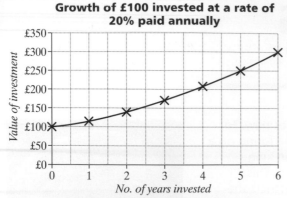

Figure 3: Graph showing the growth of £100 invested at an interest rate of 20% paid annually

Figure 4: Linear growth assumed during year 4

The method used by the Babylonians to calculate when the investment is worth twice the initial value involved supposing that during year 4 the growth is linear[1]. The problem now becomes one of finding the value that divides the interval from 3 to 4 in the same ratio as 200 divides the interval from 173 to 207 (see Figure 4).

[1]This method is often known as *linear interpolation*.

Therefore you need to solve $\dfrac{x-3}{1} = \dfrac{27}{34}$, (Equation 2)

where x is the number of years after which the investment has doubled.

This gives $x = 3 + \dfrac{27}{34} = 3.79$, which means that the target of doubling the value of the investment will be reached 290 days into the year.

The development of logarithms by Napier in the early 1600s allows the exact solution of the problem of when the investment will be doubled. The original problem was to find t where

$$£200 = £100\left(1 + \frac{20}{100}\right)^t,$$

i.e. $2 = 1.2^t$. (Equation 3)

Using logarithms gives $t = \dfrac{\log 2}{\log 1.2} = 3.80.$ (Equation 4)

So you can see the approximate method used by the Babylonians almost 4000 years before the development of logarithms was relatively accurate.

Many banks and building societies calculate interest more than once a year – they certainly charge interest more frequently than once a year if you borrow money from them!

Consider the case of a bank that instead of giving 20% interest once a year gives 10% interest twice a year. At the end of the first year £100 would be worth $£100\left(1 + \dfrac{10}{100}\right)^2$. This gives £121 opposed to £120 when 20% interest is added just once at the end of the year. In other words giving an interest payment of 10% twice a year is the same as giving an interest payment of 21% just once in the year – this is the *annual equivalent rate*, often denoted by AER. You can see by comparing the tables in Figures 2 and 5 that your investment doubles more quickly with this more frequent compounding.

End of year	Value
0	£100
1	£121
2	£146
3	£177
4	£214
5	£259
6	£314
7	£380
8	£459

Figure 5: The growth of £100 invested at an interest rate of 10% paid twice per year

In general, at the end of t years your investment would now be worth $£100\left(1 + \dfrac{10}{100}\right)^{2t}$.

What would be the effect of compounding the interest more frequently? For example, if you received 5% interest every 3 months, at the end of the first year your investment would be worth $£100\left(1 + \dfrac{5}{100}\right)^{4}$.

If you receive interest of $\dfrac{20}{n}$%, n times per year, then at the end of

the first year your investment would be worth $£100\left(1 + \dfrac{20}{100n}\right)^{n}$,

and at the end of t years it would be worth $£100\left(1 + \dfrac{20}{100n}\right)^{nt}$

What does the term $\left(1 + \dfrac{20}{100n}\right)^{n}$ become as n gets large?

For example, what if $n = 365$, representing the case of adding interest each day?

In this case $\left(1 + \dfrac{20}{100 \times 365}\right)^{365} = 1.22$ (to 3 s.f.)   (Equation 5)

What if the interest were added each hour, or each minute, or...?

The table in Figure 6 shows what happens as $n \to \infty$. You can use the final column headed $\left(1 + \dfrac{20}{100n}\right)^{n}$ to find the AER when

interest of $\dfrac{20}{n}$% is compounded n times per year.

You can see that there seems little point in compounding interest many times per year, as even when it is compounded only twelve times per year the AER is 1.22 (to 3 s.f.).

It is interesting to consider the special (if unusual) case of investing £1 at 100% interest for one year with interest compounded over n intervals. In this case your investment

becomes $I = \left(1 + \dfrac{1}{n}\right)^{n}$.   (Equation 6)

The table in Figure 7 shows what happens to I as n increases. You will recognise that in this case as $n \to \infty$, $I \to e$.

	n	$\left(1 + \dfrac{20}{100n}\right)^{n}$
no interest	0	1
annually	1	1.2
twice a year	2	1.21
4 times a year	4	1.215 506 25
monthly	12	1.219 391 085
daily	365	1.221 335 858
hourly	8760	1.221 399 97
by the minute	525 600	1.221 402 712

Figure 6: Investigating $\left(1 + \dfrac{20}{100n}\right)^{n}$ as $n \to \infty$

	n	$\left(1 + \dfrac{1}{n}\right)^{n}$
annually	1	2
twice a year	2	2.25
4 times a year	4	2.441 406 25
monthly	12	2.613 035 29
daily	365	2.714 567 482
hourly	8760	2.718 126 692
by the minute	525 600	2.718 279 243

Figure 7: Investigating $\left(1 + \dfrac{1}{n}\right)^{n}$ as $n \to \infty$

Comprehension Questions

1   Explain how an investment of £100 at 20% interest per year is $£100\left(1 + \dfrac{20}{100}\right)^{2}$ at the end of two years.

2   The article suggests that the Babylonians calculated when £100 invested at 20% compounded annually was worth twice the initial amount by assuming linear growth over the fourth year. It states, 'The problem now becomes one of finding the value that divides the interval from 3 to 4 in the same ratio as 200 divides the interval from 173 to 207'. Explain clearly how this gives rise to solving the equation $\dfrac{x - 3}{1} = \dfrac{27}{34}$.   (Equation 2)

3   Explain clearly how using logarithms allows you to proceed from **Equation 3** to **Equation 4** in the article.

4   Use logarithms to find out after how long, to the nearest day, an investment of £P at 20% interest per annum compounded just once per year trebles in value.

5   Sketch a graph, showing clearly the general trend of how the value of an investment increases as the years pass. On this graph, draw curves indicating the situation if the rate of interest is **i** higher **ii** lower. Indicate clearly which curve is which.

6   Explain how $I = \left(1 + \dfrac{1}{n}\right)^n$ (Equation 6) gives the value, £I, of an investment of £1 at 100% interest for one year with interest compounded n times per year.

7   The article suggests that the methods of linear interpolation used by the Babylonians gives 3.79 years as the length of time taken for an investment at 20% interest per annum to double. Solving the problem using logarithms gives an answer of 3.80 years. Both answers have been given correct to three significant figures. In terms of days, hours and minutes, what is the difference between these two answers? Assume that there are 365 days in a year.

BIORHYTHMS

Many events in nature are cyclical – consider, for example, the rise and fall of the ocean's tides or the times of the rising and setting sun. It is not surprising then that some people claim that human behaviour may be influenced by distinct cycles. This has led to the 'theory of biorhythms' in which it is claimed that physical, emotional and intellectual **cycles** influence our behaviour. There is no scientific basis for this 'theory', but, although (like astrology) it is without any foundation, it does allow us to attempt to explain the inexplicable and therefore has its supporters.

The idea of the 'theory' is to allow you to predict what kind of day you will have. At the moment of birth all cycles are set to zero. At any day in your life you are then able to calculate where you are in each cycle. The physical cycle has a period of 23 days, the emotional cycle has a period of 28 days and the intellectual cycle a period of 33 days.

The 'theory' was first suggested by a German, Wilhelm Fliess. He was particularly taken with the idea that every integer can be expressed as the sum (or difference) of integer multiples of the numbers 23 and 28 (the periods of the physical and emotional cycles).
This can be expressed algebraically as $n = a \times 23 + b \times 28$. For example: $5 = -1 \times 23 + 1 \times 28$ and $10 = -2 \times 23 + 2 \times 28$.
(In fact **any** two numbers that have no factors in common can be used in this way, so the numbers 23 and 28 are not special in this respect.

Figure 1 shows the emotional cycle over the first 60 days – just over two complete cycles. This can be modelled by the function $f(t) = \sin \dfrac{360t°}{28} = \sin \dfrac{90t°}{7}$.

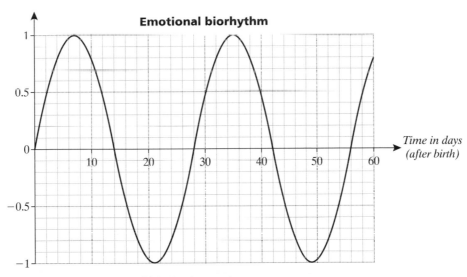

Figure 1: The emotional biorhythm cycle

After the first seven days the cycle reaches its first peak. The cycle is in a positive phase for half of the period and in a negative phase for the other half; it is in ascent for the first and last quarters and in descent in the second and third quarters.

According to the 'theory' it is not just the obvious peaks and troughs that have significance. Days on which cycles cross the zero line, whilst either ascending or descending, are 'critical' days when performance is supposedly very poor and accidents likely to occur. Days on either side of these cross-over days are also assigned as being 'critical'. The worst day of all is the 'triple critical' day when all three cycles are at a 'cross-over' day.

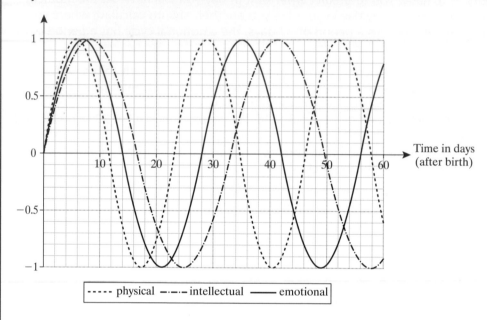

Figure 2: The physical, intellectual and emotional biorhythm cycles

A particularly significant day is when all three cycles are completed at the same time, i.e. when all three are at zero and increasing. When will this happen? Consider just two cycles with 2 and 3 day periods. Figure 3 shows these cycles over 15 days. You can see that the 2 day cycle is zero (and increasing) at 0, 2, 4, 6, 8, 10, 12, 14 … days. The 3 day cycle is zero (and increasing) at 0 (birth), 3, 6, 9, 12, 15 … days. After every 6 days the picture repeats itself.

To find when cycles of different periods repeat themselves you need to find the lowest common multiple of their periods. So for the emotional, physical and intellectual biorhythms you need to find the lowest common multiple of 23, 28 and 33. Expressing each as a product of prime factors gives:

$23 = 23$

$28 = 2 \times 2 \times 7$

$33 = 3 \times 11$

From this you can see that the lowest common multiple is in fact 23 × 28 × 33 = 21 252, since 23, 28 and 33 have no factors in common. So the significant point where the cycles repeat occurs after about 58 years and 66 days – a time of 'rebirth'.

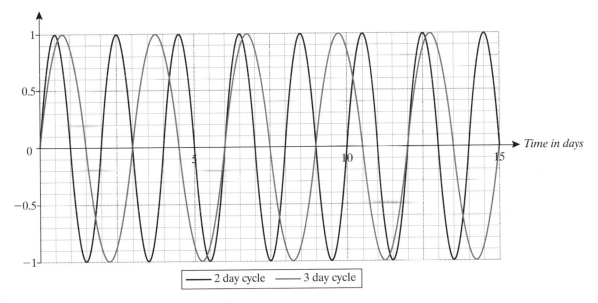

Figure 3: Cycles with 2 and 3 day periods

It has been claimed recently that other cycles also affect our behaviour: the 38 day intuitional cycle, the 43 day aesthetic cycle and the 53 day spiritual cycle.

Comprehension Questions

1 If $n = a \times 23 + b \times 28$, find a and b for
   i $n = 15$
   ii $n = 100$.

2 Approximately how many 'critical' days of the emotional biorhythm cycle are there in a year, assuming that 1 January is a 'critical' day?

3 The 'theory' of biorhythms suggests that the emotional cycle can be modelled by the function $f(t) = \sin \dfrac{90t°}{7}$.
   Explain how this function has a period of 28 days.

4 The function $f(t) = \sin \dfrac{90t°}{7}$ may be considered as a geometric transformation of the function $x(t) = \sin t$. Describe this geometric transformation.

5 a Calculate when the function $f(t) = \sin \dfrac{90t°}{7}$, used to model the emotional cycle, first has a value of $\frac{1}{2}$.
   b Use your answer to part a to deduce when the function $f(t) = \sin \dfrac{90t}{7}$ first has a value of $-\frac{1}{2}$. Explain your reasoning.

6 Find functions $g(t)$ and $h(t)$ that can be used to model
   a the physical cycle with a period of 23 days
   b the intellectual cycle with a period of 33 days.

7 a Express 28 and 38 as products of prime factors.
   b Hence or otherwise, find when the emotional and intuitional cycles first return to zero and are both increasing.

SCALING IN NATURE

Each Russian doll in the picture is a 'scaled' version of the others. The dolls are mathematically *similar* – that is, for each doll the lengths are in the same ratio. For example, the ratio *height : base radius* is the same for each doll.

Figure 1: Russian dolls

If you consider the smallest and largest dolls there is a scale factor of length, *k*. Once you know *k* and one of the dimensions of either of the dolls, you can find the corresponding dimension in the other doll.

For example, for the smallest and largest dolls in the photo, the scale factor of length, *k*, is 4.

The height of the smallest doll is 35 mm so the height of the largest doll is 35 mm × 4 = 140 mm.

The diameter of the base of the largest doll is 64 mm so the diameter of the base of the smallest doll is $\frac{64 \text{ mm}}{4} = 16$ mm.

But what about other physical features of the dolls? For example, what happens to their surface areas in such situations?

You may already know that the surface area of the largest doll is 16 ($=k^2$) times that of the smallest doll, and that the volume of the largest doll is 64 ($=k^3$) times that of the smallest doll.

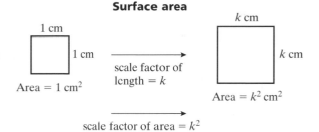

Surface area

Area = 1 cm²
scale factor of length = *k*
Area = k^2 cm²

scale factor of area = k^2

Figure 2: Scaling areas

You can come to understand why by considering how a unit area or unit volume is scaled when the scale factor of length is *k* (see Figures 2 and 3).

Following reasoning based on this understanding, biologists, until recently, argued that the *metabolic rate* of an animal, i.e. how much energy it consumes per second, should be proportional to its mass raised to the power $\frac{2}{3}$. Their reasoning was that if one animal is *k* times as tall as another, then its surface area should be k^2 times as great and its volume, and therefore its mass, should be k^3 times as great (this assumes that the animals have constant and uniform density).

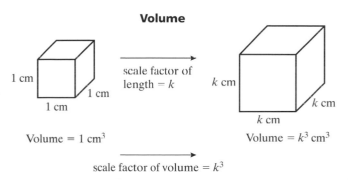

Volume

Volume = 1 cm³
scale factor of length = *k*
Volume = k^3 cm³

scale factor of volume = k^3

Figure 3: Scaling volumes

The total metabolic rate of the animal can be measured by the amount of heat it releases via its surface and so is proportional to k^2 which in turn is proportional to mass$^{\frac{2}{3}} = \sqrt[3]{\text{mass}^2}$.

The specific metabolic rate, that is the metabolic rate per unit mass, is therefore proportional to $\dfrac{1}{\sqrt[3]{\text{mass}}}$.

However, experimental data shows that metabolic rates are more closely proportional to mass raised to the power $\frac{3}{4}$ and specific metabolic rates proportional to $\text{mass}^{-\frac{1}{4}} = \dfrac{1}{\sqrt[4]{\text{mass}}}$.

This experimental 'law' or model was discovered, in 1932, by Max Kleiber, an American veterinary scientist, and is known as Kleiber's Law. His early work looked at land animals but the law is now known to hold true for the smallest micro-organism to the largest animal (the blue whale).

It seems that the 'law of quarter-power' scaling in relation to body mass is everywhere in biology. In other words, many biological variables are found to increase or decrease in proportion to $\text{mass}^{\pm\frac{1}{4}}$ or $\text{mass}^{\pm\frac{3}{4}}$. For example, lifespan is proportional to $\text{mass}^{\frac{1}{4}}$; heart rate is proportional to $\text{mass}^{-\frac{1}{4}}$, and as we have seen, metabolic rate is proportional to $\text{mass}^{\frac{3}{4}}$.

In general, the law of quarter-power scaling can be described by $y = am^b$, where y is a biological variable, m is mass, a is a constant and b is $\pm\frac{1}{4}$ or $\pm\frac{3}{4}$. The graphs in Figure 4 show the general shape of functions of this type.

In most cases the constant a depends on the group of organisms, e.g. birds, mammals or fish. Such power laws have been found throughout the physical world.

How does this law work in reality?

The table in Figure 5 gives the mass, m kg, and gestation period[1], G days, of various animals and the graph in Figure 6 shows G plotted against m.

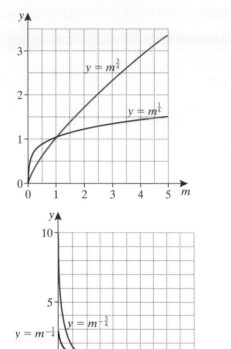

Figure 4: Graphs showing general forms of quarter-power laws

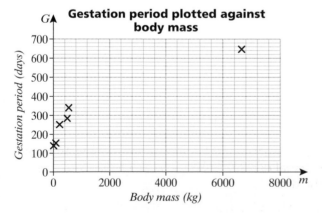

Figure 6: Graph of gestation period plotted against mass

	Body mass, m (kg)	Gestation period, G (days)
African elephant	6654	645
Cow	465	281
Goat	27.66	148
Gorilla	207	252
Horse	521	336
Sheep	55.5	151

Figure 5: Mass and gestation periods for a range of animals

[1]The gestation period is the length of time from fertilisation of an egg to birth.

The data looks as though it could be modelled by a function of the type $G = am^{\frac{1}{4}}$ or $G = am^{\frac{3}{4}}$.

To determine exactly which of these it is, and to find a, you can use a log-log plot.

Since: $G = am^b$
$\log G = \log a + b \log m$

Therefore, if $\log G$ is plotted against $\log m$ for the data and the data follows such a law, the points will lie close to a straight line with gradient b and intercept on the vertical axis $\log a$ (see Figure 7).

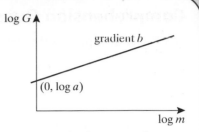

Figure 7: The features of a $\log G$ vs $\log m$ plot

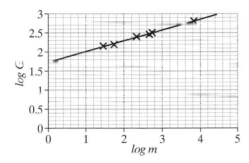

Figure 8: Graph plotting $\log G$ against $\log m$ for the animal data

The data from the table in Figure 5 has been used to plot the graph of log(gestation period) against log(mass) in Figure 8. From this graph a line of best fit can be found: its equation is $\log G = 1.73 + 0.281 \log m$. So you can deduce that $b = 0.28$ and $a = 54$. Therefore the function linking gestation period to mass is given by $G = 54m^{0.28}$.

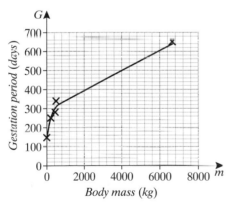

Figure 9: $G = 54\,m^{0.28}$

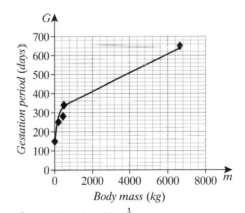

Figure 10: $G = 70\,m^{\frac{1}{4}}$

Figure 9 shows that this function gives values that closely model the actual data. Figure 10 shows that the model $G = 70m^{\frac{1}{4}}$, which is based on an actual quarter-power law, also appears to give values for the gestation period that closely fit the data.

In this case it does appear that a quarter-power law can be used.

Comprehension Questions

1   The widest part of the smallest Russian doll is 72 mm. What is the widest part of the largest Russian doll?

2   If, when using a photocopier, you use the reduction facilities so that in your copy two original A4 sheets fit onto a single A4 sheet (in other words, the area of the copy is half that of the original) what scale factor of length do you use? Explain your reasoning carefully.

3   In the novel *Gulliver's Travels*, Gulliver was 12 times the height of a Lilliputian. The Lilliputians, therefore, decided to feed Gulliver 1728 times as much food as a Lilliputian ate. Explain carefully the reasoning that the Lilliputians will have used to arrived at the figure of 1728.

4   Explain clearly how you can deduce that for an animal its specific metabolic rate is proportional to $\dfrac{1}{\sqrt[3]{\text{mass}}}$ if you assume that its metabolic rate is proportional to its mass raised to the power $\dfrac{2}{3}$.

5   The article suggests that the gestation period. G days, is related to animal mass, m kg, by the law $G = am^b$. It goes on to state that 'Since $G = am^b$, $\log G = \log a + b \log m$'. Show clearly steps that lead from $G = am^b$ to $\log G = \log a + b \log m$.

6   Explain why the gradient of the line in **Figure 7** is b and the intercept on the vertical axis is $\log a$.

7   The article derives the function $G = 54m^{0.28}$, linking the gestation period, G days, to animal mass, m kg.

   a   Find the gestation period predicted by this function of a sheep (mass 55.5 kg).

   b   Compare the value of G predicted by the function $G = 54m^{0.28}$ for this sheep (mass 55.5 kg) with the data given in the table, by expressing the difference as a percentage of the actual gestation period given by the data table in **Figure 5**.

5 Transformation of functions

You may have already met **sine waves** – they are another class of function that are very useful for modelling a wide range of situations where **oscillations** are important.

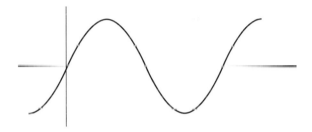

In this chapter you will learn about these functions and how you can consider all sine waves as **transformations** of the basic sine wave. The consideration of how a basic function can be **transformed geometrically** to give a function that you can use to model data is very powerful and you will learn about this here.

Sine waves can be used, for example, to describe how sound travels through the air to your ear. The human ear is incredibly sensitive – it can detect air vibrations that are of the order of a tenth of an atomic diameter. The vibrations can occur in a range of about 20 Hertz to 20 000 Hertz (where 1 Hertz is 1 cycle per second). You may like to consider how you can represent such waves algebraically and graphically.

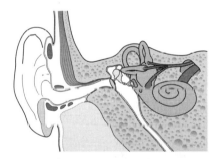

Engineers use sine waves to model all kinds of relationships – particularly in electronics and electrical engineering. Civil engineers also make use of sine waves – there are some spectacular examples of where their analysis (or lack of it) led to problems. For example, when designing the Millennium Footbridge across the River Thames in London engineers did not anticipate the oscillations that would be set up in the structure by people walking across the bridge. An even more disastrous mistake of this type was made with the design of the Tacoma Narrows Bridge in America which in 1940 oscillated itself to destruction.

5.1 Transformations of graphs

Key web search terms

transformations of graphs
stretches of graphs

translations of graphs
reflections of graphs

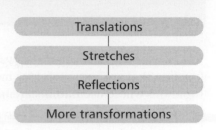

Translations

Stretches

Reflections

More transformations

Translations

You can consider graphs of quite complex functions as transformations of the graphs of the basic functions that you have met so far. For example, the graph of $y = e^x + 5$ is based on the graph of $y = e^x$. To learn about this consider the simpler case below.

You are often charged for services such as those provided by a plumber or electrician by paying a fixed call-out charge plus an hourly rate.

If an electrician charges £15 per hour, you can calculate the total charge, £C, for h hours work using the formula $C = 15h$. This assumes that there is no fixed call-out charge.

If there is an extra call-out charge of £10, $C = 15h + 10$ gives the total cost. If the call-out charge is £20, the total cost is given by $C = 15h + 20$.

The diagram shows graphs of each of these linear functions.

Each time the call-out fee is increased by £10, the graph of the straight line is moved 10 units vertically upwards.

This movement is called a **translation**.

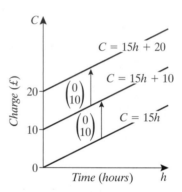

Activity 5.1A

Use a spreadsheet or graphic calculator for **questions 1 to 6**.
If you are using a graphic calculator, set the axes to show values of x from -10 to $+10$ and y from -5 to $+5$.

1 **a** Draw some graphs of curves with equations of the form $y = x^2 + a$ where a is a constant between -5 and 5 ($-5 \leqslant a \leqslant 5$). Make sure you understand the effect of altering a.

   b What translation of $y = x^2$ gives
     i $y = x^2 + 2$ **ii** $y = x^2 - 5$?

2 **a** Draw some graphs of equations of the form $y = x^3 + a$ where a is a constant between -5 and 5.
   Make sure you understand the effect of altering a.

   b What translation of $y = x^3$ gives
     i $y = x^3 + 4$ **ii** $y = x^3 - 3$?

You can use **vectors** to describe translations.

A translation of 10 units upwards is written as $\begin{pmatrix} 0 \\ 10 \end{pmatrix}$.

A translation of 10 units downwards is written as $\begin{pmatrix} 0 \\ -10 \end{pmatrix}$.

A translation of 10 units to the right is $\begin{pmatrix} 10 \\ 0 \end{pmatrix}$.

A translation of 10 units to the left is $\begin{pmatrix} -10 \\ 0 \end{pmatrix}$.

The translation $\begin{pmatrix} 3 \\ -5 \end{pmatrix}$ is a movement of 3 units to the right and 5 units downwards.

3 **a** What translation of $y = \sqrt{x}$ gives
  i $y = \sqrt{x} + 2$
  ii $y = \sqrt{x} - 2$?

   b Use a spreadsheet or graphic calculator to check your answers.

   c In general, what translation of $y = \sqrt{x}$ gives $y = \sqrt{x} + a$?

4 **a** Draw some curves with equations of the form $y = (x + a)^2$ where a is a constant between -5 and 5.
     Make sure you understand the effect of altering a.

   b Describe the transformation that takes $y = x^2$ to
  i $y = (x + 1)^2$
  ii $y = (x - 3)^2$.

5 **a** Draw some curves with equations of the form $y = (x + a)^3$ where a is a constant between -5 and 5.
     Make sure you understand the effect of altering a.

   b Describe the transformation that takes $y = x^3$ to
  i $y = (x + 2)^3$
  ii $y = (x - 4)^3$.

6 **a** What translation of $y = \sqrt{x}$ gives
  i $y = \sqrt{x + 5}$
  ii $y = \sqrt{x - 1}$?

   b Use a spreadsheet or graphic calculator to check your answers.

   c In general, what translation of $y = \sqrt{x}$ gives $y = \sqrt{x + a}$?

7 **a** Use your graphic calculator to draw $y = x^2$ and $y = (x - 3)^2 + 1$.

   b Sketch the result on paper, showing a scale on each axis.

   c What transformation takes $y = x^2$ to $y = (x - 3)^2 + 1$?

   d Predict the translation of $y = x^2$ that will give $y = (x + 4)^2 - 1$.
     Use your graphic calculator to check.

   e By completing the square, write each of the following equations in the form $y = (x + a)^2 + b$ where a and b are positive or negative constants. Use your results to draw a sketch of each.
  i $y = x^2 + 2x$
  ii $y = x^2 - 4x - 1$
  iii $y = x^2 + 5x + 9$
     Check by drawing the curves using a spreadsheet or graphic calculator using the original expressions.

Be careful when entering functions on a graphic calculator or spreadsheet. e.g. in question 6 when using a graphic calculator, enter $y = \sqrt{x + 5}$ as $y = \sqrt{(x + 5)}$. When using a spreadsheet enter the formula '=SQRT($x+5$)'.

The graph of $y = f(x) + a$ is a translation $\begin{pmatrix} 0 \\ a \end{pmatrix}$ of the graph $y = f(x)$.

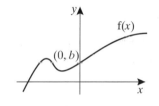

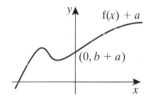

The graph of $y = f(x - a)$ is a translation $\begin{pmatrix} a \\ 0 \end{pmatrix}$ of the graph $y = f(x)$.

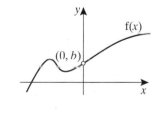

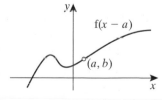

Stretches

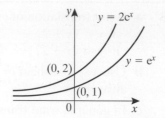

The diagram shows graphs of $y = e^x$ and $y = 2e^x$. Use a spreadsheet or graphic calculator to draw your own graphs of these functions. The curve $y = e^x$ can be transformed into $y = 2e^x$ by a **stretch** in the y direction with scale factor 2.

You can visualise this by imagining that the graph of $y = e^x$ is drawn on elastic material. With the x axis held in place, the material is stretched in the y direction so that the distance of each point from the x axis is doubled.

What do you think the curve $y = 0.5e^x$ looks like?

Use a spreadsheet or graphic calculator to check.

The scale factor of the stretch in the y direction that transforms $y = e^x$ into $y = 0.5e^x$ is 0.5.

This means that it looks as though everything has been squashed in the y direction towards the x axis.

The graph of $y = af(x)$ is a stretch parallel to the y axis with scale factor a of the graph $y = f(x)$. The x axis invariant.

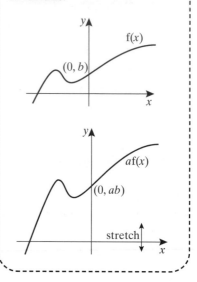

Activity 5.1B

Excel Activity

Use a spreadsheet or graphic calculator throughout.
If you are using a graphic calculator, set your calculator to show x values from -8 to $+8$ and y values from -6 to $+6$.

1 a Draw some curves with equations of the form $y = ax^2$ where a is a constant between 0 and 5.
    Make sure you understand the effect of altering a.

   b Describe how $y = x^2$ can be transformed to give

      i $y = 2x^2$ **ii** $y = \frac{1}{2}x^2$ **iii** $y = 4x^2$.

2 a Draw some curves with equations of the form $y = ax^3$ where a is a constant between 0 and 5.
    Make sure you understand the effect of altering a.

   b Describe how $y = x^3$ can be transformed to give

      i $y = 3x^3$ **ii** $y = 2x^3$ **iii** $y = \frac{1}{5}x^3$.

If we say that the x axis is **invariant** we mean that it remains where it is.

The diagram shows graphs of $y = e^x$ and $y = e^{2x}$. Use a spreadsheet or graphic calculator to draw your own graphs of these functions.

The curve $y = e^x$ can be transformed into $y = e^{2x}$ by a stretch in the x direction with scale factor $\frac{1}{2}$.

What do you think the curve $y = e^{\frac{x}{4}}$ looks like?

Use a spreadsheet or graphic calculator to check.
A stretch with scale factor 4 in the x direction stretches $y = e^x$ into $y = e^{\frac{x}{4}}$.

Discussion point
Which curve is which?
Where do the curves cut the y-axis.

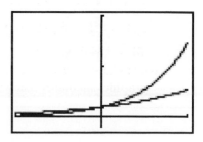

Activity 5.1C

1 a Draw some curves with equations of the form $y = (ax)^2$
   where a is a constant between 0 and 5.
   Make sure you understand the effect of altering a.

  b Describe how $y - x^2$ can be stretched in the x direction
   to give

   i $y = (2x)^2$

   ii $y = (\frac{1}{2}x)^2$

   iii $y = (3x)^2$.

2 a Draw some curves with equations of the form $y = (ax)^3$
   where a is a constant. Make sure you understand the effect
   of altering a.

  b Describe how $y = x^3$ can be transformed to give

   i $y = (2x)^3$

   ii $y = (0.1x)^3$

   iii $y = (\frac{1}{2}x)^3$.

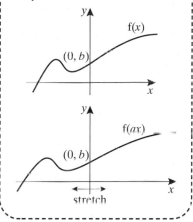

The graph of $y = f(ax)$ is a
stretch of the graph
$y = f(x)$ parallel to the x
axis with scale factor $\frac{1}{a}$ and
the y axis invariant.

Discussion point

In each case what stretch in the y
direction would also give the curve?

Can you explain why?

Reflections

The diagram shows graphs of $y = 2e^x$ and $y = -2e^x$. Use a
spreadsheet or graphic calculator to draw your own graphs of these
functions.

The graphs of the functions are **reflections** of each other in the
x axis.

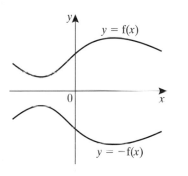

In general, the graph of
$y = -f(x)$ is a reflection
in the x axis of the graph
of $y = f(x)$.

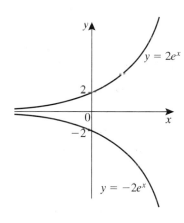

Check this by exploring graphs of functions such as

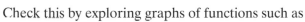

- $y = x^3$ and $y = -x^3$
- $y = \ln x$ and $y = -\ln x$.

The diagram shows graphs of $y = e^x$ and $y = e^{-x}$.

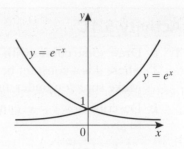

Use a spreadsheet or graphic calculator to draw your own graphs of these functions.

The graphs of the functions are reflections of each other in the y axis.

In general, the graph of $y = f(-x)$ is a reflection in the y axis of the graph of $y = f(x)$.

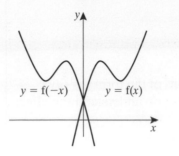

Check this by exploring graphs of functions such as

• $y = (x + 1)^2$ and $y = (-x + 1)^2$

• $y = e^{(x+1)}$ and $y = e^{(-x+1)}$.

Activity 5.1D

Use a spreadsheet or graphic calculator throughout.

1 a What transformation of $y = \sqrt{x}$ gives
  i $y = 2\sqrt{x}$
  ii $y = -\sqrt{x}$
  iii $y = -\frac{1}{2}\sqrt{x}$?

b Use a spreadsheet or graphic calculator to check your answer.

2 a Draw the curves $y = \sqrt{x}$ and $y = \sqrt{-x}$.

b Explain why $y = \sqrt{x}$ only exists for positive values of x and $y = \sqrt{-x}$ only exists for negative values of x.

c What transformation maps $y = \sqrt{x}$ onto $y = \sqrt{-x}$?

More transformations

Activity 5.1E

In this activity use your graphic calculator or a spreadsheet to check your sketches after you have drawn them.

1 a Sketch the curve $y = \dfrac{1}{x}$.

  b Sketch each of the following curves by identifying the transformation that you need to apply to $y = \dfrac{1}{x}$. In each case give a full description of the transformation.

  i $y = \dfrac{1}{x} + 4$ **ii** $y = \dfrac{1}{x + 4}$

  iii $y = \dfrac{4}{x}$ **iv** $y = \dfrac{1}{3x}$

  c Use a spreadsheet or graphic calculator to check each sketch.

2 a Sketch the curve $y = \dfrac{1}{x^2}$.

  b Sketch each of the following curves by identifying the transformation that you need to apply to $y = \dfrac{1}{x^2}$. In each case describe the transformation fully.

  i $y = \dfrac{1}{x^2} - 5$ **ii** $y = \dfrac{1}{(x - 5)^2}$

  iii $y = \dfrac{7}{x^2}$ **iv** $y = \dfrac{1}{(x + 2)^2}$

3 a Sketch the curve $y = \ln x$.

  b Sketch each of the following curves by identifying the transformation that you need to apply to $y = \ln x$. In each case describe the transformation fully.

  i $y = 2 \ln x$ **ii** $y = \ln x - 4$

  iii $y = -\ln x$ **iv** $y = \ln(-x)$

  v $y = \ln(2x)$ **vi** $y = \ln(x - 2)$

  vii $y = \ln x + 3$ **viii** $y = \ln\left(\dfrac{x}{4}\right)$

> Remember when you are asked to **sketch** a graph you need to show the main features, i.e. the shape of the graph and any intercepts with the axes or asymptotes.

Practice sheets:
Function notation

5.2 Combining transformations

In the activities in this section you will investigate how you can use a combination of transformations applied to a basic function to arrive at the complex functions you often need to model real data.

For example when a cup of tea is left to cool its temperature, $T\,°C$, after t hours may be given by $T = 70e^{-0.5t} + 20$.

You can sketch a graph of this function by starting with the basic curve $T = e^t$ and applying the following sequence of transformations. At each stage, the curve is shown sketched (intercepts with the axes, asymptotes and the curve's general shape are shown).

> Video sales
>
> A range of models

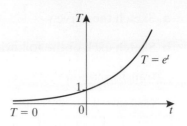

> The t-axis, i.e. $T = 0$ is an asymptote in this case.

- $T = e^t$ reflected in the T axis gives $T = e^{-t}$.

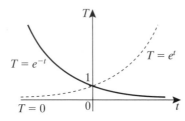

- $T = e^{-t}$ stretched in the t direction with scale factor 2 gives $T = e^{-0.5t}$.

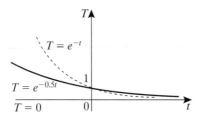

> In a sketch, stretches are sometimes difficult to show. Here, it is clear because the two curves $t = e^{-t}$ and $t = e^{-0.5t}$ are shown together.

- $T = e^{-0.5t}$ stretched in the T direction with scale factor 70 gives $T = 70e^{-0.5t}$.

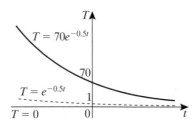

- $T = 70e^{-0.5t}$ translated by $\begin{pmatrix} 0 \\ 20 \end{pmatrix}$ gives $T = 70e^{-0.5t} + 20$.

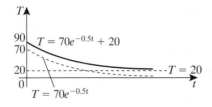

Discussion points

What was the initial temperature of the cup of tea?

What happens to the temperature eventually?

Why?

Video sales

Sales of a video in a shop during the first six weeks after its release are shown in the table and graph below.

Week	Sales
1	49
2	79
3	103
4	124
5	142
6	157

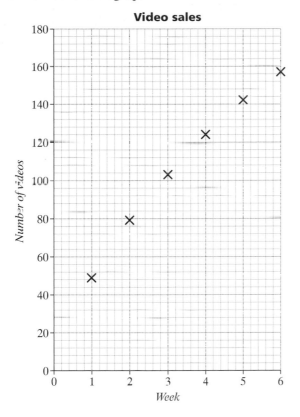

Video sales

Number of videos (vertical axis)

Week (horizontal axis)

Discussion point

What type of functions do you think would give graphs similar in shape to that of the data points?

Activity 5.2A

Excel Activity

These two functions are suggested as models for the video sales data.

Model A $y = 60\sqrt{x}$

Model B $y = 200 - 2(x - 10)^2$

In each case, y gives the number of videos sold in week x.

How well do you think each function models the data?

To help you come to a conclusion, you will consider what each model predicts will happen to sales in the long-term in **questions 1** and **2**.

1   **Model A**

   a Sketch the graph of $y = \sqrt{x}$.

   b A stretch with scale factor 60 in the y direction gives the graph of $y = 60\sqrt{x}$.

There is no need to draw another sketch – just imagine a change of scale on your $y = \sqrt{x}$ sketch. Mark the point $(1, 60)$ to give some idea of the scale of your sketch.

2 Model B

At each stage sketch a new graph after you have applied the transformation.

a Sketch the graph of $y = x^2$.

b Apply the translation $\begin{pmatrix} 10 \\ 0 \end{pmatrix}$ to give $y = (x - 10)^2$.

c Reflect the graph in the x axis to give $y = -(x - 10)^2$.

d Apply a stretch in the y direction with scale factor 2 to give $y = -2(x - 10)^2$.

e Apply the translation $\begin{pmatrix} 0 \\ 200 \end{pmatrix}$ to give $y = 200 - 2(x - 10)^2$.

3 Use your graphic calculator or graph plotting software to draw on one screen, graphs of $y = 60\sqrt{x}$ and $y = 200 - 2(x - 10)^2$, to check your sketches.
On your graph, plot the original data.

4 Which of these functions do you think is likely to be the better model for sales in the future?
Explain your answer.

Discussion point

What factors will affect the sales after 6 weeks? How are these likely to affect the graph?

A range of models

Activity 5.2B

Excel
Activity

Complete at least two of the following questions.

1 Wolves

After wolves were reintroduced into an area of the USA, the number of wolves in the population, N, could be estimated from the model $N = 20e^{0.05t}$ where t is the number of years since the wolves were reintroduced.

a Starting with the basic function $N = e^t$, apply two transformations to give the model $N = 20e^{0.05t}$.
Give a full description of each transformation you use and sketch the curve of the function at each stage. Use your graphic calculator to check you are correct.

b How many wolves were initially reintroduced?

c Use the model to estimate the number of wolves after 20 years.

d What does the model predict will happen in the long run? How realistic is this?

2   Goods delivery

A manufacturer regularly delivers goods a distance of
500 miles from a factory to a distribution centre.
It takes 2 hours to pack the goods onto the lorry and another
2 hours to unpack it. If the lorry travels at an average speed
of v miles per hour, the total time taken for the operation is
t hours, where $t = \dfrac{500}{v} + 4$.

a   Describe two transformations that can be applied to the
basic curve $t = \dfrac{1}{v}$ to give the graph of $t = \dfrac{500}{v} + 4$.

Sketch the graph at each stage.

b   For what values of v do you think it is reasonable to use
this model?

Discussion point

Can you explain how the model can
be derived from the information
given?

3   Depreciation

A car's value, £V, can be modelled by the function
$V = 9600e^{-0.25t} + 300$ where t years is the age of the car.

a   Apply a sequence of transformations to the curve $V = e^t$ to
give the graph of the model. At each stage sketch the curve
and give its equation.

b   What was the value of the car when it was new?

c   What does the model predict will happen to the value in
the long run? How well do you think this reflects what will
happen in the real situation?

4   Javelin throw

Petra Felke set a new world record at Potsdam on
9 September 1988 when she threw a javelin a distance of
80.00 metres. Sports scientists study throws such as this. They
may use a quadratic function to model the path of the javelin.

Consider the quadratic function $y = 20 - \dfrac{1}{80}(x - 40)^2$, where
y metres represents the height of the javelin above the ground
when its horizontal distance from the point from which it was
thrown is x metres.

a   Starting with the basic curve $y = x^2$, apply a sequence of
transformations that will give the graph of
$y = 20 - \dfrac{1}{80}(x - 40)^2$.
At each stage sketch the curve and give its equation.

b   According to the model what is the maximum height above
the ground reached by the javelin?

c   Comment on how realistic the model is. Describe any ways
in which you think it could be improved.

UoM4

UoM4

UoM4

5 Voltage

When an electrical circuit is switched on the voltage, V volts, increases. This can be modelled using the function $V = 12(1 - e^{-0.2t})$ where t milliseconds is the time after the switch is thrown.

a Apply a sequence of transformations to the graph of $V = e^t$ to give the graph of $V = 12(1 - e^{-0.2t})$. At each stage sketch the curve and give its equation.

b What was the voltage initially?

c What will the voltage be in the long run?

UoM4

6 Mail drop

a When mail is dropped from an aircraft its downward speed, v metres per second, during the first 5 metres of its fall can be modelled by the function $v = \sqrt{20h}$ where h metres is the distance fallen ($0 \leqslant h \leqslant 5$).

  i What are the two possible transformations of the graph of $v = \sqrt{h}$ that would give the graph of $v = \sqrt{20h}$?

  ii Sketch the graph $v = \sqrt{20h}$, then use a spreadsheet or graphic calculator to check your sketch.

  iii What would happen to the speed of the pack as h increases beyond 5? Is this likely?

b After the mail has fallen a distance of 5 metres, the parachute opens. A more realistic model for the speed after this occurs is $v = 5(1 + e^{0.1(5-h)})$ ($h \geqslant 5$).

  i Starting with the basic curve $v = e^h$, apply a sequence of transformations that will give the graph of $v = 5(1 + e^{0.1(5-h)})$. At each stage sketch the curve and give its equation. Use a spreadsheet or graphic calculator to check at each stage.

  ii What does this model predict will happen to the speed of the mail in the long run? Is this likely?

c Use the two models to draw a sketch to show how v is predicted to vary with h for a complete drop of 100 metres.

Note when entering $\sqrt{20h}$ in your graphic calculator you will need to use brackets, i.e. $\sqrt{(20h)}$.

Nuffield resources:
UoM1 Assignment 'Wave Flow'
UoM1 Assignment 'Be a Defence Wall'

5.3 Sine waves

Key web search terms

sine waves
unit circle
period (of a wave)
amplitude (of a wave)
angular speed (of a wave)

frequency (of a wave)
phase angle (of a wave)
alternating current
ferris wheel

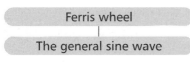

Ferris wheel

The general sine wave

In many real contexts variables follow a cyclic pattern, rising to a maximum then falling to a minimum over and over again. For example, electricity is supplied to households as alternating current (AC). The voltage and current are continually changing and plotting either of these against time gives the distinctive shape of graph known as a sine wave. Other examples of cyclic patterns include variation in temperature, the rise and fall of tides and the times of sunrise and sunset over the year.

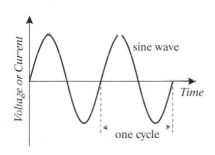

Ferris wheel

Imagine that you are a passenger on a Ferris wheel of radius 10 metres and initially your capsule is at the same height as the centre of the wheel. If the wheel rotates at 1° per second, then t seconds later the wheel will have turned $t°$.

You can use trigonometry to calculate your height above the centre of the wheel as the wheel rotates. For example, the first diagram shows the position of the capsule after one minute, when the ferris wheel has turned 60°.

If the height of the capsule above the centre is h metres then:

$h = 10 \sin t° = 10 \sin 60° \approx 8.7$

So the height is 8.7 metres, correct to 1 d.p.

The second sketch shows your position after 2 minutes, when the Ferris wheel has turned through 120°.

Using symmetry you can see that your height above the centre will again be 8.7 metres.

Check that your calculator gives $h = 10 \sin 120° = 8.7$.

The calculator is programmed to give a value for $\sin \theta$ for any value of the angle θ, including large and negative angles.

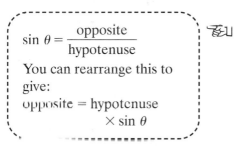

$$\sin \theta = \frac{\text{opposite}}{\text{hypotenuse}}$$

You can rearrange this to give:

$$\text{opposite} = \text{hypotenuse} \times \sin \theta$$

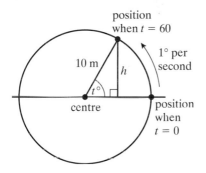

position when $t = 60$

1° per second

10 m

h

$t°$

centre

position when $t = 0$

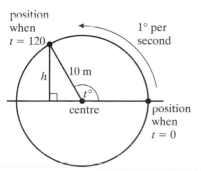

position when $t = 120$

1° per second

h

10 m

$t°$

centre

position when $t = 0$

Now imagine a point P moving round a circle with centre O and radius 1 unit – this is often referred to as a **unit circle**.

If θ is the angle between OP and the x axis, the co-ordinates of $P(x, y)$ are $\cos\theta$ and $\sin\theta$:

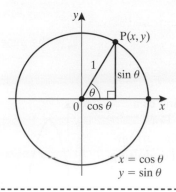

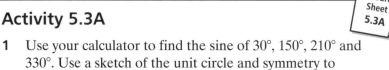

$x = \cos\theta$
$y = \sin\theta$

Values of θ greater than 360° correspond to OP completing more than one rotation.

Negative values of θ correspond to a clockwise rotation of OP.

Discussion point
What happens to the signs of $\sin\theta$ and $\cos\theta$ as θ increases from 0° to 360°?

Activity 5.3A

Resource Sheet 5.3A

1 Use your calculator to find the sine of 30°, 150°, 210° and 330°. Use a sketch of the unit circle and symmetry to explain the results.

2 Predict which of the angles 30°, 150°, 210° and 330° will have equal cosines, then use your calculator to check.

3 Find another set of angles that are related in the same way.

4 Use the relationship $h = 10\sin t°$ to complete a copy of the table giving your height as the Ferris wheel completes a circle.

5 Plot the values from the table to draw a graph of $h = 10\sin t°$.

t (seconds)	h (metres)
0	
15	
30	
45	
60	8.7
75	
90	
105	
120	8.7
135	
150	
165	
180	
195	
210	
225	
240	
255	
270	
285	
300	
315	
330	
345	
360	

Discussion point
Why are values of h negative when t lies between 180 and 360? What is happening on the Ferris wheel?

You should find that your graph is similar in shape to the graph of $y = \sin \theta$ shown here.

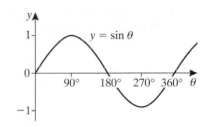

If you extend your graph beyond $t = 360$ the wave is repeated over and over again. The graph has a **period** of 360 (or 360°) because the wheel turns 1° per second.

The graph of $y = \sin \theta$ needs to be stretched by a scale factor of 10 in the y direction to give the graph of $y = 10 \sin \theta$.

The sine waves $y = \sin \theta$ and $y = 10 \sin \theta$ have the same period but different **amplitudes**.

☞ Functions that repeat themselves such as sine waves are **periodic**. The **period** is the distance along the horizontal axis for one complete wave.

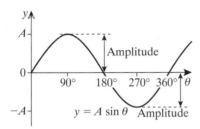

In real situations waves often repeat in time so the period is a time. In other situations the waves may repeat in distance and then the term **wavelength** is used.

The **amplitude** of a sine wave is the distance between maximum or minimum values and the mean value of the wave.

In general, the graph of $y = A \sin \theta$ has amplitude A.

Activity 5.3B

Resource Sheet 5.3B

Now imagine that the Ferris wheel travels at an **angular speed** of 3° per second instead of 1° per second.

If the wheel rotates by 3° per second, the angle it turns through in t seconds is $3t°$ and your height is given by $h = 10 \sin 3t°$.

1   What is the period of this wheel, i.e. how long does the wheel now take to complete a cycle?

2   Use a spreadsheet or graphic calculator to sketch the graph of $h = 10 \sin 3t°$.

3   What is the amplitude of this sine wave?

4   What transformations of $h = \sin t°$ would be required to give the graph of $h = 10 \sin 3t°$?

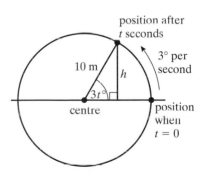

The angle the wheel turns through per unit time interval is its **angular speed**.

The diagram shows a general sine wave $y = A \sin \omega t°$.
ω tells you how many complete waves there are in 360°.
Check this statement by using your graphic calculator to plot graphs
of $y = \sin 2t°$, $y = \sin 3t°$ and $y = \sin \dfrac{t°}{2}$.

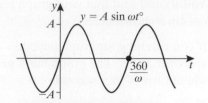

The general sine wave

(Throughout this section, t is measured in degrees.)

In the last section you used the general sine wave $y = A \sin \omega t$. In this case the y value had a mean value of zero. Although this is often the case in real situations that can be modelled by sine functions, there are some situations where the mean value is not zero. For example, the depth of the water at a harbour entrance may vary between 10 metres and 20 metres, so that the mean depth is 15 metres.

A more general form for a sine wave that may not pass through the origin is $y = A \sin(\omega t + \alpha) + c$.

The parameters α and c, like A and ω, vary from one situation to another.

Discussion point

Although the function $y = A \sin \omega t°$ is constantly varying it has a mean value of zero. Can you explain this?

A sine wave $y = A \sin \omega t°$ has a **frequency** (number of complete waves in 360°) of ω.

The wave $y = A \sin \omega t°$ has a **period** of $\dfrac{360}{\omega}$ (i.e. 360 divided by the number of complete waves in 360°).

Activity 5.3C

Excel Activity

Use a graphic calculator or a spreadsheet to investigate the general sine wave $y = A \sin(\omega t + \alpha)° + c$.
If you are using a graphic calculator, set the axes to show values of x from 0 to 360 and y from -5 to $+5$. Initially use $A = 1$, $\omega = 1$, $\alpha = 0$ and $c = 0$ so that you have a graph of $y = \sin t$. Make notes with sketches of what you find.

1 a What would you expect to happen if you increased the value of A? Check whether you are correct.

   b What would you expect to happen if you changed A from 1 to -1 to give the graph of $y = -\sin t$?
     Check whether you are correct.

   c What transformations of the curve $y = \sin t$ would give the curve $y = -0.5 \sin t$? Check by drawing this curve.

2 Return to the case where $A = 1$, $\omega = 1$, $\alpha = 0$ and $c = 0$.

   a What would you expect to happen if you increased the value of ω? Check whether you are correct.

   b What would you expect to happen if you changed ω from 1 to -1 to give the graph of $y = \sin(-t)$?
     Check whether you are correct.

   c What transformation of the curve $y = \sin t$ would give the curve $y = \sin 0.5t$? Check by drawing this curve.

In the general sine wave $y = A \sin(wt + \alpha) + c$, α is called the **phase angle**. It is the angle by which the function is shifted along the horizontal axis.

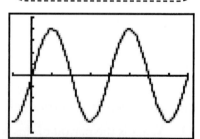

Discussion point

The graphic calculator screen shot below is of the graph $y = 4 \sin x°$. Can you determine the window used?

3 Now investigate, keeping $A = 1$, $\omega = 1$, $\alpha = 0$ and varying the value of c.

Describe what happens to the curve as c varies from -4 to $+4$.

4 a Now investigate, keeping $A = 1$, $\omega = 1$, $c = 0$ and varying the value of α.

Describe what happens to the curve as α varies
  i from 0 to 180
  ii from 0 to -180

b Repeat part **a**, but with $\omega = 2$, rather than 1.

c Repeat part **a**, but with $\omega = 3$, rather than 1.

5 Systematically investigate, using different values of A, ω, α and c to see what effect changing each parameter has on the graph $y = A \cos(\omega t + \alpha)° + c$.

Write a summary of your findings. Make sure your findings fit with what you found in **Section 5.1**.

Practice sheets:
Properties of sine waves

5.4 Fitting a sinusoidal model

Key web search terms

blood pressure (systolic/diastolic)
sunspot activity
sunrise and sunset times
tide times

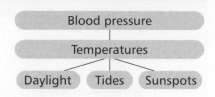

In situations that you can model using a sine wave of the form
$y = A \sin(\omega t + \alpha) + c$ you need to identify the values of the
parameters A, ω, α and c. You can find these from information such
as the maximum and minimum values of the function and when these
occur, perhaps using a graph of data collected from observations.

Blood pressure

Blood pressure is usually measured using a blood pressure cuff. This
is put around a person's arm and inflated until the blood flow is cut
off. When air is let out of the cuff two measurements (often quoted,
for example, as 'one hundred and twenty over sixty') of the blood
pressure are taken. The first of these values, called the systolic
pressure, is the pressure in mmHg (millimetres of mercury) when
the heart is contracting and blood starts to flow again. The second
value, called the diastolic blood pressure is the pressure when the
heart is relaxing and blood flows continuously. The person's blood
pressure varies between these two values as shown in the graph.

You can model the person's blood pressure, p mmHg, at time
t seconds using a function of the form $p = A \sin \omega t° + c$.

You can find the values of the parameters A, ω and c from
measurements of the person's blood pressure and heart rate.

Suppose a patient has blood pressure 120/60 and heart rate 72 beats
per minute.

The blood pressure varies between 60 and 120 mmHg.

The average of these gives the central value $c = 90$ (mmHg).

The difference between the central value and the maximum (or
minimum) gives the amplitude, 30 (mmHg), so A is 30.

ω is found from the heart rate:

A heart rate of 72 beats per minute means that the time for 1 beat is
$\frac{60}{72} = \frac{5}{6}$ seconds. This is the period of the sine wave.

Period $= \frac{360}{\omega} = \frac{5}{6}$ rearranges to give $\omega = \frac{6 \times 360}{5} = 432$.

The sinusoidal function that models this patient's blood pressure is
therefore $p = 30 \sin 432t° + 90$.

Draw the graph of this function on your graphic calculator and
check that it has the same features as the diagram above.

**Taking blood pressure using a
sphygmomanometer**

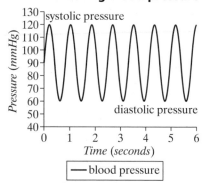

Measuring blood pressure

Blood pressure is greatest
(systolic pressure) when the
heart ventricle contracts and
least (diastolic pressure)
when the ventricle is filling
up with blood. Blood
pressure readings are quoted
as systolic pressure over
diastolic pressure, e.g.
120/60 mmHg.

Discussion point

Why is it not necessary in this case
to include the parameter α?

Activity 5.4A

Resource
Sheet
5.4A

The table gives blood pressure and pulse rate (heart rate) values for an adult male, an adult female, a baby and an elderly patient with high blood pressure.

For each patient:

a Find a function of the form $p = A \sin \omega t° + c$ to model blood pressure, p mmHg, at time t seconds.

b Use a spreadsheet or graphic calculator to assist you to draw a sketch to show how p varies with t.

c Use the trace function of your graphic calculator to find for what proportion of the time the patient's blood pressure is over 100 mmHg, assuming that at $t = 0$ the patient's blood pressure is the central value.

	Blood pressure	Pulse rate
Adult male	120/80	75
Adult female	120/80	80
Baby	70/50	120
Elderly	180/110	60

Temperatures

Temperature variation is important to workers in industries such as agriculture, tourism, power supply and many others.

Although temperature can vary widely from day to day, average monthly temperatures follow a fairly regular cyclic pattern.

The table gives average monthly temperatures in degrees Celsius (°C) at Gatwick Airport (London) and JFK Airport (New York).

The graph shows the data collected at Gatwick.

Temperature data is collected at most airports because temperature variation is important in determining when aircraft maintenance teams will need to perform tasks such as de-icing aircraft wings before they take off.

Month	Gatwick	JFK
Jan	3.8	−0.4
Feb	4.0	0.5
Mar	5.8	5.0
Apr	7.9	10.2
May	11.3	15.5
Jun	14.4	20.7
Jul	16.5	24.1
Aug	16.1	23.7
Sept	13.8	19.7
Oct	10.8	13.8
Nov	6.6	8.4
Dec	4.7	2.5

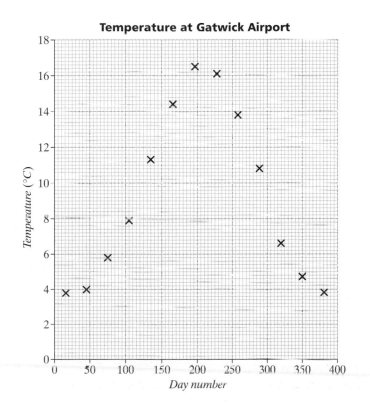

Temperature at Gatwick Airport

Discussion points

Day 1 is 1 January. Look at the points on the graph. Explain their positions.

What assumptions have been made?

Do you think the data could be represented by a sine wave?

Activity 5.4B

Resource Sheet 5.4B

You can model how the temperature, $T°C$, varies with time, t days after 31 December, using a sine wave of the form $T = A \sin (\omega t + \alpha)° + c$.

1 A, ω, α and c are parameters that depend on where in the world you are. You can find these from your own copy of the graph for Gatwick Airport by following the steps below.

   a Join the points with a smooth curve.

   b Draw a horizontal line through the 'centre' of the sine wave. Look at the point where this central line meets the temperature axis. This gives a value for c.

   c Use the graph to estimate the value of A, the amplitude.

   d Use the period of the curve to find a value for ω $\left(\text{Remember period} = \dfrac{360}{\omega} \right)$.

   e Find the value of t where the curve meets the central line (see graph alongside). This gives the **phase shift** $t = -\dfrac{\alpha}{\omega}$.

    Substitute your value of ω and calculate the value of α.

2 **a** Use your graphic calculator or computer to draw a graph of your model and compare it with the original data.

   b If necessary, adjust the values of the constants, A, ω, α and c until the graph of the sinusoidal function is a good fit of the original data.

3 Use the method in **1** above to find a sinusoidal model for the temperatures at JFK Airport.

UoM4

4 Compare the values of the parameters A, ω, α and c in the sinusoidal functions you have found to model the temperature at Gatwick and JFK Airport. Explain in real terms what the similarities and differences in them indicate.

UoM4

5 Describe ways in which the temperature models could be used and explain their limitations. Say what other information would be useful to airport personnel who need to predict the temperature.

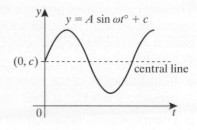

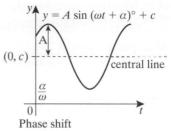

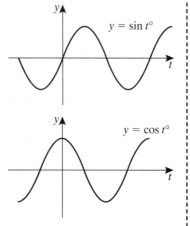

A **phase shift** of 90° converts a sine wave into a cosine wave.

Therefore $\cos t° = \sin(t + 90°)$. Check this using your graphic calculator.

Sometimes the term **phase difference** or **phase angle** is used instead of **phase shift**.

Daylight

The table gives sunrise and sunset times in Manchester.

	Sunrise and sunset times in Manchester		
Day number	Date	Sunrise (GMT)	Sunset (GMT)
0	31 Dec	08:25	15:59
10	10 Jan	08:22	16:11
20	20 Jan	08:12	16:28
30	30 Jan	07:59	16:47
40	09 Feb	07:40	17:08
50	19 Feb	07:19	17:27
60	01 Mar	06:57	17:47
70	11 Mar	06:33	18:06
80	21 Mar	06:09	18:24
90	31 Mar	05:45	18:42
100	10 Apr	05:22	19:00
110	20 Apr	04:59	19:18
120	30 Apr	04:37	19:37
130	10 May	04:18	19:54
140	20 May	04:01	20:11
150	30 May	03:49	20:25
160	09 Jun	03:42	20:35
170	19 Jun	03:39	20:41
180	29 Jun	03:43	20:41
190	09 Jul	03:52	20:36
200	19 Jul	04:04	20:25
210	29 Jul	04:19	20:11
220	08 Aug	04:37	19:51
230	18 Aug	04:54	19:30
240	28 Aug	05:11	19:08
250	07 Sep	05:29	18:44
260	17 Sep	05:46	18:19
270	27 Sep	06:04	17:55
280	07 Oct	06:21	17:31
290	17 Oct	06:40	17:08
300	27 Oct	06:58	16:47
310	06 Nov	07:18	16:27
320	16 Nov	07:36	16:11
330	26 Nov	07:54	15:58
340	06 Dec	08:09	15:51
350	16 Dec	08:19	15:50
360	26 Dec	08:25	15:55

Activity 5.4C

In this activity you can use the given data or find your own – perhaps for where you live.

You could share the work with other students and extend the investigation to include moonrise and moonset times and the number of hours of moonlight.

1   Use a graphic calculator or computer to draw graphs of the data of

   a sunrise time
   b sunset time
   c number of hours of daylight

   against day number.

2   Which days in the year do you expect to be the longest and shortest, in terms of daylight hours? Compare your answers with what the graphs show.

3   **a** Find a function of the form $y = A \sin(\omega t + \alpha)° + c$ to model each graph. Use a graphic calculator or computer to draw a graph of each model.
    b Compare your graph of each model with the graph of the original data. Adjust the values of A, ω, α and c to improve your models where possible.
    c Compare your predictions with the actual data.
    ○ Predict for how many days there will be more than 14 hours of daylight.

Tides

Tides are caused by the gravitational effect of the moon and the sun. Tables of the predicted times and heights of high and low tides are published for many locations in the UK. Such information is important for those planning activities such as navigation, fishing, water sports and engineering or construction projects in coastal locations.

The times and heights of high and low tides predicted for Barry in South Wales on a particular day are given in the table.

Time (GMT)	Height (m)
00.24	4.7
06.38	14.4
12.40	4.9
18.48	14.4

Activity 5.4D

You can model the height of the tide, h metres, at any time of day using the general sinusoidal equation $h = A \sin(\omega t + \alpha) + c$, where t is the time.

1   Find values for A, ω, α and c using the data in the table.

2   Use your graphic calculator or computer to draw a graph of h against t.

3   A boat requires a tide height of 10 metres or more of water to be able to enter a harbour. Using your calculator's trace function, find the times between which this boat could enter the harbour at Barry on this day.

Sunspots

In September 1996 a panel of experts was recruited by the NASA Office of Space Science to try to predict the extent of solar activity during Solar Cycle 23. After considering a range of prediction techniques the panel summarised their findings in the graph shown below. The graph shows predicted values for solar magnetic flux as well as the predicted number of sunspots.

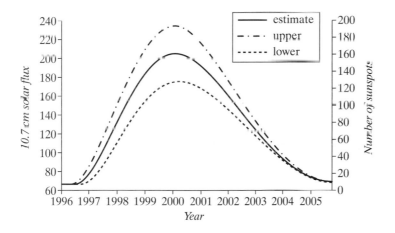

Sunspots appear as dark spots on the surface of the sun and usually last for several days. They are regions where the magnetic field strength is thousands of times greater than the Earth's magnetic field.

Sunspots have been observed for many years and it has been found that the number of sunspots follows a **cyclic pattern**, each cycle lasting approximately 11 years. We are now part-way through the 23rd cycle that has been identified since records began.

The level of solar magnetic activity is important because it can affect the operation of satellites, electric power transmission grids and high frequency radio communications.

Activity 5.4E

1 Find a sinusoidal model for the number of sunspots for each of the three curves, starting with the general sinusoidal equation. The actual number of sunspots for the months during the years 1996–2000 are given below:

	1996	1997	1998	1999	2000
Jan	10.4	10.5	43.7	82.6	112.8
Feb	10.1	11	48.9	84.6	116.6
Mar	9.7	13.5	53.4	83.8	119.8
Apr	8.4	16.5	56.5	85.4	120.7
May	8	18.3	59.4	90.4	118.9
Jun	8.5	20.3	62.5	93	118.6
Jul	8.4	22.6	65.5	94.4	119.6
Aug	8.3	25	67.8	97.5	118.4
Sep	8.4	28.3	69.5	102.3	116.1
Oct	8.8	31.8	70.5	107.7	114.4
Nov	9.8	35	73	110.9	112.7
Dec	10.4	39	77.9	111	112.1

2 Compare the values predicted by your models with the observed values.

3 a Find a sinusoidal model to represent the real data.

   b Use this new model to predict the number of days during Cycle 23 when the number of sunspots will exceed 100.

145

5.5 Solving trigonometric equations and inequalities

Key web search terms

alternating current
mathematical bungee rope models
sunrise and sunset times

In **Section 5.4** you used sine functions to model how variables such as blood pressure, the height of a tide and the number of daylight hours vary with time. You can use these sine models to make predictions such as the times when a boat can sail into a harbour or the day of the year on which there will be a particular amount of daylight. You have seen how to estimate values using your graphs. You will now learn how to use algebraic methods.

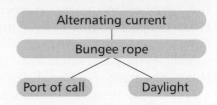

Alternating current

The current, I amps, in an electrical circuit can be modelled by the function $I = 20 \sin(18t + 30)°$ where t is the time in milliseconds. Suppose you wish to find the first and second times when the current is zero. You can do this by solving the trigonometric equation:

$$20 \sin(18t + 30)° = 0 \quad \Rightarrow \quad \sin(18t + 30)° = 0$$

The following graph shows the first two cycles of $y = \sin \theta°$ where θ is used to represent $(18t + 30)°$

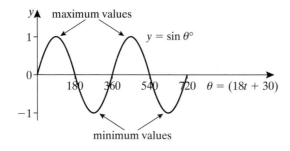

> **Discussion points**
> What are the amplitude, period, frequency and phase angle of this current?
>
> Can you describe the transformations that you would need to use to get from the function $I = \sin t°$ to the function $I = 20 \sin(18t + 30)°$?

> You could extend the basic sine graph to give more solutions if these are required.

The value of $\sin \theta°$ is zero when $\theta = 0, 180, 360, \ldots$
This gives a series of equations for t:

$$18t + 30 = 0, \quad 18t + 30 = 180, \quad 18t + 30 = 360, \ldots$$

The first of these equations gives a negative value of t:

$$18t + 30 = 0 \text{ gives } t = -\frac{30}{18} = -1\tfrac{2}{3}$$

You can find the first two positive values of t by solving $18t + 30 = 180$ and $18t + 30 = 360$:

$$t = \frac{180 - 30}{18} = \frac{150}{18} = 8\tfrac{1}{3} \text{ and } t = \frac{360 - 30}{18} = \frac{330}{18} = 18\tfrac{1}{3}$$

> **Checkpoint**
> Check that your solutions are correct by substituting back into the original equation.
> e.g.   When $t = 8\tfrac{1}{3}$
> $$20 \sin(18 \times 8\tfrac{1}{3} + 30)°$$
> $$= 20 \sin 180° = 0$$

Activity 5.5A

1 Draw the graph of $y = 20 \sin(18x + 30)°$ on a graphic calculator. Use the zoom and trace facilities to check that the values of t found above where $I = 20 \sin(18t + 30)° = 0$ are correct.

2 Find the first two times when the current $I = 20 \sin(18t + 30)°$ reaches its maximum value, i.e. when $I = 20$, so that $\sin(18t + 30)° = 1$. Calculate these values and then check your answers using your graphic calculator.

3 Find the first two times when the current $I = 20 \sin(18t + 30)°$ reaches its minimum value, i.e. when $I = -20$, so that $\sin(18t + 30)° = -1$. Calculate these values and then check your answers using your graphic calculator.

Bungee rope

Bungee ropes undergo a series of tests before they are used in a jump. In one test a heavy mass is attached to the end of the rope. The rope is held so it is taut and then the mass is released.

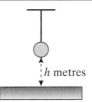

h metres

You can model the height, h metres, of the mass above the ground during the motion in this test by $h = 30 \cos 36t° + 35$, where t is the time in seconds after the mass is released.

You can use this function to predict the minimum and maximum height of the mass above the ground and the times when it is at these heights.

Since $\cos 36t°$ varies between -1 and 1, $30 \cos 36t°$ varies between -30 and 30, so the value of h varies between 5 and 65.

To find when the mass will be at its minimum height of 5 metres solve $\cos 36t° = -1$:

$\cos \theta° = -1$ when $\theta = 180, 540, 900, \ldots$ (see graph below)

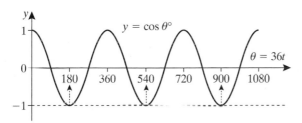

The corresponding times are found by solving the equations

$36t = 180, \quad 36t = 540, \quad 36t = 900, \ldots$

i.e. $t = \dfrac{180}{36} = 5, t = \dfrac{540}{36} = 15, t = \dfrac{900}{36} = 25$

Discussion points
What are the amplitude, period and mean value of
$h = 33 \cos 36t° + 38$?

How can these be used to check the minimum and maximum height of the mass above the ground and the times when it is at these heights?

Discussion point
How often does the model predict that the mass will return to this minimum height?

Activity 5.5B

1   Draw the graph of $y = 30 \cos 36x° + 35$ on your graphic calculator.
    Check that the values calculated above are correct using the zoom and trace facilities of your graphic calculator.

2   Calculate the times when the model predicts that the mass will be at the maximum height of 65 metres above the ground. Check your answers using your graphic calculator.

Discussion point

In what ways will the actual motion of the mass of a bungee jumper differ from that predicted by this model?

Port of call

Suppose that:

- A ship can only enter a harbour when the water is at least 5 metres deep at the harbour entrance.
- The height of water, d metres, at the entrance to a particular harbour can be modelled over the 24 hours of a day by $d = 4 \sin 30t° + 7$, where t is the number of hours after midnight.

The times at which the ship can enter the harbour are therefore given by the trigonometric inequality $4 \sin 30t° + 7 \geqslant 5$.

Use your graphic calculator to draw the graphs of $y = 4 \sin 30x° + 7$ and $y = 5$ for $0 \leqslant x \leqslant 24$.

This will show that there are four times during the day when the depth of the water is exactly 5 metres.

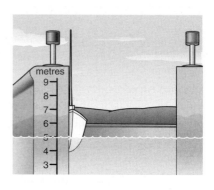

Discussion point

Can you describe the transformations that map the function $d = \sin t°$ onto $d = 4 \sin 30t° + 7$?

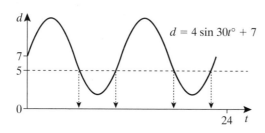

You can find the times by solving $4 \sin 30t° + 7 = 5$
(subtracting 7) $4 \sin 30t° = -2$
(dividing by 4) $\sin 30t° = -0.5$

You can find one value for $30t$ that satisfies this equation using $\sin^{-1}(-0.5)$ on your calculator.

Try this now. The value given on your calculator should be -30.

This gives $30t = -30$, leading to $t = -1$, which is not in the set of values of t that we are using ($0 \leqslant t \leqslant 24$).
You can find other more useful solutions using the graph of

$y = \sin \theta°$ where θ represents $30t$.

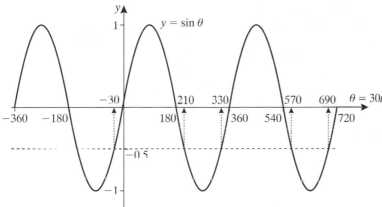

The sketch shows the solution $\theta = -30$ given by your calculator and also the first four positive solutions for the angle.

The symmetry of the curve gives the values of θ:

$\theta = 180 + 30 = 210$ $\qquad$ $\theta = 360 - 30 = 330$
$\theta = 540 + 30 = 570$ $\qquad$ and $\qquad$ $\theta = 720 - 30 = 690$

Equating these values to $30t$ gives the times when the depth of water is 5 metres:

$30t = 210 \Rightarrow t = 7$ $\qquad$ $30t = 330 \Rightarrow t = 11$
$30t = 570 \Rightarrow t = 19$ $\qquad$ and $\qquad$ $30t = 690 \Rightarrow t = 23$

The times are shown below on the sketch graph of $d = 4 \sin 30t° + 7$.

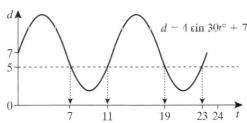

The ship can enter the harbour when $4 \sin 30t° + 7 \geqslant 5$. Looking for the points on the curve where d is greater than or equal to 5 gives the time intervals $0 \leqslant t \leqslant 7$, $11 \leqslant t \leqslant 19$ and $23 \leqslant t \leqslant 24$.

The ship can therefore enter the harbour before 7 am, between 11 am and 7 pm and after 11 pm on that particular day.

Checkpoint

Use your graphic calculator to find the values of x where the graphs $y = 4 \sin 30x + 7$ and $y = 5$ intersect.

Check that these agree with the times found above by calculation.

Activity 5.5C

A larger ship wishes to enter the harbour described above on the day concerned. This ship requires a water depth of 8 metres.

Find the times when this ship can enter the harbour.

Nuffield resources
UoM 1 Assignment 'Tides'
UoM1 Assignment 'Coughs and sneezes'

Daylight

The number of hours of daylight, N, on any day during the year in Manchester can be modelled approximately by
$N = 12.7 - 4.3 \cos(n + 10)°$, where n is the day number, with day 1 taken to be 1 January.

Therefore the days during the year when there are predicted to be less than 15 hours of daylight are given by the trigonometric inequality $12.7 - 4.3 \cos(n + 10)° < 15$.

Use your graphic calculator to draw the graphs of
$y = 12.7 - 4.3 \cos(x + 10)°$ and $y = 15$ for $0 \leqslant x \leqslant 365$.

The sketch below shows that there are two days during the year when daylight is predicted to last for 15 hours.

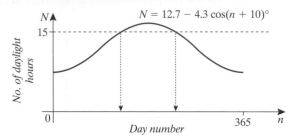

You can find these days by solving $\quad 15 = 12.7 - 4.3 \cos(n + 10)°$
(rearranging) $\quad\quad\quad\quad 4.3 \cos(n + 10)° = -2.3$
(dividing by 4.3) $\quad\quad\quad\quad \cos(n + 10)° = -0.5349$
(using $\cos^{-1}$ on a calculator) $\quad\quad n + 10 = 122$
$\quad\quad\quad\quad\quad\quad\quad\quad\quad\quad\quad n = 112$

This corresponds to 22 April. The graph shows that there will be less than 15 hours of daylight on any day before 22 April.

> **Discussion point**
> Can you describe the transformations that map the function $y = \cos x°$ onto $y = 12.7 - 4.3 \cos(x + 10)°$?

> **Discussion points**
> What is the period of $N = 12.7 - 4.3 \cos(n + 10)°$?
>
> How does this compare with the period you would expect in the number of daylight hours?
>
> What adjustment would be needed to the function to give a more accurate result?

Activity 5.5D

You can find the other day on which there are 15 hours of daylight by considering the symmetry of the graph of $y = \cos \theta°$. The second value of $(n + 10)$ is 112 less than 360.

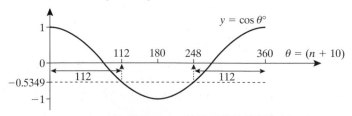

1. Solve $n + 10 = 248$ to find the second day during the year when there are predicted to be 15 hours of daylight. Write down the period of the year when there are less than 15 hours of daylight.

2. Use the model $N = 12.7 - 4.3 \cos(n + 10)°$ to predict the periods of the year during which there are:
   a less than 10 hours of daylight
   b more than 16 hours of daylight.

> **Checkpoint**
> Use the trace facility on your graphic calculator to check the predictions.

> **Practice sheets:**
> **Solving trigonometry equations**

5.6 Revision summary

Graphs of families of functions (e.g. quadratic, exponential) have characteristic shapes. The characteristic shape stays the same when a graph is translated, stretched or reflected. The equation of the transformed graph tells you the transformations used.

Simple transformations

Translations

When a graph is translated it does not change shape, size or orientation; it just moves relative to the axes.

A translation with vector $\begin{pmatrix} a \\ b \end{pmatrix}$ means that the graph is moved a units to the right and b units upwards.

If the function $y = f(x)$ is transformed to $y = f(x - a)$ the effect is to give the graph a translation with vector $\begin{pmatrix} a \\ 0 \end{pmatrix}$ – i.e. to move it a units to the right.

If the function $y = f(x)$ is transformed to $y = f(x) + a$ the effect is to give the graph a translation with vector $\begin{pmatrix} 0 \\ a \end{pmatrix}$ – i.e. to move it a units upwards.

Stretches

A stretch is a transformation that enlarges the graph in one direction only.

A stretch of scale factor a in the y direction multiplies all the y co-ordinates by a whilst leaving the x co-ordinates unchanged; a stretch of factor a in the x direction multiplies all the x co-ordinates by a whilst leaving the y co-ordinates unchanged.

If $0 < a < 1$, the graph will 'shrink'.

If the function $y = f(x)$ is transformed to $y = f\left(\dfrac{x}{a}\right)$ the effect is to stretch the graph parallel to the x axis with factor a.

If the function $y = f(x)$ is transformed to $y = af(x)$ the effect is to stretch the graph parallel to the y axis with factor a.

Reflections

The graph $y = f(x)$, when reflected in the x axis, becomes $y = -f(x)$, which has the effect of reversing the signs of all the y co-ordinates. (Negative co-ordinates become positive and positive, negative.)

When reflected in the y axis, $y = f(x)$ becomes $y = f(-x)$, which has the effect of reversing the signs of all the x co-ordinates. If the y axis is a line of symmetry of the original graph, the reflection has no apparent effect.

Combinations of transformations

Simple transformations can be combined to produce complex transformations of a graph; for example, the graph of $y = 5 - 2(x + 8)^2$ can be produced from the simple graph $y = x^2$ by:

- a stretch in the y direction with scale factor 2 giving $y = 2x^2$
- a translation $\begin{pmatrix} -8 \\ 0 \end{pmatrix}$ giving $y = 2(x + 8)^2$
- reflection in the x axis giving $y = -2(x + 8)^2$
- translation $\begin{pmatrix} 0 \\ 5 \end{pmatrix}$ giving $y = 5 - 2(x + 8)^2$

Sine waves

Sine waves can be used to model everyday situations such as height above the ground on a Ferris wheel or sunrise and sunset times. Cosine waves can also be used; both types have the same shape but are translations of one another in the x direction.

Definition of sine and cosine

If P is on a circle radius 1 and centre $(0, 0)$, the x co-ordinate of P is the cosine of the angle the radius OP makes with the positive direction of the x axis and the y co-ordinate is the sine of this angle.

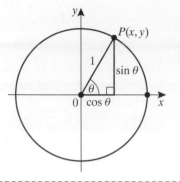

Period and amplitude

$y = \sin \theta°$ and $y = \cos \theta°$ are periodic functions. They repeat themselves every 360°, which is the period of the functions. Minimum and maximum values of the functions are -1 and $+1$, so the amplitude is 1.

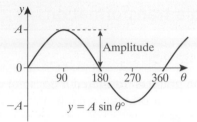

The period and the amplitude of the basic sine and cosine functions can be altered by transformations.

The general sine graph

The period, amplitude and position of the graph $y = \sin t°$ are changed by transformations.

The graph of $y = \sin \omega t°$ is a stretch of $y = \sin t°$ in the x direction with stretch factor $\dfrac{1}{\omega}$. It repeats itself ω times every 360°, i.e. it has a period of $\dfrac{360°}{\omega}$.

The graph of $y = A \sin t°$ is a stretch of $y = \sin t°$ in the y direction. It has amplitude A.

The graph of $y = \sin (t + \alpha)°$ is a translation of $y = \sin t°$ with vector $\begin{pmatrix} -\alpha \\ 0 \end{pmatrix}$ and the graph of $y = \sin t° + c$ is a translation of $y = \sin t°$ with vector $\begin{pmatrix} 0 \\ c \end{pmatrix}$.

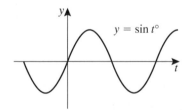

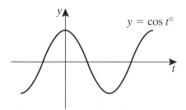

The graph of $y = \sin(t + 90)°$ is equivalent to the graph of $y = \cos t°$.

Combining transformations gives the equation of the general sine graph, $y = A \sin(\omega t + \alpha)° + c$. Any sine graph can be obtained from any other by transformations.

Fitting sine graphs to data

The parameters A, ω, α and c in the function $y = A\sin(\omega t + \alpha)° + c$ determine the amplitude, period and position of the graph. To fit a sine function to a suitable set of data, you need to find the values of these parameters.

The place where the central line cuts the y axis gives the value of c.

The distance of the maximum and minimum points of the graph above and below the central line is the amplitude, which is the value of A.

The value of ω is $\dfrac{360}{\text{period of graph}}$.

You can find the phase angle α by finding the translation of the graph.

$y = A\sin(wt + \alpha)° + c$ is a translation of $y = A\sin wt° + c$ by $\begin{pmatrix} -\alpha/w \\ 0 \end{pmatrix}$.

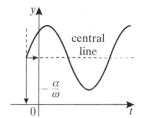

Solving trigonometric equations and inequalities

Trigonometrical functions are periodic and therefore equations and inequalities can have an infinite number of solutions.

A sketch of the graph and the required values of the variable shows how many solutions there are in the required range and their approximate values.

Using the $\sin^{-1}$ function on a calculator will give a solution in the range -180 to $+180$; the sketch shows how these should be used to calculate values in the required range.

For example, to solve the equation $3\sin\left(\dfrac{t}{2} - 10\right)° + 5.2 = 6.5$,

sketch the graph of $y = 3\sin\left(\dfrac{t}{2} - 10\right) + 5.2$ and the line $y = 6.5$.

This shows that the first two solutions are approximately 80 and 320.

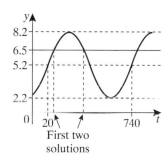

$$3\sin\left(\frac{t}{2} - 10\right)° + 5.2 = 6.5$$

$$\therefore \qquad 3\sin\left(\frac{t}{2} - 10\right)° = 1.3$$

$$\therefore \qquad \sin\left(\frac{t}{2} - 10\right)° \approx 0.4333$$

$$\therefore \qquad \frac{t}{2} - 10 = \sin^{-1} 0.4333\ldots \approx 25.679 \text{ (from calculator)}$$

$$\therefore \qquad \frac{t}{2} = 25.679 + 10 = 35.679$$

$$\therefore \qquad t = 71.358 \approx 71.4$$

The other solution is therefore $200 + (200 - 71.358) \approx 328.642 \approx 329$.

5.7 Preparing for assessment

Your coursework portfolio

Any of the functions you have used to model data can be considered as transformations of one of the basic functions. For example, any exponential function can be transformed into any other exponential function by the application of translations, stretches and reflections.

In your portfolio, show how you use considerations of transformations to help you find a function with the best possible fit to your data, once you have decided which type of function to use, choosing from:

- linear
- quadratic
- power
- exponential
- logarithmic
- trigonometrical

You could use primary or secondary data from different but related situations, such as the high and low tide times in different places (or times in the same place at different times of the year). You could then compare the different versions of the same function (probably trigonometric for tide times) that will best fit the different data sets.

Collect a data set(s) – conduct experiments, use data from another subject that you study, get data from the Internet, etc. – and graph the data using a spreadsheet or graphic calculator.

Find a function(s) that fits the data well. Consider the transformations of the basic function (e.g. $y = \sin t$ or $y = e^x$) that are needed to make it fit your data set well. Explain carefully how you determine which transformations to use. Consider whether a different combination of transformations could have the same effect.

Perhaps consider the transformations that are needed to make the model of one data set fit the model of another data set. Explain in terms of the real situation what this tells you about the similarities and difference of the data sets you are modelling.

Nuffield Resources
UoM1 Assignments: Coughs and Sneezes, Sea Defence Wall, Tides, Water flow.

Practice exam questions

(UoM1) Ferris Wheel

Data

1   In Space World at Fukuaka in Japan there is
    a Ferris wheel with a diameter of 80 metres.
    A ride on this wheel takes 15 minutes.

    The graph shows the height, h metres, of
    one of the pods above the centre of the
    wheel during the ride.

    The equation of the graph is $h = 40 \cos 24t°$,
    where t minutes is the time since the start of
    the ride.

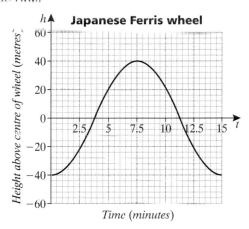

Japanese Ferris wheel

Time (minutes)

Height above centre of wheel (metres)

Question

a   The function $h = -40 \cos 24t°$ is based on
        the basic function $h = \cos t°$.
        State the geometric transformations that
        should be applied to the graph of
        $h = \cos t°$ to give the graph of
        $h = -40 \cos 24t°$.

b   Solve the equation $-40 \cos 24t° = 30$ for
        $0 \leqslant t \leqslant 15$ to find at what times the pod
        is at least 30 metres above the centre of
        the wheel.

c   Find for how long the pod is 30 metres
        above the lowest point of the wheel in one
        complete revolution of the wheel.

d   Write down a formula that would give
        the height, h metres, of this pod above
        the ground assuming that at its lowest
        point a pod is at the ground.

The London Eye is a Ferris wheel with a
diameter of 67 metres. The time for a
complete revolution of the wheel is
30 minutes.

c   Sketch a graph to show the distance, d
        metres, of one of the pods of the London
        Eye above the centre of the wheel during
        a 30-minute ride, assuming that at $t = 0$
        the pod is at its lowest point.
        Write the equation connecting d and t.

(UoM4) Life expectancy

2   The graph shows how the life expectancy at
    birth for males and females in England and
    Wales increased during the 20th century.

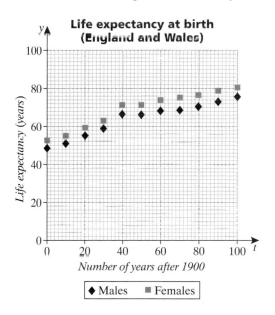

Life expectancy at birth
(England and Wales)

Life expectancy (years)

Number of years after 1900

◆ Males   ■ Females

The quadratic function
$y = 51 + 0.5t - 0.002t^2$, where y years
represents life expectancy at birth and t
represents the number of years after 1900,
can be used to model the data for females.

a   Life expectancy for females born in
        England and Wales in the year 2000,
        when $t = 100$, was 80.3 years.
        Find the value predicted by the
        model.

b   **i**   Show clearly that the model
            $y = 51 + 0.5t - 0.002t^2$ can be written
            as $y = -0.002[(t - 125)^2 - 41\,125]$

    ii What is the maximum life expectancy
            at birth predicted by this model and in
            what year after 1900 is it predicted to
            occur?

155

c   The life expectancy at birth for males
can be modelled by the quadratic function
$y = 48 + 0.44t - 0.002t^2$.

The models suggest that there was one
year when the life expectancy at birth for
males was equal to that for females. Find
this year.

It is proposed that the life expectancy at
birth for females could alternatively be
modelled by the exponential function
$y = 52(2 - e^{-0.008t})$.

The graph of this model can be sketched
by starting with the curve $y = e^t$ and
applying a sequence of transformations.

Graph of $y = e^t$

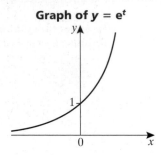

d   The equation of each curve in the
sequence is given below. In each case
describe fully the transformation that has
been applied and sketch the curve.

i $y = e^{-t}$

ii $y = e^{-0.008t}$

iii $y = -e^{-0.008t}$

iv $y = 2 - e^{-0.008t}$

v $y = 52(2 - e^{-0.008t})$.

e   The two models for life expectancy for
females at birth in England and Wales
are given again below.

Quadratic Model:
$$y = 51 + 0.5t - 0.002t^2$$

Exponential Model:
$$y = 52(2 - e^{-0.008t})$$

Compare the two models by
commenting on what each model
predicts will happen:

i   when $t = 0$

ii when $t \to \infty$

iii when $t \to -\infty$.

6 Finding a Good Model

Throughout much of your work in this book you have been looking at how you can use mathematical functions to model real data. Once you have such a model you can use it to solve problems and make predictions for situations for which you have no data. This is one way in which mathematics puts you in a powerful position to make sense of the world. In this chapter you will learn to apply some of the mathematics you already know to help you find mathematical models more easily.

As an example of what you will learn to do, consider the data a scientist may have about the weight of the massive claw, C milligrams, of a fiddler crab and the weight of the rest of its body, B milligrams. It looks from a graph of the data that a power relation of the form $B = aC^n$ may be suitable.

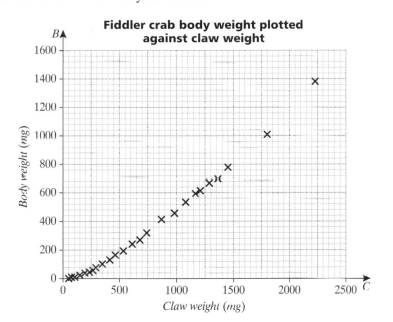

In this chapter you will learn to find the parameters a and n using logarithmic techniques. This method suggests that the model $B = 0.014C^{1.5}$ will be a good fit to the data. You may like to investigate this.

Claw weight (mg)	Body weight (mg)
57.6	5.3
80.3	9.0
109.2	13.7
156.1	25.1
199.7	38.3
238.3	52.5
270.0	59.0
300.2	78.1
355.2	104.5
420.1	135.0
470.1	164.9
535.7	195.6
617.9	243.0
680.6	271.6
743.3	319.2
872.4	417.6
983.1	460.8
1079.9	537.0
1165.5	593.8
1211.7	616.8
1291.3	670.0
1363.2	699.3
1449.1	777.8
1807.9	1009.1
2235.0	1380.0

6.1 Transforming variables

Key web search terms

linearising data (or linearizing data)
inverse square law

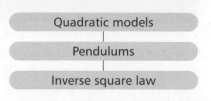

Quadratic models
|
Pendulums
|
Inverse square law

Quadratic models

In **Section 2.1** you explored using $d = kt^2$ to model how the distance, d metres, increases with time, t seconds, for a car accelerating from rest.

When you can model data by a **quadratic function** of the form $y = kx^2 + c$, plotting y against x^2 rather than x will give you a good **straight line fit** and allow you to find the parameters k and c.

t	t^2	d
0.0	0.00	0.00
0.1	0.01	0.04
0.2	0.04	0.23
0.3	0.09	0.69
0.4	0.16	1.45
0.5	0.25	2.57
0.6	0.36	4.00
0.7	0.45	5.60
0.8	0.64	7.62
0.9	0.81	10.12
1.0	1.00	12.77

Activity 6.1A

In this activity use graph paper.
This table shows the data for the accelerating car that you met in **Chapter 2**. It is repeated with an extra column for values of t^2.

1   Draw a graph of d against t^2.

2   Draw an approximate straight line of best fit on your graph.

3   Find the equation of this line by finding its gradient, m. (Its intercept with the vertical axis, c, should be zero in this case.)

| **Discussion point**
Your straight line should go through the origin. Why?

You should find that the gradient of the straight line is approximately 12 so the equation of the straight line is $d = 12t^2$.

In **Section 2.1** you also found quadratic models for the braking distances and stopping distances for cars travelling at different speeds, shown in the *Highway Code* table opposite. In the next activity you will find a quadratic model using the method above.

Speed (mph)	Thinking distance (m)	Braking distance (m)	Stopping distance (m)
20	6	6	12
30	9	14	23
40	12	24	36
50	15	38	43
60	18	55	73
70	21	75	96

Activity 6.1B

a   Plot d against v^2, where d metres is the stopping distance and v mph is the speed.

b   Draw a straight line through the points.

c   Find the values of the gradient, m, and the intercept with the vertical axis, c, for your line.

d   The quadratic model of the data is $d = mv^2 + c$. Substitute your values of m and c and check that this closely models the data in the table.

| **Discussion point**
Is the model similar to the one you found in **Section 2.1**?

Pendulums

Galileo (1564–1642), the great Italian scientist and artist, was particularly interested in the back and forth motion of a suspended weight – a **pendulum**. Some trace this to his observation of a lamp swinging back and forth in the cathedral of Pisa when he was a student. His interest in this is not surprising, as he needed a timing device to assist him in his experiments concerning motion. A friend of Galileo's, Santorio Santorio, a physician in Venice, soon began using a short pendulum, which he called 'pulsilogium', to measure the pulse of his patients.

The table shows time taken, T seconds, for a complete oscillation of a pendulum for various lengths, l metres, of string. Throughout the experiment the same bob (the weight on the end of the string) was used and it was released with the string at the same angle.

The **time period** is the time for one complete swing of the pendulum. (The bob returns to its initial position.)

Length of pendulum, l (metres)	Time period from experiment, T (seconds)
0.05	0.44
0.10	0.64
0.20	0.89
0.30	1.05
0.40	1.24
0.50	1.41
0.60	1.55
0.70	1.62
0.80	1.78
0.90	1.82
1.00	2.09

Discussion point

What factors might affect the time period of a swinging pendulum?

Discussion point

What type(s) of function do you think could be used to model this data?

Consider linear, quadratic, logarithmic, exponential, etc.

Activity 6.1C

Carry out an experiment of your own to collect data about the time period of a pendulum and its length.

Use your graphic calculator or spreadsheet to plot a graph of your data.

There are some features of this data that indicate that a logarithmic model may be suitable, but the mechanics of the situation mean that a model of the form $T = k\sqrt{l}$, where k is a constant, is better.

You could experiment with different values of k until you get a good fit. This is a worthwhile activity and not time-consuming if you use a graphic calculator or graph plotting software on a computer.

An alternative way of finding k is to transform the data to a linear form. In this case, instead of plotting T against l, plot T against $\sqrt{l}$ – you will do this in the next activity.

Activity 6.1D

In this activity either use your own data or the data given here. Use graph paper to draw graphs for parts **a**, **b** and **c**.

a Draw up a table that gives the original data (pendulum length, l metres; time period, T seconds) and includes a new column of values for $\sqrt{l}$.

b Plot a graph of T against $\sqrt{l}$ (T on the vertical axis and $\sqrt{l}$ on the horizontal axis).

c Draw an approximate straight line of best fit to the $(T, \sqrt{l})$ data and use it to find the parameter k in the model $T = k\sqrt{l}$.

d Go back to your graph of the data (T, l) and plot the model $T = k\sqrt{l}$ using the value of k that you found. Check that your model lies close to the original data.

Length of pendulum, l (metres)	$\sqrt{l}$	Time period from experiment, T (seconds)
0	0	0
0.05		0.44
0.10		0.64
0.20		0.89
0.30		1.05
0.40		1.24
0.50		1.41
0.60		1.55
0.70		1.62
0.80		1.78

Discussion point

Your graph should go through the origin. Can you explain why?

Inverse square law

This table shows the amount of radiation, in milli-roentgens per hour, measured at various distances from a source of radioactivity.

You can see immediately that, as the distance away from the source increases, the radiation decreases.

Distance from source (metres)	Radiation (milli-roentgens per hour)
3.1	2100
6.5	500
8.6	270
9.2	240
13.2	110
18.5	60
30.8	20
33.8	17
36.9	15
43.1	11
49.2	8
61.5	5
70.8	4

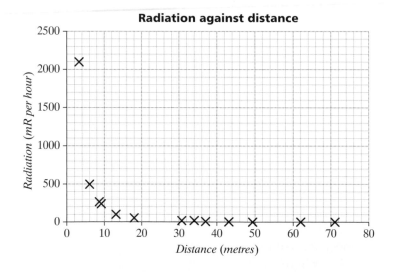

Situations of this kind can often be modelled well by an **inverse square law**, where one quantity is inversely proportional to the square of the other. In this case, radiation could be inversely proportional to the square of the distance from the source of radiation. So the function relating the radiation, R mR/h, to distance, d m, from the source could be $R = \dfrac{k}{d^2}$ where k is constant.

Activity 6.1E

1 Test whether the function $R = \dfrac{k}{d^2}$ fits the data by plotting R against $\dfrac{1}{d^2}$ to see if this gives a straight line.

2 Draw an approximate line of best fit and find its equation. Hence find the value of k in the equation $R = \dfrac{k}{d^2}$.

Discussion point

Do you know other situations in which an inverse square law applies?

In this section you have seen that if data can be modelled by a function of the form $y = kx^n + c$ then plotting y against x^n will give a straight line with gradient k and intercept on the y axis at $(0, c)$.

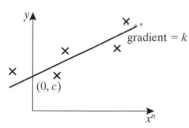

Practice sheets:
Transforming variables

6.2 Using logarithms

Key web search terms

logarithms
Johannes Kepler

Hot drink?

In this section you are going to use another linearisation technique to find parameters of functions that you may wish to use to model data.

The data for the cooling coffee from **Section 3.2** is repeated below but in this case, $T°C$ is now the temperature of the coffee above room temperature ($19°C$) t minutes after the start of observations. In the next activity you will find an exponential function of the form $T = T_0 e^{-kt}$ that closely fits this data.

To reduce this model to linear form you have to use some of the log theory that you met in **Chapter 3**.

If $\qquad T = T_0 e^{-kt}$
then $\quad \ln T = \ln(T_0 e^{-kt})$ (the log of T must be equal to the log of $T_0 e^{-kt}$)
$\therefore \qquad \ln T = \ln T_0 + \ln(e^{-kt})$
$\therefore \qquad \ln T = \ln T_0 - kt \ln(e)$
$\therefore \qquad \ln T = \ln T_0 - kt$

> The laws of logarithms are used here – see **Section 3.5**.

> This process is sometimes known as 'taking logarithms of both sides'.

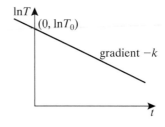

This is of the form $y = mx + c$ (the general equation of a straight line), where $\ln T = y$, $-kt = mx$ and $\ln T_0 = c$.

So if you plot a graph of $\ln T$ against t, you will get a straight line.

The intercept of the line with the vertical axis will be $\ln T_0$.

The gradient of the straight line will be $-k$.

Complete the following activity to find these.

Activity 6.2A

a   Plot a graph of the data with $\ln T$ on the vertical axis and t on the horizontal axis.

b   Draw a straight line of best fit to the data.

c   Find the equation of the straight line, by finding the gradient ($-k$) and the y intercept ($\ln T_0$).
    Hence express $\ln T$ in terms of t.

d   Use your value of $\ln T_0$ to find T_0
    Find an equation for T in terms of t in the form $T = T_0 e^{-kt}$.

Time, t (minutes)	Temperature (degrees C)
0	67
10	56
20	47
30	39
40	32
50	27
60	22
70	18
80	15
90	12
100	10
110	9
120	8
130	7
140	6
150	5

Activity 6.2B

Here is data about the population of the world from 1650 to 2000.

Year, t	Population in millions, P
1650	500
1700	600
1750	700
1800	900
1850	1300
1900	1700
1950	2500
1976	4000
2000	7000

1 **a** Use your graphic calculator to plot a graph of the data to check that it can be modelled by a function of the form $P = P_0 e^{kt}$, where P is the population at t years and P_0 is the population when $t = 0$.

b If $P = P_0 e^{kt}$, show that $\ln P = \ln P_0 + kt$.

c Find the natural logarithm of the population values and plot these against year on graph paper.

d Draw a straight line of best fit through the points.

e Find the equation of the line of best fit and use this to find the parameters k and P_0, so you now have a model of how the population increases with time in the form $P = P_0 e^{kt}$.

f Check that your model closely fits the data by using your graphic calculator to superimpose $P = P_0 e^{kt}$ on the graph of your original data.

Discussion point

Would it be appropriate to use different models for different parts of this data set?

2 Here is data about the number of AIDS cases in the U.K. from 1984 to 1995.

End of year	t	No. of AIDS cases (UK)	Cumulative No. of AIDS cases (UK), N
1984	0	161	161
1985	1	247	408
1986	2	474	882
1987	3	680	1562
1988	4	905	2467
1989	5	1081	3548
1990	6	1242	4790
1991	7	1387	6177
1992	8	1574	7751
1993	9	1783	9534
1994	10	1846	11380
1995	11	1753	13133

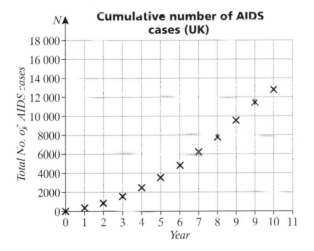

The graph suggests that the number of AIDS cases may be modelled by an exponential function $N = N_0 e^{kt}$, where N is the cumulative number of AIDS cases and t is the number of years after 1984 ($t = 0$ in 1984) year.

a Show that $\ln N = \ln N_0 + kt$, where N_0 is the population when $t = 0$.

b Plot the logarithm of the cumulative number of AIDS cases against t and draw a straight line of best fit.

c Find the equation of your straight line and use it to find an exponential model for the cumulative number of AIDS cases.

d Check that your exponential model closely fits the data by superimposing the data on a graph of your function.

3 The mass (m kg) of a substance that dissolves in one litre of water at different temperatures ($t°C$) was found. The results are shown in the table.

$t°C$	10	20	30	40	50
m kg	35.5	39.1	43.2	47.7	52.8

It is thought that the mass and the temperature are connected according to the law $m = ae^{kt}$.

a Show that the law can be transformed to give $\ln m = kt + \ln a$.

b Plot a graph of $\ln m$ against t and comment on the suitability of the law for modelling the results of the experiment.

c Use your graph to find the approximate values of a and k.

d Use your answer to **c** to estimate the value of m when $t = 60$.

Feed the birds

You can also use the process of taking logarithms if the function that you are trying to find is a power relation such as $y = ax^n$.

In this case, taking logarithms of each side gives $\ln y = \ln(ax^n)$. Applying the rules of logarithms gives $\ln y = \ln a + n \ln x$. So a graph of $\ln y$ against $\ln x$ will be a straight line with gradient n and y intercept $\ln a$.

Now follow how this works with some real data to find a relationship between the lengths and the masses of different birds.

The scatter diagram of mass against length shows some general positive correlation (i.e. longer birds generally have greater mass) but the connection is not linear.

Bird	Total length (cm)	Mass (g)
Aquatic warbler	13	13
Marsh warbler	13	13
Kingfisher	17	40
Spotted sandpiper	19	36
Skylark	19	43
Common sandpiper	20	52
Mandarin duck	31	628
Sparrowhawk	33	144
Chukar	33	536
Razorbill	38	610
Pintail	59	851
Egyptian goose	68	2500

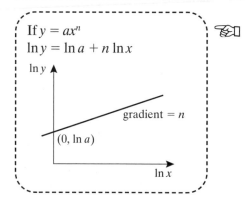

If $y = ax^n$
$\ln y = \ln a + n \ln x$

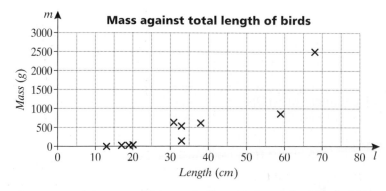

In the next activity you will investigate whether a function of the form $m = al^n$, where m grams is the mass of a bird of length l centimetres, can be used to model the data.

Activity 6.2C

Resource Sheet 6.2C

1 Assuming that $m = al^n$, show that $\ln m = \ln a + n \ln l$.

2 Find the logarithms of the length of the birds and the logarithms of their masses and add these to a copy of the table of the data.

3 Draw a scatter diagram of $\ln m$ plotted against $\ln l$.

4 Draw a straight line of best fit on your scatter diagram and find its equation.

5 Find the function $m = al^n$ that can be used as a power model and use a graphic calculator to see how well it fits the original mass/length data.

6 Red-legged partridges have a mean length of 33 cm. Use your model to estimate the mean mass of red-legged partridges. Comment on the likely accuracy of your estimate.

If you cannot read off the value of the y intercept because your line of best fit does not cross the y axis before it goes off the page, you have two options:

1 Re-draw your graph so that the line does cross the y axis.

OR

2 Calculate the y intercept by using the general straight line equation $y = mx + c$. (You need to know the gradient first.) Substitute the x and y values of any point on the line into this equation and rearrange to find the value of c.

You can use this method on some of the data you met earlier in this chapter, such as the radiation data leading to the inverse square law in **Section 6.1**.

Activity 6.2D

Plot $\ln R$ against $\ln d$ for the radiation data in the Inverse Square Law section. Draw a straight line of best fit, find its equation and hence find the relationship between R and d.
Compare your result with the one you found earlier by the other method.

A man's best friend

Dogs come in all shapes and sizes. This table shows the heights and weights of dogs of a variety of breeds. Is there a connection between height and weight?

Activity 6.2E

Assume the data fits a model of the form $W = kH^p$, where W kg is the weight and H cm is the height of the dog.

1 Use your graphic calculator to plot a graph of the data to check that this is likely.

2 Use logarithms to reduce the data to linear form and then use a graph to find a function for W in terms of H.

3 Check that this function closely models the data.

Height at shoulder (cm)	Weight (kg)
70	40
44	12.5
41	10.5
80	57.5
76	47.5
74	55
68	34
70	50
65	40
52	22
16	3
65	26
60	20
25	6
56	23
70	64

Kepler's laws

Johannes Kepler (1571–1630) investigated data about planetary motion and eventually developed three laws:

1   The orbits of planets around the Sun are ellipses with the Sun at one focus.

2   Lines joining planets to the Sun sweep out the equal areas in equal time intervals.

3   The squares of the times taken for planets to orbit the Sun are proportional to the cubes of the mean distance from the Sun.

The third law indicates a power function of the form $T^2 = kW^3$ or $T = AW^{\frac{3}{2}}$.

The data on which Kepler based his work was collected by Tycho Brahe.

The planets Uranus, Neptune and Pluto had not been discovered when Kepler devised his three laws.

Activity 6.2F

Resource Sheet 6.2E

1   Use logarithms to show that $T = AW^{\frac{3}{2}}$ can be written in the form $Y = \frac{3}{2}X + C$ where $Y = \ln T$, and $X = \ln W$ and $C = \ln A$.

2   Investigate how closely this form of Kepler's third law fits the data in this table by plotting the logarithm of the time for one orbit against the logarithm of the mean distance from the Sun.

Planet	Time (in years) for one orbit	Mean distance from Sun (in millions of kilometres)
Mercury	0.24	58
Venus	0.62	108
Earth	1.00	150
Mars	1.88	228
Jupiter	11.90	778
Saturn	29.50	1427
Uranus	84.01	2871
Neptune	164.79	4497
Pluto	248.40	5914

Girls' heights and weights

This table gives the average heights and weights of girls at different ages.

	Average heights and weights of girls	
Age (years)	Average height (inches)	Average weight (pounds)
0.3	24.5	14.5
0.6	26.8	18.5
0.9	28.8	20.5
1.3	30.7	23.5
1.8	32.0	24.8
2.0	35.0	29.0
3.0	38.5	33.3
4.0	41.8	38.8
5.0	44.0	42.5
6.0	46.0	47.5
7.0	48.0	53.5
8.0	50.8	60.8
9.0	53.3	69.0
10.0	55.5	77.0
11.0	58.5	87.5
12.0	60.5	94.0
13.0	61.3	103.0

The graph below shows the logarithm of the girls' average weights plotted against the logarithm of the average heights.

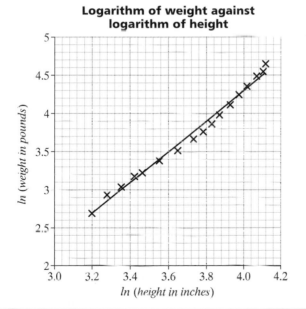

Logarithm of weight against logarithm of height

Activity 6.2G

1 Comment on how closely the straight line fits the data.

2 Use the logarithmic graph and the straight line of best fit to find a model linking the girls' weights and heights.

Nuffield resources:
UoM1 Starter 'Log Graphs'
UoM1 Assignment 'Smoke Strata'
UoM4 Comprehension 'Mortality'

Note:
Throughout these activities you have used natural logarithms – you could equally have used logarithms in base 10. You could try this for this last activity. Can you explain why this is the case?

Practice sheets:
log plots

6.3 Revision summary

Linearising data

A graph of raw data may suggest the type of function that you can use to model the data. Experimenting with parameters might then give a good fit.

For example, the data shown below may suggest a function of the form $y = ax^2 + b$.

(**Note:** Other functions are possible.)

Transforming the data so that it lies close to a straight line is an alternative method. If $y = ax^2 + b$ is a good fit, plotting y against x^2 will give a straight line. It is easier to draw a straight line than a curve.

Finding the gradient and intercept of the straight line on the y axis then gives values for the parameters a and b.

Trying different values for a and b might give a model that fits the data well

$a = \text{gradient}$
$= \dfrac{\text{change in } y}{\text{change in } x}$

Examples of other functions
To check whether $y = ax^3 + b$ is a good model plot y against x^3 (gradient $= a$ and y intercept $= b$).
To check whether $y = a\sqrt{x} + b$ is a good model plot y against $\sqrt{x}$ (gradient $= a$ and y intercept $= b$).

Fitting an exponential function

To fit a function of the form $y = ae^{kt}$ use natural logarithms.

$$\ln y = \ln(ae^{kt})$$
$$\therefore \ln y = \ln a + \ln(e^{kt})$$
$$\therefore \ln y = \ln a + kt \ln(e)$$
$$\therefore \ln y = \ln a + kt$$

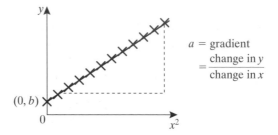

This is of the form $y = mx + c$.

Plotting a graph of $\ln y$ against t should give a straight line.

The gradient of the straight line is k.

The intercept of the line with the vertical axis is $\ln a$.

In the case of exponential growth, k is positive. In exponential decay, k is negative.

Fitting a power function

If the function used to model the data is a power relation, $y = ax^n$, take logarithms. (You can use either natural logarithms or logarithms to base 10.)

Taking natural logarithms, $\ln y = \ln(ax^n)$.

Applying the rules of logarithms gives

$$\ln y = \ln a + n \ln x.$$

A graph of $\ln y$ against $\ln x$ should be a straight line with gradient n and intercept $\ln a$. If the intercept is c, then $\ln a = c$ gives $a = e^c$.

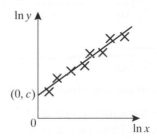

6.4 Preparing for assessment

Your coursework portfolio

For your coursework portfolio you need to produce a report of a piece of work where you find a model for data using the techniques you have just covered in this chapter.

First select some non-linear data that interests you. This may be from work you have carried out in another subject.

Plot a graph of this to identify the type of function that will be most useful in modelling all or part of your data set. This will give you an opportunity to revise what you know about a range of functions such as quadratic and other power functions (Chapter 2), exponential (Chapter 3) and trigonometric (Chapter 5) functions.

You may wish to check that the function you choose is a good choice – you may do this by considering if a transformation of one or both variable(s) will allow you to plot a straight line graph. For example, if you believe that your data may be modelled by a function of the form $y = A \sin t + c$, a graph of y plotted against values of $\sin t$ should give a straight line. This line will allow you to find values for A and c.

If you believe that the data will best be modelled by a power function of the form $y = Ae^{kt}$ or $y = ax^n$ you can use logarithmic techniques to find values for the unknown parameters.

Remember to show clearly:
- tables of data and any transformations of variables;
- all of your mathematical working, taking care to present this clearly using correct notation;
- all graphs that you draw including a final diagram that shows how well the model you find fits your original data.

Don't forget to show evidence of where you check your working.

Finally, summarise what you have done, paying particular attention to assessing how good your model is for the data you have and what it predicts will happen in the long run.

Practice exam questions

(UoM1) Light intensity

Data

1   The graph shows the results of an experiment in which the intensity of light, in milliwatts per square centimetre, was measured at distances between 100 cm and 200 cm from the source.

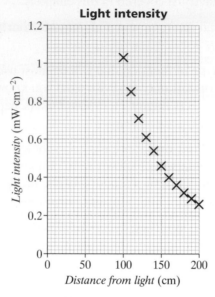

The table gives the data used to draw the graph of light intensity against distance.

Distance, x (cm)	Light intensity, y (mW cm^{-2})
100	1.03
110	0.85
120	0.71
130	0.61
140	0.54
150	0.46
160	0.40
170	0.36
180	0.32
190	0.29
200	0.26

a   Calculate the percentage decrease in the light intensity as the distance increases from 1 metre to 2 metres.

b   The function $y = ax^n$ can be used to model the data.
Show that applying the rules of logarithms to this function gives $\ln y = \ln a + n \ln x$.

c The graph below shows the result when ln y is plotted against ln x.

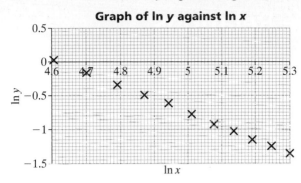

Graph of ln y against ln x

Resource Sheet 6.4Q

i What feature of the graph suggests that the function $y = ax^n$ is a suitable model for the data?

ii On a copy of this graph, draw the line of best fit and use it to show that $n \sim -2$ and $a \approx 10\,400$.

d **i** Use the model $y = 10\,400x^{-2}$ to find the value of y when $x = 150$.

ii Calculate the error in the value you found in part **d i** expressed as a percentage of the actual light intensity at a distance of 150 cm.

e **i** What does the model $y = 10\,400x^{-2}$ predict will happen to y as $x \to \infty$?

ii According to the model $y = 10\,400x^{-2}$, what would happen to y as $x \to 0$?

iii How do your answers to parts **e i** and **e ii** compare with what you would expect to happen to the light intensity in reality?

(UoM1) Resistance and voltage

Data

2 In an experiment the following values of resistance, R Ohms, and voltage, V millivolts, were taken in an electrical circuit.

R (Ohms)	45.3	49.8	52.4	57.6	62.3
V (millivolts)	113	102	96	86	79
$\dfrac{1}{V}$					

It is thought that R and V are connected by a law of the form $R = \dfrac{a}{V} + b$.

a Complete the table, giving the values of $\dfrac{1}{V}$.

b Plot a graph of R against $\dfrac{1}{V}$.

c Find the gradient and y intercept for your graph.

d Use your values from **c** to find the approximate values of a and b.

7 Recurrence Relations

▶ Contents

In this final chapter you will learn about a further method of developing powerful mathematical models that you can use to make sense of situations. One area in which these methods are particularly useful is in modelling growth – you have seen throughout this book that modelling growth can be of concern to a wide range of people including scientists, economists and social scientists. In this chapter you will look, for example, at how the growth of a sunflower may be modelled using **recurrence relations**.

You may have grown a sunflower as a child – they grow particularly tall and quickly. However, as you can see from this data and its graph, the functions you have met so far will not be suitable for modelling its growth effectively over the entire range.

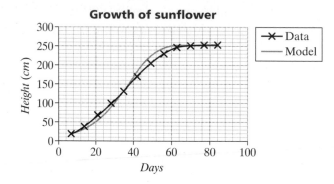

Days	Height (cm)
7	17.9
14	36.3
21	67.7
28	98.1
35	131.0
42	169.5
49	205.5
56	228.3
63	247.1
70	250.5
77	253.8
84	254.5

Recurrence relations tell you how to get from one value to the next. For example, a simple model for growth in this case is $H_n = H_{n-1} + 0.75H_{n-1}$. Taking $H_0 = 18$ cm, then $H_1 = 31.5$ cm, $H_2 = 55.1$ cm, and so on.

A more complex recurrence relation is

$$H_n = H_{n-1} + 0.8H_{n-1}\left(1 - \frac{H_{n-1}}{255}\right).$$

You can see from the graphs of the data and this model above that this is very effective at modelling the growth. Although this recurrence relation may look complicated, you will see in this chapter that it is relatively easy to work with, particularly when you use a spreadsheet to do the calculations.

7.1 Basic recurrence relations

Key web search terms

recurrence relations
difference equations

Who wants to be a millionaire?

In your interest   Population growth

In this section, you will return to explore, using new mathematical techniques, some of the examples of growth that you first met in Section 3.1.

Who wants to be a millionaire? – Revisited

Think back to the growth of prize money in the *Who wants to be a millionaire?* TV quiz show that you first investigated in **Section 3.1**.

At most stages the prize money doubles, but there are a few steps where this is not the case, so that the final prize is a million.

The model introduced in **Section 3.1** looked at the case of *always* doubling to get from one prize to the next. The first few values of prize money resulting from this model are shown in the spreadsheet opposite. $£P_n$ is the value of the nth prize.

Since you always double to get from one prize to the next,
$P_2 = 2 \times P_1$
$P_3 = 2 \times P_2$ and so on.

In general, $P_{n+1} = 2 \times P_n$.

Equations such as these are called **recurrence relations** because you can use them repetitively to find subsequent values from a given starting value. They are also known as **difference equations** because they also allow you to find the difference between each term and the next.

To use a recurrence relation to generate a sequence of numbers you need to know the relationship and a starting value.

Spreadsheets are particularly useful when using recurrence relations because you can 'fill down' to calculate successive values.

	A	B
1	Prize number	Prize value
2	n	$£P_n$
3	1	100
4	2	200
5	3	400
6	4	800

Discussion point

Do you understand this statement? Can you explain it to someone else?

	A	B
1	Prize number	Prize value
2	n	$£P_n$
3	1	100
4	2	300
5	3	900
6	4	2700

Spreadsheet for $P_{n+1} = 3 \times P_n$

	A	B
1	Prize number	Prize value
2	n	$£P_n$
3	1	100
4	=A3+1	=3*B3
5	=A4+1	=3*B4
6	=A5+1	=3*B5

Activity 7.1A

1 Investigate the prize money you would obtain on the quiz show if $P_{n+1} = 3P_n$ and $P_1 = 100$.
   Use a spreadsheet to do this.
   The first few rows of the spreadsheet are shown in the margin. The second diagram shows the formula in each cell.
   Note:
   • The formula in cell A4 is '=A3+1'. This calculates the prize number by adding one to the previous prize number.
   • The formula in cell B4 is '=3*B3'. The prize money is three times the previous prize money, reflecting the recurrence formula $P_{n+1} = 3 \times P_n$.

2 Use a spreadsheet to investigate the effect of varying the multiple, k, used to get from the value of one prize to the next where $P_{n+1} = kP_n$.
Try $k = 1.5$, $k = 2.5$ and $k = 5$.

3 *A challenge*: Can you find a value of k that would result in a final prize of one million?

Savings revisited

In **Section 3.1** you investigated a model for the growth of savings. Each year, interest of 4% was added to the amount in the account so that at the end of a year the amount in the account was given by:

amount at end of year = amount at start of year + interest for year

The interest for the year is 4% (or 0.04) of the amount in the account at the start of the year, so:

amount at end of year = 1.04 × amount at start of year

If £A_n denotes the amount in the account at the end of the nth year, you can write this using symbols as $A_{n+1} = 1.04 A_n$.

Activity 7.1B

1 Check that the recurrence relation $A_{n+1} = 1.04 A_n$, with $A_0 = 40$, gives the same value for A_{10} that you found in **Activity 3.1B**.

2 How much interest would your investment of £40 have earned after 10 years?

3 Explain why the amount of interest earned at the end of $(n+1)$ years, £I_{n+1}, is given by $I_{n+1} = 1.04 A_n - 40$.

4 a Set up a spreadsheet to calculate successive values of A_n and I_n.

	A	B	C
1	End of year	Amount	Interest
2	n	£A_n	£I_n
3	0	40	0
4	1	41.6	1.6

b Use your spreadsheet to find how many years it would take to
i earn £20 interest
ii double your money.

Population growth revisited

In **Section 1.5** you investigated the model proposed by Thomas Malthus that the population of Great Britain would double every 25 years. He made the statement in 1798, when the population was 7 million.

Activity 7.1C

1 Write down a recurrence relation to find successive values, P_n, of the population for successive periods of twenty-five years.

2 You can use a spreadsheet to calculate successive values of year and population. Take $Y_0 = 1798$ and $P_0 = 7\,000\,000$.

	A	B	C
1	n	Year	Population
2		Y_n	P_n
3	0	1798	7000000
4	1	1823	14000000
5	2	1848	28000000

a Explain why in the spreadsheet the formula:
   i in cell B4 is '=B3+25'
   ii in cell C4 is '=2*C3'.

b Complete a spreadsheet such as that above to calculate the growth of the population of Great Britain from 1798 to the present day.

c Draw a graph that contrasts Malthus' model with the actual data.

d Write a paragraph that compares and contrasts predictions made by Malthus' model with the data.

Year	England and Wales population (thousands)
1811	10 164
1821	12 000
1831	13 897
1841	15 914
1851	17 928
1861	20 066
1871	22 712
1881	25 974
1891	29 002
1901	32 612
1911	36 136
1921	37 932
1931	39 988
1941	41 748
1951	43 815
1961	46 196
1971	49 152
1981	49 634
1991	51 099
2001	52 211

7.2 More complex examples of recurrence relations

Credit cards

Credit cards

Predator–prey relationships

Supermarket trolleys

If you use a credit card to buy goods you get a bill each month. You are charged interest on the amount not paid back the previous month and you must pay a minimum amount depending on the outstanding balance.

Example:
Suppose that you use a credit card to buy a hi-fi system costing £500. The credit card company will charge you 1.5% interest each month. At the end of each month you must pay a minimum of 3% of the outstanding balance or £5, whichever is the larger amount. Suppose, however, you pay back £50 each month and do not buy any more goods using this card.

Row 2 of the spreadsheet shows that you owe the company £500.

	A	B	C	D	E	F
	End of month	Interest	Balance on bill	Minimum payment	Actual payment	Remaining balance
2	0		£ 500.00			£ 500.00
3	1	£ 7.50	£ 507.50	£ 15.23	£ 50.00	£ 457.50

Row 3 shows that at the end of the first month:
- you are charged £7.50 interest (0.015 × £500)
- the balance on your bill is £507.50 (£500 + £7.50)
- the minimum payment is £15.23 (0.03 × £507.50)
- you actually pay £50
- the balance remaining at the end of the month is £457.50 (£507.50 − £50).

The balance remaining at the end of each month, $£B_{n+1}$, is given by
$$B_{n+1} = B_n + 0.015B_n - 50$$

(the balance at the end of the previous month + interest charged − £50 payment).

Simplifying this gives $B_{n+1} = 1.015B_n - 50$.

Activity 7.2A

1 Write down the spreadsheet formula in cell
   a B3
   b C3
   c D3
   d E3
   e F3.

2 Set up a spreadsheet such as that above to investigate this situation. Use the 'fill down' facility of the spreadsheet to investigate what happens in successive months.

---

3 **a** How long would it take to pay back the £500 you borrowed from the credit card company?

   b What is the total interest you would pay to the credit card company?

   c Express the total interest you would pay as a percentage of the initial loan.

Activity 7.2B

The table shows the different monthly rates of interest charged by a range of credit cards. Use a spreadsheet to investigate the difference in the length of time it takes to pay back a debt of £1000 at £100 per month for the cards with the highest and lowest interest rates.

Card	APR (%)	Monthly interest rate (%)
Smile	12.9	1.016
Alliance and Leicester	17.4	1.346
Halifax	17.9	1.382
Bank of Scotland	19.9	1.524
Sainsburys	15.9	1.237
Marbles	14.9	1.164
MBNA	14.9	1.164
Barclays	18.9	1.453
Natwest	18.9	1.453
NextGold	25.9	1.938
Marks and Spencer	18.9	1.453

Source: Moneyfacts, correct as at November 2001

Discussion points
Find some current interest rates charged by credit cards. Do they represent good value?

Predator–prey relationships

Populations of different animal species are affected by many factors, some of which can be modelled using recurrence relations.
For example, suppose there is a population of 1000 mice in a wood and, if there were no predators, the population would increase by 20% each year. The number of mice, M_n, after n years, is given by $M_n = M_{n-1} + 0.2M_{n-1}$.

Discussion points
Can you explain why this recurrence relation models the population?

Is this a realistic model? What factors could affect the numbers of mice in the wood?

Activity 7.2C

1 **a** Set up a spreadsheet using the model
      $M_n = M_{n-1} + 0.2M_{n-1}$ to calculate the number of mice over 20 years, where M_0 is 1000.

   b How long does it take the population of mice to double?

2 a How does changing the number 0.2 in the formula affect the number of mice over 20 years?

b How does changing M_0 affect the number of mice over 20 years?

c Sketch graphs to illustrate your answers to parts **a** and **b**.

One of the factors affecting the number of mice in the wood is the fact that there are predators that kill and eat mice. Suppose that there are owls in the wood that kill 180 mice a year.

3 a Change your spreadsheet to reflect this situation.

b How does it affect the number of mice over 20 years?

c By changing the number of mice killed each year by owls, can you wipe out the population of mice within 20 years?

d How many mice would the owls have to kill each year for the population to remain stable?

This is, of course, still a very simple model of a complex situation; many other factors are involved in reality. For example, the number of owls living in the wood will depend on the number of mice and vice versa.

In the next activity you will investigate a more complex model.

Assume that:
- initially there are 10 owls
- each year the number of owls is 1% of the number of mice in the previous year
- each owl kills 18 mice a year
- initially there are 1000 mice
- mice reproduce so that their numbers increase by 20% each year.

The spreadsheet shows the numbers of mice and owls for the first 5 years.

B3	▼	=	=B2+0.2*B2−18*C2

	A	B	C
1	Year	Number of mice	Number of owls
2	0	1000	10
3	1	1020	10
4	2	1044	10
5	3	1069	10
6	4	1095	11
7	5	1122	11

Note
This spreadsheet has been formatted to only show integer values in each cell.

Activity 7.2D

1 a The formula in cell B3 is '=B2+B2*0.2−18*C2'. Explain each element of this formula.

 b Write down what this formula would be if the population of mice were increasing by 30% each year and if every owl killed 25 mice each year.

 c What is the formula in cell C3?

2 a Set up a spreadsheet to reproduce the one above.

 b What happens to the number of mice over 20 years?

 c Change the values of the parameters in your formulae and note what happens. Illustrate your answers with sketch graphs.

Supermarket trolleys

Customers arriving at a supermarket pick up trolleys either in the car park or at the entrance to the supermarket.

Of the trolleys picked up in the car park, 80% are returned there and the remaining 20% are returned to the supermarket entrance.

Of the trolleys picked up at the supermarket entrance, 60% are returned there and the remaining 40% are returned to the car park.

Assume that:
- at the start of the day there are 150 trolleys in each location
- in any hour, all trolleys in a location at the beginning of the hour are picked up by customers
- customers return trolleys to either location at the end of the hour.

Activity 7.2E

1 a Explain why $C_n = 0.8C_{n-1} + 0.4E_{n-1}$, where C_n is the number of trolleys in the car park at the end of the nth hour and E_n is the number of trolleys at the entrance to the supermarket at the end of the nth hour.

 b Write a similar recurrence relation for E_n.

 c Make a table to show what happens to the number of trolleys in both locations during the day.

 d Experiment with different starting numbers of trolleys and with different proportions of trolleys being returned to the two different locations.

2 This model is not very realistic. Say why, and suggest some ways in which it could be made more realistic. Can you write some improved recurrence relations?

7.3 More sophisticated models

A basic model

The table and graph show the growth of the population of England and Wales over the last two hundred years. Initially the growth is quite rapid but, as you can see, this rate of growth is now slowing down. You can use recurrence relations to model this growth. To take account of the long term slowdown in growth requires a quite complex equation – the logistic equation. You will learn about this in this section.

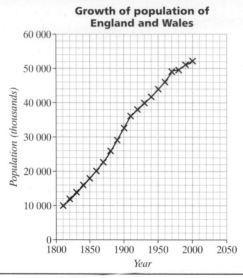

Growth of population of England and Wales

A basic model
The logistic equation

Year	England and Wales population (thousands)
1811	10 164
1821	12 000
1831	13 897
1841	15 914
1851	17 928
1861	20 066
1871	22 712
1881	25 974
1891	29 002
1901	32 612
1911	36 136
1921	37 932
1931	39 988
1941	41 748
1951	43 815
1961	46 196
1971	49 152
1981	49 634
1991	51 099
2001	52 211

Activity 7.3A

Excel Activity

Develop a spreadsheet like that below so that you can investigate the growth of the population of England and Wales, using the data in the table.

Points to note:
- Column B has been added to allow you to use notation such as P_n.
- In column D, calculate the increase in population ($P_n - P_{n-1}$) by subtracting the previous population (ten years earlier) from the current population.
- In column E, calculate the fractional increase in population by dividing the increase by the previous population.

Make sure your spreadsheet is complete for the years 1811–2001.

	A	B	C	D	E
1	Year		England and Wales population (thousands)	Increase	Fractional increase
2					
3		n	P_n	$P_n - P_{n-1}$	$(P_n - P_{n-1})/P_{n-1}$
4	1811	0	10 164		
5	1821	1	12 000	1 836	0.18
6	1831	2	13 897	1 897	0.16
7	1841	3	15 914	2 017	0.15

Discussion points

How might a population such as that of England and Wales grow?

What factors might affect growth?

What do you think will happen in the long run?

For the first one hundred years the fractional increase in the population is relatively constant when compared with more recent values.

Activity 7.3B

Excel Activity

1   Investigate how well the recurrence relation, $P_n = P_{n-1} + 0.13P_{n-1}$, with $P_0 = 10\,164$, models the population data. Do this by using a new spreadsheet. Into this, copy the first three columns from the spreadsheet above and in column D, calculate the population predicted by the recurrence relation.

	A	B	C	D
1	Year		England and Wales	Model 1
2			population (thousands)	
3		n	P_n	$P_n = P_{n-1} + 0.13*P_n$
4	1811	0	10 164	10 164
5	1821	1	12 000	11 485
6	1831	2	13 897	12 978

2   Draw a graph of the data together with the model. Confirm that the model closely matches the data for the first one hundred years but after this there is considerable divergence.

3   Use your spreadsheet to investigate how well the recurrence relation $P_n = P_{n-1} + rP_{n-1}$ models the population data for various values of r. Draw graphs to illustrate your investigations. What do you conclude?

4   In general what is the long-term behaviour of models of the form $P_n = P_{n-1} + rP_{n-1}$?

Discussion point
The recurrence relation has been written as $P_n = P_{n-1} + 0.13P_{n-1}$. It could equally have been written as $P_{n+1} = P_n + 0.13P_n$ (with $P_1 = 10\,164$) Can you explain why?

Discussion points
Why is $P_n = P_{n-1} + rP_{n-1}$ (where r is a constant that depends on the population and other factors) unlikely to be a reasonable model for the growth of a population where P_n is the population at the end of the nth time interval?

Would models of the form $P_n = P_{n-1} + rP_{n-1}$ be suitable over a restricted range?

The logistic equation

You can use models of the form $P_n = P_{n-1} + rP_{n-1}$ to model the growth of a population when there is relatively **rapid** and **unrestricted growth**. However, in the long term, populations usually reach a **steady** or **equilibrium value**. In reality a population will fluctuate about this 'steady' value.

In 1946, a Belgian scientist, Verhulst, developed a more sophisticated model to reflect this. He did this by reasoning that population growth depends not only on the size of the current population but also on how far the current size is away from an upper limit called the carrying capacity.

The general equation introduced by Verhulst is:

$$P_n = P_{n-1} + rP_{n-1}\left(1 - \frac{P_{n-1}}{K}\right)$$

This is sometimes called the **Verhulst equation** or the **logistic equation.**

The **carrying capacity, K**, is the maximum population size that can be supported. This limit may depend on a range of factors, e.g. how much food can be produced, how much space members of the population require and so on.

Activity 7.3C

1   Use a spreadsheet to investigate the logistic equation for the growth of the population of England and Wales using: $P_0 = 10\,164$ (population in 1811), $r = 0.18$ (the growth factor for the population growing between 1811 and 1821), and $K = 60\,000$ (estimated carrying capacity).

	A	B	C	D
1	Year		England and Wales population (thousands)	Model 2
2				
3		n	P_n	$P_n = P_{n-1} + 0.18*P_{n-1}(1 - P_{n-1}/60000)$
4	1811	0	10 164	10 164
5	1821	1	12 000	11 684
6	1831	2	13 897	13 377

Spreadsheet formulae:

	A	B	C	D
1	Year		England and Wales population (thousands)	Model 2
2				
3		n	P_n	$P_n = P_{n-1} + 0.18*P_{n-1}(1 - P_{n-1}/60000)$
4	1811	0	10 164	10 164
5	=A4+10	=B4+1	12 000	=D4+0.18*D4(1−D4/60000)
6	=A5+10	=B5+1	13 897	=D5+0.18*D5(1−D5/60000)

2   Draw a graph that shows both the data and model.

3   Comment on how this logistic model compares with the basic model you explored in **Activity 7.3B**.

4   Investigate how the logistic equation $P_n = P_{n-1} + rP_{n-1}\left(1 - \dfrac{P_{n-1}}{K}\right)$ can be used to model the growth of the population of England and Wales by experimenting with different values of r and K. Base your choice of values on information you have from the data.

Activity 7.3D

You have investigated the growth of the population of England and Wales using

• the basic recurrence relation $P_n = P_{n-1} + 0.13P_{n-1}$

(Activity 7.3B)

• the logistic equation $P_n = P_{n-1} + rP_{n-1}\left(1 - \dfrac{P_{n-1}}{K}\right)$

(Activity 7.3C).

The two equations differ by the multiplying term $\left(1 - \dfrac{P_{n-1}}{K}\right)$.

What effect does this have?

1   **a**   When $P_{n-1} = P_0$, so P_{n-1} is considerably smaller than K, what happens to the term $\left(1 - \dfrac{P_{n-1}}{K}\right)$?

     b   What happens to the logistic equation in this case?

2   **a**   When $P_{n-1} \approx K$, what happens to the term $\left(1 - \dfrac{P_{n-1}}{K}\right)$?

     b   What happens to the logistic equation in this case?

7.4 Revision summary

Recurrence relations

Sometimes a sequence of terms can be described by giving a starting value and the relationship between consecutive terms. Such a relationship is called a **recurrence relation**.

Relationships of this type are also known as **difference equations** because they give the difference between successive terms in a sequence.

Examples:

$P_{n+1} = 2P_n$ with $P_1 = 100$ gives the sequence of prizes when the first prize is £100 and the prize money doubles from each prize to the next.

$A_{n+1} = 1.05A_n$, with $A_0 = 70$ gives the amount in an account at the end of the nth year if £70 is invested at a fixed rate of interest at 5% per annum.

$B_{n+1} = B_n + 0.015B_n - 50$, with $B_0 = 600$ gives the balance at the end of each month when £600 is spent on a credit card account charging interest at 1.5% per month if a payment of £50 is made at the end of each month.

Modelling growth

Basic model of population growth

The population at the end of the nth time interval is given by $P_n = P_{n-1} + rP_{n-1}$, where r is the percentage increase during each time interval (written as a decimal).

Models of this form result in unlimited exponential growth, but can be useful in modelling reality over a restricted range.

Example:

A population growing at 9% per year from an initial population of 5000 can be modelled by

$P_n = P_{n-1} + 0.09P_{n-1}$ with $P_0 = 5000$.

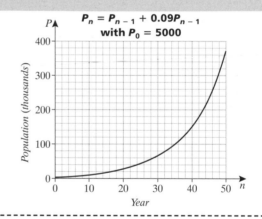

The logistic equation

The **Verhulst equation** or **logistic equation** is:

$$P_n = P_{n-1} + rP_{n-1}\left(1 - \frac{P_{n-1}}{K}\right)$$

The carrying capacity, K, is the maximum population size that can be supported. K may depend on a range of factors, e.g. availability of food and space.

Example:

A population growing at 9% per year from an initial population of 5000 with a carrying capacity of 20 000 can be modelled by

$$P_n = P_{n-1} + 0.09P_{n-1}\left(1 - \frac{P_{n-1}}{20\,000}\right)$$ with $P_0 = 5000$.

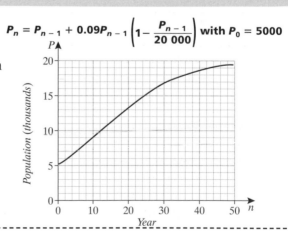

7.5 Preparing for assessment

Practice exam question

(UoM4) **Credit card**

A holidaymaker has paid for a holiday costing £640 using her credit card. She makes regular monthly payments to pay off this debt and does not buy anything else using the card until the debt is cleared.

The recurrence relation $A_{n+1} = A_n + \dfrac{r}{100}A_n - M$ can be used to find the amount owed at the end of each month. £A_n represents the amount owed at the end of the nth month, $r\%$ is the monthly interest rate and £M is the fixed amount paid by the holidaymaker each month.

a   i   If the holidaymaker pays £50 each month and the interest rate is fixed at 1.25% per month, show that the recurrence relation can be written as $A_{n+1} = 1.0125A_n - 50$.

    ii   Show that after 2 months the holidaymaker owes £555.48.

    iii   The table below shows the amount owed at the end of each month. Use the recurrence relation to complete a copy of the table. Extend the table until the amount owed at the end of a month becomes less than £10. When this occurs the holidaymaker pays off the remaining debt.

End of month	Amount owed
0	£640.00
1	
2	£555.48
3	
4	
5	

iv   What is the total amount of interest paid by the holidaymaker?

b   i   Draw a graph on graph paper to show the amount owed at the end of each month.

    ii   Explain briefly, using a sketch, how the graph would change if the interest rate were greater than 1.25%

c   If the holidaymaker did not pay off £50 per month, the recurrence relation giving the amount owed at the end of each month would be $A_{n+1} = 1.0125A_n$.

    i   In this case, write A_{12} in terms of A_0.

    ii   The APR is the annual percentage rate of interest. Use your answer to **c i** to find the APR for this credit card.

Using Technology

Throughout this course you will find it useful to use technology to help you not only find the solutions to problems but also to investigate situations and to learn new mathematics.

In addition to your **graphic calculator**, for some topics you will find it useful to use a **spreadsheet** and at other times you may use **graph plotting software** on a computer. Spreadsheets and graph plotting software are particularly useful when you want to print out your work.

You need to have a graphic calculator when you are working through this book – and also when you are preparing work for your coursework portfolio and when you are sitting the written examination papers.

Graphic calculators

You will find a graphic calculator helpful when carrying out all calculations – but particularly useful when investigating graphs of functions (e.g. when you try to find a function to model data), or when working with recurrence relations.

Plotting graphs

You need to learn how to use your graphic calculator to plot graphs of functions. When doing this it is important to use notation appropriately so that you get a plot of the correct graph. For example, you need to use brackets when entering trigonometrical functions such as $y = \sin(2x + 30)$. You also need to make sure that you view the graph using a suitable 'window'.

The graphic calculator draws graphs using small rectangular elements of the screen called pixels. For this reason the graph may look 'blocky'.

You may find it useful to use some of the features of your graphic calculator such as the **Trace** facility, which allows you to find the coordinates of points on a graph. Be warned that this facility only allows you to find pixels that the graphic calculator has used, so if you want to find where a function intersects the y axis you may not be able to use the trace facility to find y when x is exactly zero.

Discussion point

Consider the following graphic calculator screen. Is it a graph of $y = x^2$?

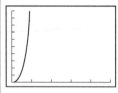

It is viewed in the window

```
WINDOW
 Xmin=0
 Xmax=50
 Xscl=10
 Ymin=0
 Ymax=1000
 Yscl=100
 Xres=1
```

whereas if you view it with the window

```
WINDOW
 Xmin=-50
 Xmax=50
 Xscl=10
 Ymin=-1000
 Ymax=1000
 Yscl=100
 Xres=1
```

it becomes clear that it is the graph of $y = x^3$.

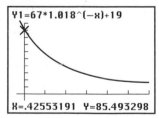

Finding where the curve of the function $y = 67 \times 1.018^{-x} + 19$ crosses the y axis

In this case, using the **Zoom** facility can give you a more accurate result: the first diagram alongside shows the identification of a 'zoom box' that becomes the whole screen in the second diagram.

When asked to make a **sketch** of a graph make sure that your drawing includes all the important features, such as where the graph crosses the axes.

Graphic calculator screen: Sketch:

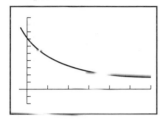

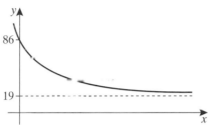

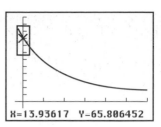
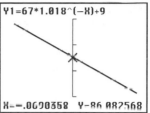

Zooming in using a 'zoom box'

Working with recurrence relations

You can use your graphic calculator very effectively to find successive terms using a recurrence relation. In **Section 7.3** you modelled the growth of the population of England and Wales using the recurrence relation $P_n = P_{n-1} + 0.13P_{n-1} = 1.13P_{n-1}$ with $P_0 = 10\,164$. To do this with your graphic calculator input 10 164 and press ENTER. On the next line enter 'Ans $\times$ 1.13'. Repeatedly pressing ENTER will give you successive terms in the recurrence relation. Not all recurrence relations are as simple as this, but in most cases using the ANS and ENTER keys intelligently can save work.

```
10164
Ans*1.13        10164
                11485.32
                12978.4116
                14665.60511
                16572.13377
```

Spreadsheets

A spreadsheet is particularly useful for printing out graphs and for quickly finding successive terms generated by recurrence relations.

Plotting graphs

You can plot very good graphs of both data and functions using a spreadsheet but you need to take care so that you get the graph that you want. It is best to use the 'XY (Scatter)' option.

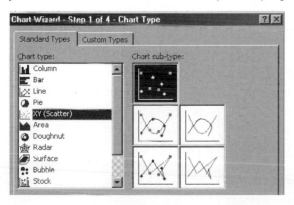

To draw a graph of the function $y = x^2$, you need to set up a table of x and y values.

Here successive x values have been found by adding 1 to the previous value and starting with $x = 0$ (in cell A2). The 'fill down' command has been used based on the formula in cell A3 to get the next nine x terms.

	A	B
1	x	y
2	0	0
3	1	1
4	2	4
5	3	9
6	4	16
7	5	25
8	6	36
9	7	49
10	8	64
11	9	81
12	10	100

You can use the formatting options to make your graph look more conventional.

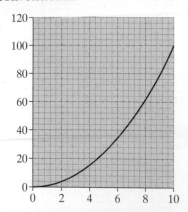

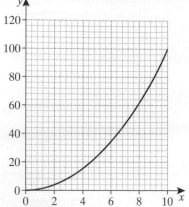

Be careful not to use the 'Line' option when drawing your graph.

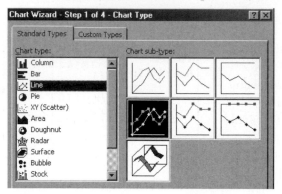

Each value of y has been found by squaring the corresponding x value – again the formula was first entered in one cell (B2) and 'fill down' used.

	A	B
1	x	y
2	0	=A2^2
3	=A2+1	=A3^2
4	=A3+1	=A4^2
5	=A4+1	=A5^2
6	=A5+1	=A6^2
7	=A6+1	=A7^2
8	=A7+1	=A8^2
9	=A8+1	=A9^2
10	=A9+1	=A10^2
11	=A10+1	=A11^2
12	=A11+1	=A12^2

Discussion point

Can you explain how the 'Line' option gives rise to the graph shown here?

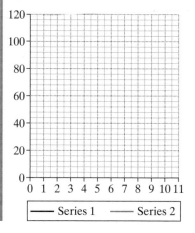

Working with recurrence relations

'Filling down' in a spreadsheet allows you to find successive terms generated by a recurrence relation. In **Section 7.3**, when you explore how the recurrence relation $P_n = 1.13P_{n-1}$ can be used to model the growth in the population of England and Wales, you can set up a spreadsheet by inputting the data and the recurrence formula only once.

	A Year	B n	C Population (thousands)	D Model
2	1811	0	10,164	10164
3	1821	1	12,000	11485
4	1831	2	13,897	12978
5	1841	3	15,914	14666
6	1851	4	17,928	16572
7	1861	5	20,066	18727
8	1871	6	22,712	21161
9	1881	7	25,974	23912
10	1891	8	29,002	27020
11	1901	9	32,612	30533
12	1911	10	36,136	34502
13	1921	11	37,932	38988
14	1931	12	39,988	44056
15	1941	13	41,748	49783
16	1951	14	43,815	56255
17	1961	15	46,196	63568
18	1971	16	49,152	71832
19	1981	17	49,634	81170
20	1991	18	51,099	91723
21	2001	19	52,211	103647

Notice how you only need to input the data in column C.

You can calculate:
- each successive year after you have input the start year in cell A2;
- each successive value of n after you have input the initial value in cell B2;
- each successive value of P_n after you have input the initial value (the actual population in 1811) in cell D2.

	A	B	C	D
1	Year	n	Population (thousands)	Model
2	1811	0	10164	10164
3	=A2+10	=B2+1	12000	=1.13*D2
4	=A3+10	=B3+1	13897	=1.13*D3
5	=A4+10	=B4+1	15914	=1.13*D4
6	=A5+10	=B5+1	17928	=1.13*D5
7	=A6+10	=B6+1	20066	=1.13*D6
8	=A7+10	=B7+1	22712	=1.13*D7
9	=A8+10	=B8+1	25974	=1.13*D8
10	=A9+10	=B9+1	29002	=1.13*D9
11	=A10+10	=B10+1	32612	=1.13*D10
12	=A11+10	=B11+1	36136	=1.13*D11
13	=A12+10	=B12+1	37932	=1.13*D12
14	=A13+10	=B13+1	39988	=1.13*D13
15	=A14+10	=B14+1	41748	=1.13*D14
16	=A15+10	=B15+1	43815	=1.13*D15
17	=A16+10	=B16+1	46196	=1.13*D16
18	=A17+10	=B17+1	49152	=1.13*D17
19	=A18+10	=B18+1	49634	=1.13*D18
20	=A19+10	=B19+1	51099	=1.13*D19
21	=A20+10	=B20+1	52211	=1.13*D20

You may need to use 'absolute' cell references when filling down. This means that the value used in a formula remains constant. For example, in the formulae in the cells in column D, the value of 0.15 in cell F2 is always used.

	A	B	C	D	E	F
1	Year	n	Population (thousands)	Model		
2	1811	0	10164	10164	r=	0.15
3	=A2+10	=B2+1	12000	=(1+$F$2)*D2		
4	=A3+10	=B3+1	13897	=(1+$F$2)*D3		
5	=A4+10	=B4+1	15914	=(1+$F$2)*D4		
6	=A5+10	=B5+1	17928	=(1+$F$2)*D5		
7	=A6+10	=B6+1	20066	=(1+$F$2)*D6		
8	=A7+10	=B7+1	22712	=(1+$F$2)*D7		
9	=A8+10	=B8+1	25974	=(1+$F$2)*D8		
10	=A9+10	=B9+1	29002	=(1+$F$2)*D9		
11	=A10+10	=B10+1	32612	=(1+$F$2)*D10		
12	=A11+10	=B11+1	36136	=(1+$F$2)*D11		
13	=A12+10	=B12+1	37932	=(1+$F$2)*D12		
14	=A13+10	=B13+1	39988	=(1+$F$2)*D13		
15	=A14+10	=B14+1	41748	=(1+$F$2)*D14		
16	=A15+10	=B15+1	43815	=(1+$F$2)*D15		
17	=A16+10	=B16+1	46196	=(1+$F$2)*D16		
18	=A17+10	=B17+1	49152	=(1+$F$2)*D17		
19	=A18+10	=B18+1	49634	=(1+$F$2)*D18		
20	=A19+10	=B19+1	51099	=(1+$F$2)*D19		
21	=A20+10	=B20+1	52211	=(1+$F$2)*D20		

Discussion point

The spreadsheet shown here is the one above modified to investigate different growth factors without making many changes.

Can you explain how this is done?

Graph plotting software

You can use graph plotting software on a computer to carry out work towards this qualification. Again this is useful if you want to print out your work. Software such as *Autograph* allows you to plot both data and functions easily and has some powerful functions for statistical work.

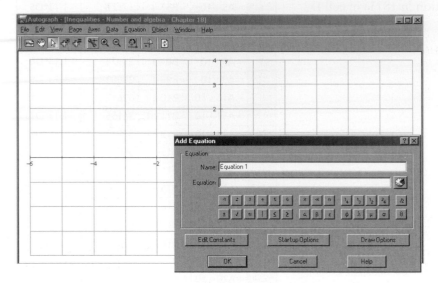

Answers

1 Rules, Laws and Models

1.1 Models of Direct Proportion

1.1A

a, b

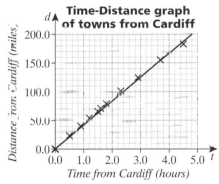

Time-Distance graph of towns from Cardiff

c The car starts off in Cardiff.

d Using points $(0, 0)$ and $(4, 170)$, the gradient is $170/4 = 42.5$.

e The gradient is defined to be 'difference in y divided by difference in x, between two different points on the line'.

f miles/hour.

g

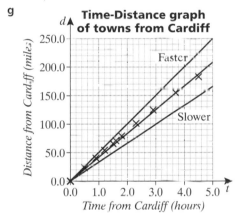

Time-Distance graph of towns from Cardiff

1.1C

1 a

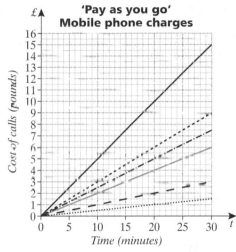

'Pay as you go' Mobile phone charges

··· Standard (Std)   ——— Same network (Std)
— Other networks (Std) ·········· Standard (Off-peak)
– Same network   ·–·–· Other networks
  (Off-peak)   (Off-peak)

b Gradients are the rates shown in the table, but given in £/minute rather than pence/minute.

2 $C = 0.01mt$ for each line, where m is the tariff in pence/minute as given in the table.

1.1D

1

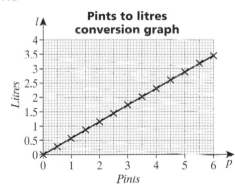

Pints to litres conversion graph

2 ab In the form $y = kx$, the conversion is given by $p = 0.57l$, with $k = 0.57$.

1.1E

1 $N = \dfrac{1}{4.448}F$

1.1F

1 Government against business: $k = 0.5$.

2 Fat against flour: $k = 0.5$.

3 VAT against price before: $k = 0.175$.

1.1G

1

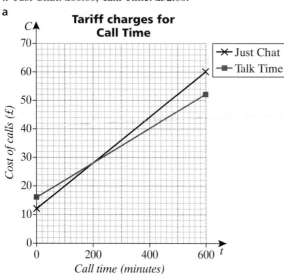

2 $E = 110Y$

3 $E = 0.9S$

4 $Y = 0.00818S$

5 $S = 122.22Y$

1.2 Linear Models

1.2A

1 i Just Chat: £16.80, Talk Time: £19.60.
  ii Just Chat: £60.00, Talk Time: £52.00.

2 a

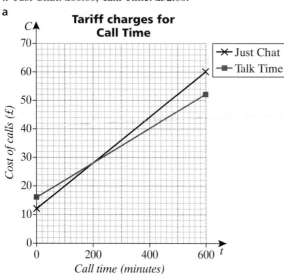

b Just Chat: 0.08, Talk Time: 0.06.
  The gradient of each line represents the call time for each tariff (in £/min).

c Just Chat: 12, Talk Time: 16.
  The intercept of the lines with the cost axis represents the line rental (in £'s).

d $(t, C) = (200, 28)$ – this represents the call time at which both tariffs charge the same.

3 i Just Chat: $C = 12 + 0.08t$
  Talk Time: $C = 16 + 0.06t$
  ii $t = 200$, $C = 28$.

4 Answers in **2d** and **3** are the same.

1.2C

1 400 gallons.

2 a

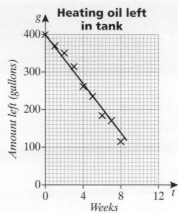

b Gradient is approximately -32.5.

c The gradient is negative indicating a loss in oil with time, and the number represents the oil loss/week.

3 a $g = 400 - 32.5$ **b** 9 weeks.

1.2D

2 a $c = 1.77$ **b** $y = 0.08x + 1.77$

1.2F

1 a Let £C be the charge and t be the number of hours for a call-out.
  $C = 25 + 20t$

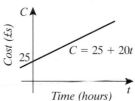

This is a good model that can be extended in the long term.

b Let £L be the size of the loan owing and w be the number of weeks into paying back the loan.
  $L = 120 - 18w$

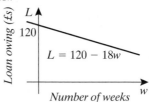

This is a good model that is used commonly, but this particular model is only valid for $0 \leqslant w \leqslant 7$.

c Let $v \, \text{ms}^{-1}$ be the speed of the car and t seconds be the time that it has been accelerating.
  $v = 25 + 0.5t$

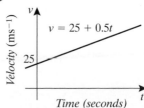

This could be possible because acceleration depends on the car model, but $25 \, \text{ms}^{-1}$ is 90 kph and is unlikely to continue accelerating for more than about one minute.

d Let H cm be the height of the candle and t be the number of hours it burns for.

$H = 20 - 1.6t$

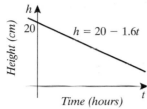

This is a good model, but is only valid for $0 \leqslant t \leqslant 13$.

e Let $T°C$ be the temperature of the joint and h be the number of hours it has been defrosting.

$T = -18 + 1.5h$

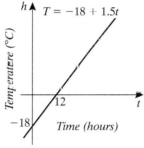

This could model this for a *limited* length of time because cooling actually depends on the temperature difference between the joint and the surrounding air.

1.2II

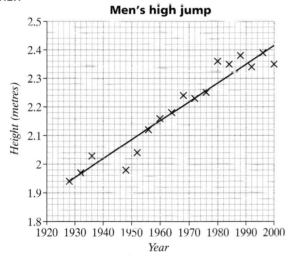

Using the points (1930, 1.95) and (1980, 2.29):

$H = 0.0068Y - 11.174$

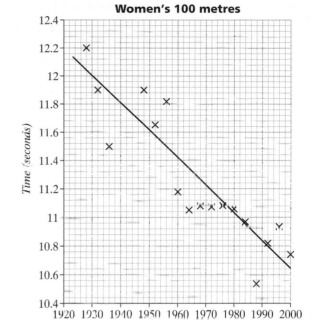

Using the points (1930, 12) and (1980, 11.4):

$T = -0.012Y + 35.16$

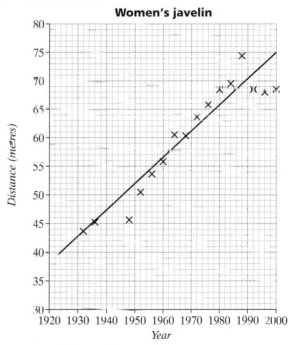

Using the points (1940, 47) and (1990, 70):

$D = 0.46Y - 845.4$

In the long term, these linear models do not have limits. These are also the best performances of the year and not world records, so will fluctuate between years, but the overall trend will be for all 3 events, times/heights/distances to level off:

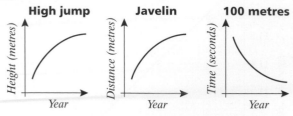

1.2I(a) & 1.2I(b)

1 The demand decreases as the price increases. Moreover, the rise in price is *directly related* to the drop in demand.

2

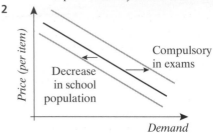

Whatever the price, fewer pupils will mean less demand for calculators. If calculators are compulsory, then demand will increase.

Half price competitor model's will be more desirable, so less demand for this particular model.

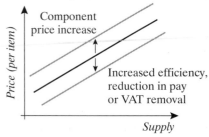

VAT removal will lower the supply line by the equivalent of the VAT increased efficiency or reduction in the pay of workforce lowers production costs.

1.2I(c)

At price £B, supply meets demand.
At the lower price £C, demand far outstrips supply and there will be a shortage. The price is likely to rise to lower demand/raise supply.

1.2I(d)

1 Demand: $P = 100 - 0.001n$, Supply: $P = 0.00125n$.
2 £55.56 to the nearest pence.

1.3 More complex linear models

1.3A

1 $T = 0, 0 \leqslant I \leqslant 5000$
$T = 0.1(I - 5000), 5000 \leqslant I \leqslant 7000$
$T = 0.22(I - 7000) + 200, 7000 \leqslant I \leqslant 37\,000$
$T = 0.4(I - 37\,000) + 6800, I \geqslant 37\,000$

1.3B

1 $C = 40, 0 \leqslant t \leqslant 400$
2 a m = 0.05 £/min
 b c = 20, $C = 0.05t + 20$
3 For the cheapest at t minutes, choose:
Just Chat for $t \leqslant 200$
Talk Time for $200 \leqslant t \leqslant 400$
Talk 400 for $t \geqslant 400$.

1.3C

2

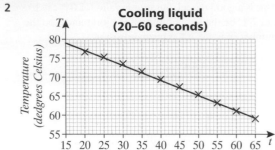

Using the points, (18, 78) and (56, 62): $T = 85.2 - 0.4t$

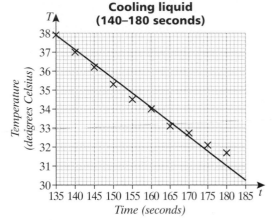

Using the points, (140, 36.8) and (180, 31.4),
$T = 55.7 - 0.135t$

3 a First model: $T = 85.2 - 0.4t$
When $t = 20$, $T = 77.2$ (76.7)
When $t = 40$, $T = 69.2$ (69.4)
When $t = 60$, $T = 61.2$ (61.0)

Second model: $T = 55.7 - 0.135t$
When $t = 140$, $T = 36.8$ (37.0)
When $t = 160$, $T = 34.1$ (34.0)
When $t = 180$, $T = 31.4$ (31.6)

The models are accurate to within 0.3 degrees Celsius for most of each range.

The models are inaccurate in the other's range, for example:
First model: $T = 85.2 - 0.4t$
When $t = 150$, $T = 25.2$ (35.3)
Second model: $T = 55.7 - 0.135t$
When $t = 40$, $T = 50.3$ (69.4)

3 b First model: $T = 85.2 - 0.4t$
When $t = 0$, $T = 85.2$
And $T = 0$ when $t = 213$

Second model: $T = 55.7 - 0.135t$
When $t = 0$, $T = 55.7$
And $T = 0$ when $t = 412.6$

Although the two models are accurate over their limited range of time, it is clear that they give completely different predictions at the extreme values.

4 A better linear model for the whole data set can be found by using as large a range of temperatures as possible, where there is data, and the line crosses close to the majority of the points.

1.3D

1

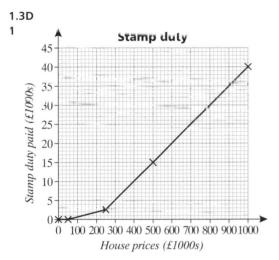

Stamp duty

y-axis: Stamp duty paid (£1000s), marked 0, 5, 10, 15, 20, 25, 30, 35, 40, 45

x-axis: House prices (£1000s), marked 0, 100, 200, 300, 400, 500, 600, 700, 800, 900, 1000

2 0%, $S = 0$, $0 \leqslant H \leqslant 60\,000$
1%, $S = 0.01H$, $60\,000 < H \leqslant 250\,000$
3%, $S = 0.03H$, $250\,000 < H \leqslant 500\,000$
4%, $S = 0.04H$, $H > 500\,000$

1.3E

1 A. Using (0, 0) & (4, 30): $v = 7.5t$
B. Using (5, 35) & (7, 47): $v = 5 + 6t$
C. Using (9, 54) & (12, 65): $v = 21 + 3.7t$

2 a Coefficient a is the gradient of the line in the graphs, so has units mph/s.

b Acceleration of the car during each phase, i.e.
Phase A, $a = 7.5$
Phase B, $a = 6$
Phase C, $a = 3.7$

3 a The value u mph represents the initial speed the car must initially have at $t = 0$, if it is to reach the speeds in each phase (at each phase's constant acceleration).
Phase A, $u = 0$ (starts from rest)
Phase B, $u = 5$
Phase C, $u = 21$

3 b Values for u in phases B and C do not model the car from rest at $t = 0$.

4 $t = 8$ seconds
Actual time taken is 10.8 seconds.
This tells us that this car cannot accelerate at the same rate through its different gears, and more specifically, it has progressively slower accelerations with each gear.

5 See Q4.

1.4 Representing rules, laws and models in different ways

1.4A

1 'Nine-fifths of the Celsius temperature and add thirty-two'.

2 $C = 0$, $F = 32$ (approx. 30), when $C = 100$, $F = 212$ (approx 230).

3 a $C = \frac{1}{9}(F - 30)$

4 $C = 10$

5 $K = C + 273$

1.4B

2 Temperature conversion
$F = \frac{9}{5}C + 32$
In the form $y = mx + c$
$m = \frac{9}{5}°F°C^{-1}$ and $c = 32°F$
m gives the change in the number of degrees Fahrenheit for a change of one degree Celsius, c is just the temperature on the Fahrenheit scale for zero degrees Celsius.

Men's 100 m fastest times
$T = 28.00729 - 0.00909Y$

In the form $y = mx + c$
$m = -0.00909s$ and $c = 28.00729s$
m gives the yearly improvement in the fastest times
c represents the (predicted) fastest time set in the year 0.

In the form $y = kx$.
Cost of petrol: $k = $ approx. 70p/litre unleaded
Currency conversion: $k = 0.9$€
Concorde flight: $k = $ approx. 1300 km/hr

1.5 How good is the model?

1.5A

1 $7 \times 2^8 = 1792$ million

3 Q1 shows that the model is not suitable for long term predictions, and Q2 shows that it took 50 years to double from 1900 to 1950, and to almost double again, in the next 50 years.

4 Surface area of the earth in acres:
$150\,000\,000 \times 247.1 = 3.7065 \times 10^{10}$ acres
Malthus' model is for a sixfold increase in wheat production for each year.
$(1 \times 6^{13} \approx 1.3 \times 10^{10}$ acres)
$1.6^{14} \approx 7.8 \times 10^{10}$ acres

1.5B

1

Time, t (hrs)	Height, h (m)
7	1.7
8	1.7 + 0.225 = 1.925
9	1.925 + 0.450 = 2.375
10	2.375 + 0.675 = 3.050
11	3.050 + 0.675 = 3.725
12	3.725 + 0.450 = 4.175
13	4.175 + 0.225 = 4.400

2

t	h (data)	h (rule)	diff.	% diff
7	1.7	1.700	–	–
8	1.8	1.925	0.125	6.9%
9	2.3	2.375	0.075	3.3%
10	3.1	3.050	−0.050	−1.6%
11	3.8	3.725	−0.075	−2.0%
12	4.3	4.175	−0.125	−2.9%
13	4.4	4.400	0.000	0.0%

1.5C

1 1975: $28.00729 - 0.00909 \times 1975 = 10.05454$ s
1981: $28.00729 - 0.00909 \times 1981 = 10$ s
2001: $28.00729 - 0.00909 \times 2001 = 9.8182$ s

2 When $Y = 0$, $T = 28.00729$ seconds.
This represents the fastest time taken to run 100 m in the year 0, as predicted by the model.

3 $T = 0$ when $Y = \dfrac{28.00729}{0.00909} \approx 3081$
This represents the year in which it will take no time to run 100 m, as predicted by the model.

4 The model is reasonably accurate over the years in the graph, although extending it *far* beyond where you have data leads to obviously incorrect/impossible results.

1.7 Practice exam questions

1 a i 340
  ii 1960 km
  b i Because the number of litres of fuel in the tank is decreasing.
  ii $-\frac{1}{4}$ (or equivalent)
  iii The average change per mile of the number of litres in the tank.
  c i $y = 490 - \frac{1}{4}x$ (or equivalent)
  ii The number of litres of fuel in the tank at the start of the journey.

2 a ii £105 200
  iii Unlikely to be very accurate as the last few data points appear to be departing from the linear model.
  b That average house prices increase by the same amount each quarter over the whole time period shown.

2 c i $y = \frac{3125}{2}x + 50\,000$
  ii The average house price rise, in pounds, per quarter.
  d i Sensible straight line.
  ii Depends on line drawn: maybe about £11 500.
  iii This estimate is larger as the second line has a greater gradient. The second estimate is likely to be more accurate as the line represents the more recent data better than the single straight line.
  e Single linear model is simple and easy to find and use. The two-line model is more complicated to calculate and use but fits the data rather more closely. Neither model is a very good fit to the data.

2 Quadratic and other models

2.1 Quadratic models

2.1B

6 a $x = 3, 5$
  b $x = 4, -4$
  c $x = 2\frac{1}{2}, 7$
  d $x = -3, 2$

2.1D

A $y = 2x(x + 3)$
B $y = -(x + 2)^2 - 1$
C $y = -3 - 2x^2$
D $y = \frac{1}{2}x^2 + 4$
E $y = (x - 1)^2 + 2$
F
G $y = 4 - x^2$
H
I used as example
J $y = (x - 2)(x - 4)$
K $y = (x - 2)^2$
L $y = 3x^2$
M $y = (x + 4)^2 + 3$
N $y = (x + 2)(x - 5)$
O $y = -(x + 1)^2 + 3$

2.1E

2 a $t = \sqrt{\dfrac{d}{k}}$

2.1H

1 linear

2

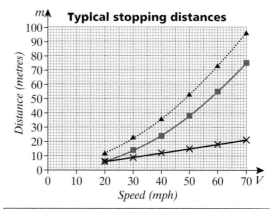

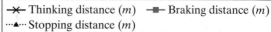

4 $B = 0.015V^2$

5 a $D = 0.015V^2 + 0.3V$
  b 44 mph, to nearest mph.

6 All increase stopping distance:
night – increased thinking distance;
wet – increased braking distance;
older drivers – increased thinking distance.

2.1I

a $T = 0.48V$; $D = 0.015V^2 + 0.48V$
b Further stopping distances because of increased thinking distance (braking distances basically unchanged).

2.1J

1 minimum at $(-2, 0)$

2.1L

4 a minimum at $(-3, -1)$ **b** minimum at $(2, -14)$

2.1M

2 51.5 mm at day 35.

3 From day 35 onwards, the height will decrease towards and then below 0 mm, making no physical sense.

2.1N

3 a Day 52: 4.65 hrs, i.e. 04:39 GMT

b Model has the time of sunrise increasing after around day 50 and from day 304, $t > 24$ which makes no physical sense.

2.1P

3 a Day 52: 21.17 hrs, i.e. 21:10 GMT

4 With decreasing accuracy: May Day, Valentine's Day, Christmas Day.

2.1Q

1 a $x = -4, 1$ **b** $x = 1\frac{1}{2}, -1$
   c $x = 3, -1$ **d** $x = 0, 5$
   e $x = \frac{1}{2}, -4$ **f** $x = -2, 5$
   g $x = -3, 7$ **h** $x = -3, 4$
   i $x = -4, \frac{1}{2}$ **j** $x = -5, \frac{1}{2}$

2 a $x = -11.745, -0.255$ **b** $x = 0.438, 4.562$
   c $x = -1, 2$ **d** $x = -1.106, 1.356$
   e $x = -0.01, -9.99$ **f** $x = -4.449, 0.449$

3 a $x = -7, 11$ **b** $x = -8.472, 0.472$
   c $x = -4, 6$ **d** $x = -4.5, 3.5$
   e $x = -0.207, 1.207$ **f** $x = -5, 1$
   g $x = -2, 8$ **h** $x = -7, 13$
   i $x = -4, 3$ **j** $x = -5.690, 3.690$

2.1R

1 a $n = -0.882, 70.882$
   b $h = 11.82, 58.18$

2 $n = 16, 84$, to nearest day after April 30th

3 $n = 28, 72$, to nearest day after April 30th

2.1S

4 £11 025 (when $x = 10.5$)

2.2 Basic curves

2.2A

3 a 1000, 100, 10, 1, 0.2

b y values will also be negative

4 a i and **ii**. Very small and positive.
   iii and **iv**. Very large and positive.

2.2B

1 B   **2** D   **3** A   **4** C   **5** E

2.2C

1 a i 21.16   **ii** 8.41   **iii** 1.44

b minimum of 0, when $t = 270.6$ to 1 dp.

c ii values of d become negative – no physical interpretation possible.

2 a i 10.70   **ii** 5.73
   b i 12.07   **ii** yes
   c i 13.72   **ii** yes

2.2D

1 994

2 a 4

3 a i 0.620   **ii** 1.061   **iii** 1.337

4 a £2.24

5 a i 7.54   **ii** 6.24

2.3 Gradients

2.3A

1 Approximate values:

Time, t (hrs)	0	50	100	150	200	250
Leak Rate (m/s^{-1})	−14	−10	−7.5	−5.8	−2.5	0

2.3B

1 a 11 degrees Celsius/hour

b 4.8 degrees Celsius/hour

2 a 8 degrees Celsius/hour (note positive, since question asks for the rate at which the temperature is *falling*).

b 3.3 degrees Celsius/hour

c 0.8 degrees Celsius/hour

3 At 5 hours, 15 hours, 30 hours and 39 hours.

2.3C

1 $(15, -9), (39, -8)$

2 a 25 hours

b 24 hours

c around 24–23 hours from the graph. (Actually about 24 hours 39 minutes long.)

2.3D

1 35 m

2 a $(4, 2)$

b After 4 seconds, the height of the flyer is at its minimum height of 2 m from the ground.

3 a i 28   **ii** 26   **iii** 24

4 a i −7.5 m/s   **ii** 5.75 m/s   **iii** −5.5 m/s

b Gradients give the speed of the ride at the times given.

5 The ride starts from its minimum height is pulled back up by the cables, accelerating it upwards before gravity brings it back down at which point the cable slows the ride down to a minimum height of 2 m.

2.3E

2 49

3 a 3 hours 38 minutes

b 60.7 units/hour

4 Slow start, highest rate of production in the middle half of shift, and a steady drop in work rate as the shift comes to an end.

5 b Very poorly. The productivity rate actually picks up rapidly and finishes at about 130 units/hour!

2.4 Using simultaneous equations

2.4A
1 $2g = s$; $g + s = 12$ **2** $g = 4$; $s = 8$

3

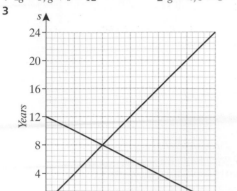

2.4B
1

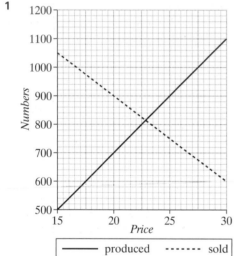

2 £22.86; 814 copies   **3** £18 608.04

2.4E
3

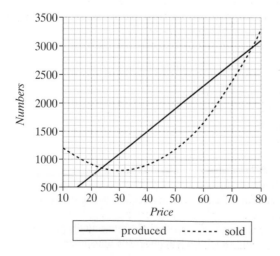

2.5 Linear inequalities

2.5A
1 Yes: $P \geqslant 15$ and $P \leqslant 33.33$.

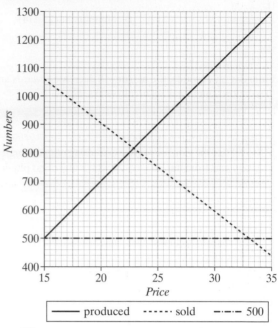

2 $t < 200$

2.5B
1

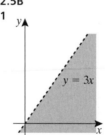

2 $5 \leqslant x <$

3 a

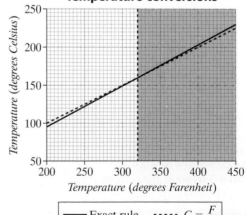

b $\dfrac{F}{2} < \dfrac{5}{9}(F - 32)$

c $F > 320$

4 a $d = 70t$ and $d = 60t$

b $d < 70t$ and $d > 0$

4 c

d $d < 70t$ and $d > 60t$

5 a $L = 500 - 0.5m$ **c** $L \geqslant 50$

2.7 Practice exam questions

1 a 206 feet

b 24.0 feet/second

c $t = 0$ and $t = 8.5$

d i 15 ft/s   **ii** 34 ft/s   **iii** 14 ft/s

e Around $t = 6$

f The emergency stop occurred at the time given in 1e.

2 a i $t = 2$ **ii** Accelerating quicker at lower speeds.

b i Between 3.15 and 4.0; between 6.5 and 6.8.

ii Gear change, and the emergency stop respectively.

c i -19 mph/s

ii $v = 161.5 - 19t$

iii the gradient would be more negative.

3 a £4500   **b** 5.5, 0.5

c ii £12 500   **iii** 3 years

d i

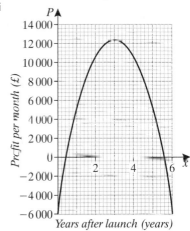

Years after launch (years)

ii Negative profit means a real life loss.

e 5 years and 5 months, to nearest month.

3 Modelling Growth

3.1 Exploring basic models of growth

3.1A

1

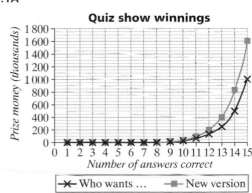

2 £1 638 400

3.1B

1 a £40

b $0.04 \times 1040 \times 41.60$

c $1000 \times 1.04^{10} = 1480.24$

2

3.1C

1 a 1040.40, 1040.00

b 1082.43; 1081.60

c 1485.95; 1480.24

2 Money grows more quickly because your savings' interest is itself earning interest more quickly – half-yearly, rather than yearly.

3.1D

1 The total amount at the end of each year includes what was in the account at the beginning of the year plus any interest earned, i.e. an increase by a factor of (1 + percentage).

2 29 years (£5116.02).

3 b The starting amount, 2500 here, is just a constant. The second term gives the factor by which the amount has increased with t, so for the same interest rate, the time taken to double will be the same, whatever the starting amount.

c Increase the percentage interest, or increase the frequency at which interest is added over each year.

3.1E

Assumptions of honesty is moving names up the list, no aliases (i.e. trying to get paid twice), people actually paying as well as moving names up the list.

You can expect £39 060 if all assumptions hold.

3.1F

1

Time, t (years)	Amount of carbon-14 (grams)	Radioactivity (disintegrations per minute per gram)
0	1	15.3
5730	0.5	7.65
11 460	0.25	3.825
17 190	0.125	1.9125
22 920	0.0625	0.95625
28 650	0.03125	0.478125
34 380	0.015625	0.2390625

2

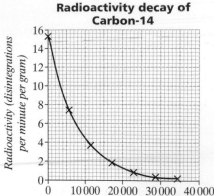

Radioactivity decay of Carbon-14

Radioactivity (disintegrations per minute per gram) vs *Time, t (years)*

3.2 Exponential growth and decay

3.2A

1 1, 2, 4, 8, 16, 32, 64, 128, 256, 512, 1024, 2048, 4096

3 $k = 1, a = 2, m = 0.05$

4 a 4   **b** 64   **c** 4096

5 a 262 144   **b** 6.872×10^{10}

6 a 4.72×10^{21} **b** 4 720 000 kg

7   **i** decay towards 0
     ii growth
     iii growth

     The difference between **ii** and **iii** is that the rate of growth is greater in **iii**.

3.2B

1

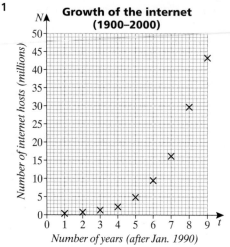

Growth of the internet (1900–2000)

Number of internet hosts (millions) vs *Number of years (after Jan. 1990)*

2 $k = 0.21, a = 1.84, m = 1$

3 a

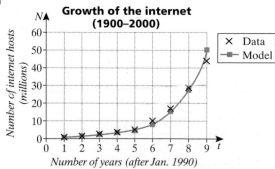

Growth of the internet (1900–2000)

× Data
■ Model

Number of internet hosts (millions) vs *Number of years (after Jan. 1990)*

b i 1993–1994   **ii** 1995–1998

c i 1999   **ii** −17.4%

4 a $N = 0.21$

     0.21 million hosts in 1990 is entirely possible, because you'd expect between 0 and 0.375 (in 1991).

     b $N = 1970$

     1.97 billion hosts in 2005 is less likely because the hosts will get more powerful, and the figure will mean a host for every third person on Earth!

     c $N = 1.85 \times 10^7$

     1.85×10^7 million hosts in 2020, seems very unrealistic because that would mean the equivalent 100 s of hosts per person on the planet!

     d $N = 4.72 \times 10^{-4}$

     472 hosts in 1980 is possible depending on when you interpret the birth of the internet as we know it (late '70s possibly, although 1983 is often quoted).

     e $N = 1.06 \times 10^{-6}$

     1 host in 1970 is not realistic, because the internet had not been invented yet!

5 Seems to fit well *for the data available*, except the data towards the ends of the range.

3.2C

1

Number of half-lives	Time, t (thousands of years)	Amount of plutonium, y (grams)
0	0	1000
1	24	500
2	48	250
3	72	125
4	96	62.5
5	120	31.25
6	144	15.625
7	168	7.8125
8	192	3.90625

2

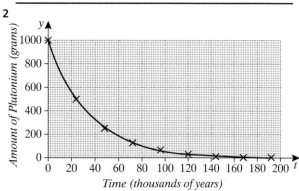

Amount of Plutonium (grams) vs *Time (thousands of years)*

3 About 80 years.

3.2D

1 $k = 1000, a = 1.029, m = -1$

2 a 751 g

3 a 229 737 g   **b** 1972 kg

4 0.930 g

5 a 0.0977%   **b** 9.54×10^{-5}%

6   **i** decay
     ii decay (slower than **i**)
     iii growth

7

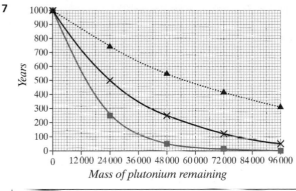

Mass of plutonium remaining

— ✕ — Plutonium ── ■ ── Lower half-life ···▲··· Higher half-life

3.2E

2 **a** around 20°C.
   b room temperature.

3 Model fits the data quite well, *except* for an hour in the middle (from 40 mins to 100 mins).

4 **a** 86.0, 30.3, 20.9, 19.3, 19.1
   b The temperature will remain at 19°C.

5 All three models have different long term temperatures, and model C has a different starting temperature from models A and B, and the recorded initial temperature. However, model C fits best the recorded temperatures over the whole range from 0 to 150 minutes.

3.3 Exponential & logarithmic functions

3.3A

2 $2^{3x} = (2^3)^x = 8^x$

3 $0.5 \times 8^x = 0.5 \times (8^x) \neq (0.5 \times 8)^x$
   $(0.5 \times 8)^x = 0.5^x \times 8^x = 4^x$

4 $y = 3 \times a^{bx}$ where $a^b = 9$, e.g. $y = 3 \times 3^{2x}$

3.3B

2 $y = 1000^x = 10^{3x}$
   $y = 100^x = 10^{2x}$
   $y = 10^x = 1000^{x/3}$

3.3C

1 End of 1st half year: £1 × 1.5 = £1.50
   End of 2nd half year: £1.50 × 1.5 = £2.25

2 At the end of each month, you will have what you started the month with and a further $\frac{1}{12}$ from the interest, i.e. you will have in any month, $(1 + \frac{1}{12})$ times as much as you had the previous month. Over a year, this factoring up, gives the formula.

3 In general, the investment at the end of the year is given by $£\left(1 + \frac{1}{n}\right)^n$, where n is the number of times interest is compounded over the year.
   As n increases, (i.e. the interest is added more frequently), the final investment tends to £2.72 – no matter how large n gets.

3.3D

a As k varies, the graph is stretched in the y-direction.
b As m varies, the graph is stretched in the x-direction.

3.3E

1 $e^{\ln p} = p$, for all positive p.
2 $\ln(e^p) = p$, for all positive p.
3 Q1 will only work when working in 'COMPLEX' mode (in 'REAL' mode the natural log of a negative number returns an error). Q2 will work for negative p.
4 They are inverse functions of one another.
5 Sketch of a log graph with: the curve crossing the x-axis at $(1, 0)$, $y \to -\infty$ as $x \to 0^+$, and y continually increasing with positive values of x.
6 There are no points in the region $x < 0$, and the graph doesn't cross the y-axis, so it looks like it is not defined for $x = 0$, leaving $\ln x$ (seemingly) defined only for $x > 0$.
7 $y = e^x$ and $y = \ln x$ are reflections of each other in the line $y = x$.

3.3F

1 $y = \log_{10} x$ and $y = \ln x$ both cross the x-axis at $x = 1$ and tend to infinity as x tends to 0 (from positive x). One is a stretch of the other in the y-direction.
2 $y = 10^x$ and $y = \log_{10} x$ are reflections of each other in the line $y = x$.

3.3G

1 Graph C – intercept of 1, graph tending to 0 as x gets very negative.
2 Graph E – intercept of 3 and graph tends to $y = 2$ as x gets very negative.
3 Graph B – intercept of 1, reflection in y-axis.
4 Graph G – intercept of 1, y becomes large and negative as x gets large and positive.
5 Graph F – intercept at 2, double the values of $y = e^x$ for each x.
6 Graph A – intercept at 3, y becomes large and negative as x gets large and positive.

3.4 Implications of models

3.4A

1 ±10 mega tonnes.

2 **a**

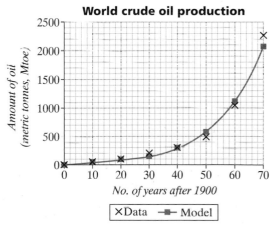

World crude oil production

No. of years after 1900

✕ Data ── ■ ── Model

b The model fits the data reasonably well except for the last data point for 1970.

3 **a** 4090 Mtoe
   b 7804 Mtoe

4 **a** −37.4%
   b −142%

5 a As $t \to \infty, y \to \infty$

b In practice, oil production will reach a maximum and then tail off because there is a limited supply of oil.

6 a 12.2 Mtoe (1890)

b 0.922 Mtoe (1850)

3.4B

1 a 1920–1970

b 1900–1910, 1980–2000

2 a 5.65 billion

b 7.1% to 1 d.p.

3 When $t = -100, y = 2.2 \times 10^{-12}$, so the model predicts less than one person alive in the year 1800!

4 Since t is the year, taking $t = 0$, the model predicts 8.7×10^{-12} billion people as the world population in the year 0; i.e. less than one person.

5 a As $t \to \infty$, the model predicts that the world population will also increase without limit at an every increasing rate.

b In the long run, the world population has a physical limit based on the land area available. Also, as countries become more developed, the birth rate generally decreases leading to near zero population growth as seen in Europe, Japan and the USA.

Functions to model this levelling of could be exponentials of the form $P = L - Ae^{-kt}$, where L is the long term population limit.

6 a 2042

b 1365

c 400

7 a 2072

b 2749

3.4C

1 & 2a

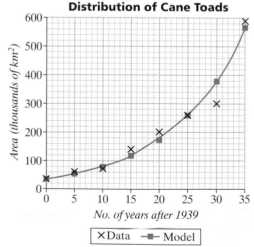

Distribution of Cane Toads

No. of years after 1939

✕ Data — ■ — Model

2 b 1969

c −25.3% percentage error

3 a $a = 0.486, b = -1.26, c = 32.8$

b When $t = 30$, i.e. 1969, as well.

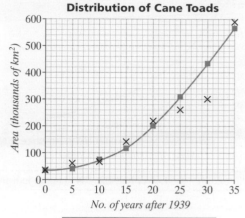

Distribution of Cane Toads

No. of years after 1939

✕ Data — ■ — Quadratic model

c −43.7%

4 a

Year	t	Exponential model	Quadratic model
1935	−4	26.7	45.6
1936	−3	28.9	41.0
1937	−2	31.2	37.3
1938	−1	33.7	34.5

b The exponential model is more realistic because we are not told that the toads had trouble settling in or there were any reasons as to why its population should drop from 1935–1938 before picking up again, as the quadratic model suggests.

5 a Exponential: $t = 68$, year 2007, Quadratic: $t = 127$, year 2066

b Neither is reasonable, because Australia will not all be suitable for the toads, and as they are also considered pests, their population spread will also be controlled by man.

6 a Both models predict an unlimited expansion of the area in which cane toads will reach.

b Long term, area occupied will stabilize – see Q5b.

3.4D

1 $\dfrac{(530 - 505)}{505} \times 100 = 5.0\%$

2 Not exponential, because increase in waste is not constant for constant time intervals (yearly, in this case).

3 &

4

Waste disposal

Number of years after 1992

✕ Data — ■ — Model A — ▲ — Model B

5 a Model A, because it is fitting the data well, including those at the ends of the range.

b Model B; because it predicts less waste for negative t, whereas Model A predicts that the waste had been falling in the years before 1992.

6

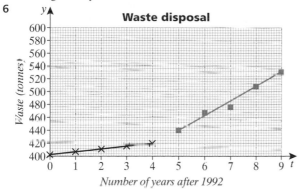

Number of years after 1992

3.4E

1 a

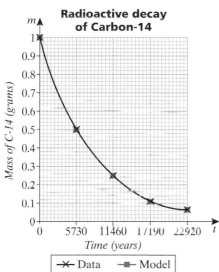

b $m \to 0$ as $t \to \infty$ and the model reflects this because the exponential term will continue to decrease towards zero: $m = e^{-0.000121t} = (e^{-0.000121})^t = 0.999879^t$

2 $k = -1.21 \times 10^{-4}$

3.4F

1 a $5^6 = 15\,625$ **b** $2 \times 5^6 = 31\,250$

2 a x^n **b** Px^n

3 Women Only (£11 110), Make Money (£3768)

4 a

Stage	New Recruits	Total Participants
1	1	1
2	10	11
3	100	111
4	1000	1111
5	10 000	11 111
6	100 000	111 111
7	1 000 000	1 111 111
8	10 000 000	11 111 111
9	100 000 000	111 111 111
10	1 000 000 000	1 111 111 111

b Very unlikely as the next stage will involve 10 billion, and the letters are meant to involve women only!

5 a Level 1: 2 new recruits
Level 2: 4 new recruits
Level 3: 8 new recruits and these contribute the £24 000.

5 b

Level	New Recruits	Total Participants
1	1	1
2	2	3
3	4	7
4	8	15
5	16	31
6	32	63
7	64	127
8	128	255
9	256	511
10	512	1023
11	1024	2047
12	2048	4095
13	4096	8191
14	8192	16 383
15	16 384	32 767
16	32 768	65 535
17	65 536	131 071
18	131 072	262 143
19	262 144	524 287
20	524 288	1 048 575
21	1 048 576	2 097 151
22	2 097 152	4 194 303
23	4 194 304	8 388 607
24	8 388 608	16 777 215
25	16 777 216	33 554 431

c As can be seen from the table, the scheme can only last 16 rounds if restricted to the Isle of Wight, and 25 rounds for the whole female population of the UK. In reality, this will be less, because people will (eventually) recognise or be warned off these pyramid schemes.

3.5 Solving exponential and logarithmic equations

3.5A

1 6.9 days

2 1991

3 1948, to nearest year.

4 5728 years, to nearest year.

3.5B

1 $t = \dfrac{\ln\left(\dfrac{m}{1000}\right)}{-0.000121}$

2 a 5728 years
b 11 457 years
c 17 185 years
d 22 914 years
e approx. 5730 years.

3.5C

Richter magnitude	Amplitude, A (millimetres)
0	1
1	10
2	100
3	1000
4	10 000
5	100 000
6	1 000 000
7	10 000 000
8	100 000 000
9	1 000 000 000

3.5D

1 $\ln 1 = 0$
$\ln 2 = 0.6931$
$\ln 3 = 1.0986$
$\ln 4 = \ln(2 \times 2) = \ln 2 + \ln 2 = 2 \times 0.6931 = 1.386$
$\ln 5 = 1.6094$
$\ln 6 = \ln(2 \times 3) = \ln 2 + \ln 3 = 1.792$
$\ln 7 = 1.9459$
$\ln 8 = \ln 2^3 = 3\ln 2 = 3 \times 0.6931 = 2.079$
$\ln 9 = \ln 3^2 = 2\ln 3 = 2 \times 1.0986 = 2.197$
$\ln 10 = \ln(2 \times 5) = \ln 2 + \ln 5 = 2.303$
$\ln 11 = 2.3979$
$\ln 12 = \ln(2 \times 2 \times 3) = 2\ln 2 + \ln 3 = 2.485$
$\ln 13 = 2.5649$
$\ln 14 = \ln(2 \times 7) = \ln 2 + \ln 7 = 2.639$
$\ln 15 = \ln(3 \times 5) = \ln 3 + \ln 5 = 2.708$
$\ln 16 = \ln 2^4 = 4\ln 2 = 4 \times 0.6931 = 2.773$
$\ln 17 = 2.8332$
$\ln 18 = \ln(2 \times 3 \times 3) = \ln 2 + 2\ln 3 = 2.890$
$\ln 19 = 2.9444$
$\ln 20 = \ln(2 \times 2 \times 5) = 2\ln 2 + \ln 5 = 2.996$

2 a 0.602   **b** 0.778   **c** 0.903   **d** 0.954
   e 1.079   **f** 1.204   **g** 1.380   **h** 2.158

3.5E

1 a $t = \dfrac{\ln N}{0.05 \times \ln 2}$ **b** 199 minutes

2 b $t = 59.66$, i.e. 1999 to the nearest year.

3 a $t = \dfrac{\ln\left(\dfrac{y}{1000}\right)}{-\ln 1.029}$

   b $t = 24.247$, i.e. approx 24 000 years.

4 a 75°C   **b** $t = \dfrac{\ln\left(\dfrac{\theta}{75}\right)}{-\ln 1.02}$

5 a 6.40   **b** 1×10^{-7}
   d A comment on how the graph has a very small gradient for small concentrations, which means that they are further apart on the pH scale.

6 a 60 dB
   b 10^{-14} watts/cm^2
   c 10^{-2} watts/cm^2
   d Sketch of a log curve crossing the x-axis at $(10^{-16}, 0)$ with y increasing without limit as x increases. Also needs *at least* one other point to indicate the different scales on the axes, e.g. $(10^{-10}, 60)$ from part a).

3.7 Practice exam questions

1 a i When $t = 0$, $N = N_0 e^{kt} = N_0 e^0 = N_0 = 20$
   b

Day t	Number of flies, N	
	Data	Model
0	20	20
9	35	64
12	95	95
15	138	141
18	205	208
21	355	307
24	429	453

c

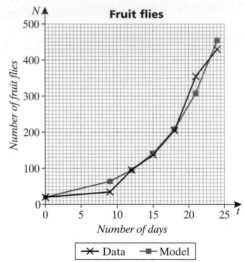

d -82.9%
e i 1 105 416   **ii** Limited food available.
f 1.139 to 3 dps.

2 b ii 0.144 to 3 dps
   iii 5 hours before it was first found.
   c i temperature will fall to a steady 20 degrees Celsius.
   ii Room temperature
   d Best when temperature is not too close to 37 or 20 degrees Celsius, and depends largely on how accurate/reliable temperature readings are.

4 Simulations

4.1 Random events

Use the spreadsheets to check individual answers.

4.2 Random numbers

4.2A

1 b Random number between 0 and 4.9
   INT(RAND)+1
   INT(4*RAND)
   Random integer 0, 4
   INT(3*RAND)−1

2 b Random number between 0 and 9.9
   Random integer 0 to 9 inclusive
   Random integer 1 to 0 inclusive
   Random integer −1, 0, 1
   =INT(5*RAND())
   =INT(5*RAND())+1
   =INT(100*RAND())+1

4.2B

1

Call number	Call time	Random number	Time taken (minutes)	Query start	Query end	Wait time (minutes)	Queue length at time of call
1	9:00	8	4	9:00	9:04	0	0
2	9:02	9	5	9:04	9:09	2	0
3	9:04	6	3	9:09	9:12	5	0
4	9:06	9	5	9:12	9:17	6	1
5	9:08	4	2	9:17	9:19	9	2
6	9:10	7	3	9:19	9:22	9	2
7	9:12	0	1	9:22	9:23	10	2
8	9:14	4	2	9:23	9:25	9	3
9	9:16	7	3	9:25	9:28	9	4
10	9:18	6	3	9:28	9:31	10	4
11	9:20	4	2	9:31	9:33	11	4
12	9:22	6	3	9:33	9:36	11	4
13	9:24	9	5	9:36	9:41	12	4
14	9:26	8	4	9:41	9:45	15	4
15	9:28	3	2	9:45	9:47	17	4
16	9:30	1	1	9:47	9:48	17	5
17	9:32	7	3	9:48	9:51	16	5
18	9:34	6	3	9:51	9:54	17	5
19	9:36	5	2	9:54	9:56	18	5
20	9:38	6	3	9:56	9:59	18	6
21	9:40	6	3	9:59	10:02	19	7
22	9:42	0	1	10:02	10:03	20	7
23	9:44	4	2	10:03	10:05	19	8
24	9:46	1	1	10:05	10:06	19	8
25	9:48	2	2	10:06	10:08	18	7
26	9:50	3	2	10:08	10:10	18	8
27	9:52	9	5	10:10	10:15	18	8
28	9:54	9	5	10:15	10:20	21	8
29	9:56	4	2	10:20	10:22	24	8
30	9:58	8	4	10:22	10:26	24	9

3 Run the simulation of a number of times before drawing conclusions.

Calls are unlikely to be as regular as every 2 minutes (busy and quiet periods).

Could simulate callers hanging up and leaving the queue either at the start (e.g. if they are told what number they are in the queue) or hang up after waiting a certain time (e.g. simulate patience as another random number!)

4

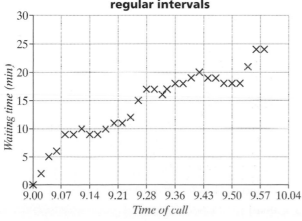

Wait times as calls come in at regular intervals

Time of call

Waiting time (min)

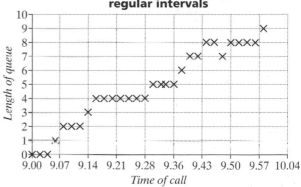

Queue build up as calls come in at regular intervals

Length of queue

Time of call

4.2C

Use spreadsheet to help check individual simulations.

4.3 More complex simulations

4.3A, B, C

Use spreadsheet to help check individual simulations.

4.3D

1 Description that the nucleus decays with probability 0.5, (e.g. if the random number is even/odd, or falls in the range 0–4 etc.) and must also note that once decayed the nucleus stays in a decayed state.

2 $\ln x$ and e^x are inverse functions of each other.

3 After each time interval, the proportion of atoms *remaining* is 0.9 of the nuclei at the start of the time interval. To find how many successive time intervals, n, pass before the proportion is down to 0.5, we must solve $0.9^n = \frac{1}{2}$

4 $0.9^n = \frac{1}{2}$

$\therefore \ln(0.9^n) = \ln\frac{1}{2}$

$\therefore n \ln 0.9 = \ln\frac{1}{2}$

$\therefore n = \dfrac{\ln\frac{1}{2}}{\ln 0.9}$

5 After one time interval, there will theoretically be 0.8 (80%) of the original number of nuclei, so:

$0.8 = e^{-k}$

$\therefore \ln 0.8 = -k$

$\therefore k = -\ln 0.8 = 0.223$

4.5 Practice exam question

1 a

Time (min)	9	10	11	12	13
Probability	0.1	0.4	0.3	0.1	0.1
Random number	0	1, 2, 3, 4	5, 6, 7	8	9

Or equivalent.

Assuming the random numbers have been assigned as above.

b

Student number	Arrival time	Random number	Time taken (minutes)	Time start	Time end	Wait time (minutes)
1	14:00	3	10	14:00	14:10	0
2	14:10	1	10	14:10	14:20	0
3	14:20	9	13	14:20	14:33	0
4	14:30	1	10	14:33	14:43	3
5	14:40	0	9	14:43	14:52	3
6	14:50	6	11	14:52	15:03	2
7	15:00	5	11	15:03	15:14	3
8	15:10	0	9	15:14	15:23	4
9	15:20	8	12	15:23	15:35	3
10	15:30	5	11	15:35	15:46	5
11	15:40	3	10	15:46	15:56	6
12	15:50	8	12	15:56	16:08	6

c 3 minutes

d i 10 minutes

   ii Comparing the *mode* from the table to the *mean* of the distribution (10.7).

e e.g. simulate promptness (minutes early late for interview), work with times to nearest half minute, periods between interviews when interviewers write up their notes.

5 Transformations of functions

5.1 Transformation of graphs of functions

5.1A

1 b i $\begin{pmatrix} 0 \\ 2 \end{pmatrix}$ **ii** $\begin{pmatrix} 0 \\ -5 \end{pmatrix}$

2 b i $\begin{pmatrix} 0 \\ 4 \end{pmatrix}$ **ii** $\begin{pmatrix} 0 \\ -3 \end{pmatrix}$

3 a i $\begin{pmatrix} 0 \\ 2 \end{pmatrix}$ **ii** $\begin{pmatrix} 0 \\ -2 \end{pmatrix}$

  c $\begin{pmatrix} 0 \\ a \end{pmatrix}$

4 b i $\begin{pmatrix} -1 \\ 0 \end{pmatrix}$ **ii** $\begin{pmatrix} 3 \\ 0 \end{pmatrix}$

5 b i $\begin{pmatrix} -2 \\ 0 \end{pmatrix}$ **ii** $\begin{pmatrix} 4 \\ 0 \end{pmatrix}$

6 a i $\begin{pmatrix} -5 \\ 0 \end{pmatrix}$ **ii** $\begin{pmatrix} 1 \\ 0 \end{pmatrix}$

  c $\begin{pmatrix} -a \\ 0 \end{pmatrix}$

7 c $\begin{pmatrix} 3 \\ 1 \end{pmatrix}$ **d** $\begin{pmatrix} -4 \\ -1 \end{pmatrix}$

  e i $y = (x + 1)^2 - 1$

    ii $y = (x - 2)^2 - 5$

    iii $y = (x + 2\frac{1}{2})^2 + 2\frac{3}{4}$

5.1B

1 b Stretch in y-direction, scale factors:

  i 2   **ii** $\frac{1}{2}$ **iii** 4

2 b Stretch in y-direction, scale factors:

  i 3   **ii** 2   **iii** $\frac{1}{5}$

5.1C

1 b Scale factors:

  i $\frac{1}{2}$ **ii** 2   **iii** $\frac{1}{3}$

2 b Stretch in x-direction, scale factors:

  i $\frac{1}{2}$ **ii** 10   **iii** 2

5.1D

1 b Stretch in the y-direction, scale factors:

  i 2

  ii −1 (or just reflection in x-axis)

  iii −$\frac{1}{2}$

2 b There are no (real) roots for negative numbers.

  c Reflection in the y-axis.

5.1E

1 b i Translation $\begin{pmatrix} 0 \\ 4 \end{pmatrix}$

  ii translation $\begin{pmatrix} -4 \\ 0 \end{pmatrix}$

  iii Stretch in the y-direction by factor 4 OR stretch in the x-direction by factor 4

  iv Stretch in the x-direction by factor $\frac{1}{3}$ OR stretch in the y-direction by factor $\frac{1}{3}$

2 b i Translation $\begin{pmatrix} 0 \\ -5 \end{pmatrix}$

  ii Translation $\begin{pmatrix} 5 \\ 0 \end{pmatrix}$

  iii Stretch in the y-direction by factor 7.

  iv Translation $\begin{pmatrix} -2 \\ 0 \end{pmatrix}$

3 b i Stretch in the y-direction by factor 2

  ii Translation $\begin{pmatrix} 0 \\ 4 \end{pmatrix}$

  iii Reflection in x-axis.

  iv Reflection in y-axis.

  v Stretch in the x-direction by factor $\frac{1}{2}$ or translation $\begin{pmatrix} 0 \\ \ln 2 \end{pmatrix}$

  vi Translation $\begin{pmatrix} 2 \\ 0 \end{pmatrix}$

  vii Translation $\begin{pmatrix} 0 \\ 3 \end{pmatrix}$ or stretch in the x-direction by factor e^{y-3}.

  viii Translation $\begin{pmatrix} 0 \\ \ln \frac{1}{4} \end{pmatrix}$ or stretch in the x-direction by factor 4.

5.2 Combining transformations

5.2B

1 a Stretch in the x-direction by factor 20 and stretch in the y-direction by factor 20.

  b 20

  c 54

  d The model increases exponentially without limit.

2 a Stretch in the x-direction by a factor of $\frac{1}{500}$ and a translation of $\begin{pmatrix} 0 \\ 4 \end{pmatrix}$.

  b Given the rules (2 hrs to pack/unpack) the model works for all *v*. However, *v* will be limited to realistic speeds for the lorry.

3 a Stretch in the x-direction by factor 4, stretch in the y-direction by factor 9600 and translation $\begin{pmatrix} 0 \\ 300 \end{pmatrix}$.

3 b £9900   **c** £300

4 a Translation $\begin{pmatrix} 40 \\ 0 \end{pmatrix}$, stretch in the *y*-direction by factor $\frac{1}{80}$

and translation $\begin{pmatrix} 0 \\ 20 \end{pmatrix}$

4 b 20 m

c It is possible to throw the same distance at different speeds and angles, but neither factor is included in the function explicitly.

5 a Stretch in the *t*-direction by factor $\frac{1}{5}$, reflection in the *y*-axis, stretch in the *V* direction by factor 12, reflection in the *t*-axis, translation $\begin{pmatrix} 0 \\ 12 \end{pmatrix}$

b 0 V

c 12 V

6 a i Stretch in the *x*-direction by factor $\frac{1}{20}$ or stretch in the *y*-direction by factor $\sqrt{20}$.

iii Greater values of *h* lead to greater downward speeds, but this does not take into account air resistance/terminal velocity.

b i Stretch in the *h*-direction by factor 10, reflection horizontally, translation $\begin{pmatrix} 0 \\ 0.5 \end{pmatrix}$, stretch in the *v*-direction by factor 5, translation $\begin{pmatrix} 0 \\ 5 \end{pmatrix}$

ii Long term speed of 5 ms^{-1}

iii

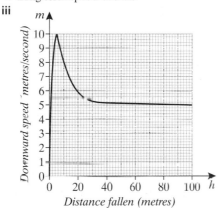

Distance fallen (metres)

5.3A

1 $\sin(30°) = \sin(150°)$ and $\sin(210°) = \sin(330°)$.
By symmetry about the *y*-axis, but $\sin(30°) = -\sin(330°)$ and $\sin(150°) = -\sin(210°)$ by reflection in the *x*-axis.

2 $\cos(30°) = \cos(330°)$; $\cos(150°) = \cos(210°)$.

3 Any set of angles: {, °, 180−, °, 180+, °, 360−, °}

4

t (seconds)	h (metres)
0	0
15	2.6
30	5
45	7.1
60	8.7
75	9.7
90	10
105	9.7
120	8.7
135	7.1
150	5
165	2.6
180	0
195	−2.6
210	5
225	−7.1
240	−8.7
255	9.7
270	−10
285	−9.7
300	−8.7
315	−7.1
330	−5
345	−2.6
360	0

5

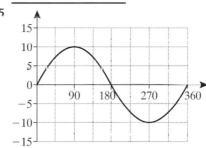

5.3B

1 120 s

2

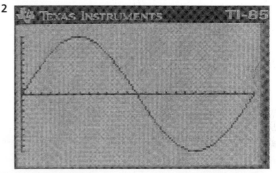

3 Amplitude = 10 m

4 Stretch of scale factor 10 in the *y*-direction and scale factor 3 in the *x*-direction.

5.3C

1 c Stretch in the *y*-direction by factor 0.5 and reflection in the *t*-axis.

2 c Stretch in the *t*-direction by factor 2.

5.4A

Adult male

$p = 20 \sin 450t + 100$

over 100 mmHg: half the time.

Adult female

$p = 20 \sin 480t + 100$

over 100 mmHg: half the time.

Baby

$p = 10 \sin 720t + 60$

over 100 mmHg: none of the time.

Elderly

$p = 35 \sin 360t + 145$

over 100 mmHg: none of the time.

5.4B

1 b $c = 10.2$

   c $A = 6.4$

   d $\omega = \frac{360}{365} = 0.986$, to 3 dps

   e $\alpha = -\omega t = -0.986 \times 25 = -24.65$

4 Both have the same period but temperatures ranges and phase difference, reflect their different geographical locations.

5 Useful for calculating heating/cooling costs of current/new buildings.

There is a limitation in that it is based on monthly averages – is a moderate, average temperature because of very high day, and much cooler night temperatures, or are the days and nights both moderate?

Additional information useful includes how much cloud cover is expected, wind strengths and directions.

5.4C

2 Winter solstice (21st December) and Summer solstice (21st June).

3 c 13 days on which there will be more than 14 hrs daylight in Manchester.

5.4D

1 $h = 4.8 \sin(15t - 52.5)° + 9.6$

3 $t = 3.819$ hours $= 03:49$; $t = 15.181$ hours $= 15:11$

5.4E

1 Let the formula be of the form $N = A \sin(\omega t + \alpha)° + c$, where N is the number of sunspots and t is the year number.

All 3 estimates peak in 2000, so one possible value for α is given by

$\alpha = 90 - 2000 = -1910$

Since sine waves repeat every 360°, it is more usual to find $-180 \leqslant \alpha < 180$, in which case, $\alpha = -110$.

With a minimum, 6 years later in 2006 (or 4 years earlier in 1996) this means $60 \leqslant \omega \leqslant 90$.

Upper

$A = (190 - 10)/2 = 90$

$c = (190 + 10)/2 = 100$

Middle

$A = (160 - 10)/2 = 75$

$c = (160 + 10)/2 = 85$

Lower

$A = (130 - 10)/2 = 60$

$c = (130 + 10)/2 = 70$

3 a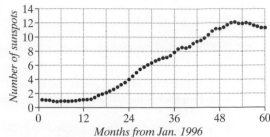

Months from Jan. 1996

From the real data, the model will be approximately, $N = 55 \sin(3.75t - 112.5) + 65$, where N is the number of sunspots and t is the number of months since Jan 1996.

b Using the model, $N > 100$ between $t = 40.5$, 67.5 months after Jan '96, i.e. over 27 months (around 820 days).

5.5A

2 $t = 3.33$, 23.33 milliseconds.

3 $t = 13.33$, 33.33 milliseconds.

5.5B

2 Every 10 seconds, $t = 10, 20, \ldots$ seconds.

5.5C

$0.5 \leqslant t \leqslant 5.5$ and $12.5 \leqslant t \leqslant 17.5$

i.e. from 12:30 am to 5:30 am & from 12:30 pm to 5:30 pm.

5.5D

1 26th August.

There will be less than 15 hours of daylight after 26th August.

2 a $n = 41, 319$ (10th Feb, 15th Nov)

   b $n = 130, 230$ (10th May, 18th Aug)

5.7 Practice exam questions

1 a Stretch in y-direction by scale factor 40 and stretch in t-direction by factor 1\24 (order unimportant).

   b 3 minutes 27 seconds (solutions are 5.7746 and 9.2254 mins).

   c 8 minutes 42 seconds (solutions are 3.1467 and 11.8532 mins).

   d $h = 40(1 - \cos 24t)$

   e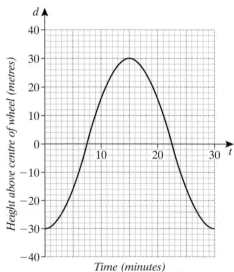

Time (minutes)

2 a 81 years
  b ii 82.25 years
  c 1850 ($t = -50$)
  d i Reflection in y-axis (stretch in t-direction scale factor of -1).
    ii Stretch in the t-direction, scale factor 125.
    iii Reflection in t-axis.
    iv Translation $\begin{pmatrix} 2 \\ 0 \end{pmatrix}$
    v Stretch in the y-direction, scale factor 52.
  e i 51 and 52 years.
    ii Quadratic becomes very large and negative, but the exponential model tends to 104.
    iii Both become very large and negative.

6 Finding a Good Model

Note: the answers in this section will be approximate, because they will depend on how the lines of best fit have been drawn.

6.1 Transforming variables

6.1A
3 m approx. 12.7.

6.1B
1a & 1b

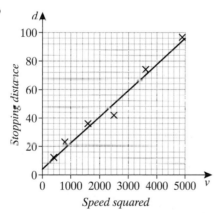

  c gradient, $m = 0.018$; intercept $c = 4.46$.
  d $d = 0.018v^2 + 4.46$.

6.1D
a

l	$\sqrt{l}$	T
0	0	0
0.05	0.2236	0.44
0.10	0.3162	0.64
0.20	0.4472	0.89
0.30	0.5477	1.05
0.40	0.6325	1.24
0.50	0.7071	1.41
0.60	0.7746	1.55
0.70	0.8367	1.62
0.80	0.8944	1.78
0.90	0.9487	1.82
1.00	1	2.09

b

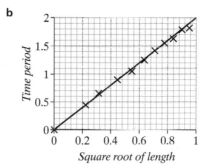

  c k approx. 2.

6.1E
1

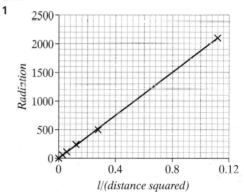

2 k approx. 18 750.

6.2 Using logarithms

6.2A
a & b

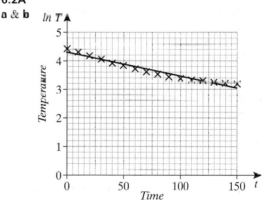

  c (approx.) y-intercept $= 4.3$ and gradient $= 0.0083$
  So, $\ln T = 4.3 - 0.0083t$
  d $T_0 = 73.7$, $T = 73.7e^{-0.0083t}$

6.2B

1 c & d

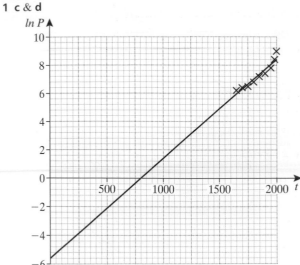

e Gradient, $k = 0.007$; intercept, $\ln P_0 = -5.5$, so
$P_0 = 0.0041$ and $P = 0.0041e^{kt}$

2 b

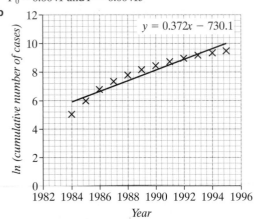

$y = 0.372x - 730.1$

c Gradient, $k = 0.37$, so $\ln N = \ln N_0 + 0.37t$
Because it is impractical to extend the graph back to year
zero, substitute into this equation, values for t and $\ln N$
from a point which lies on the line to find $\ln N_0$.
$\ln N_0 = -730$, so $N_0 = e^{-730}$
Hence, $N = e^{-730}e^{0.28t} = e^{(0.28t - 730)}$

3 b

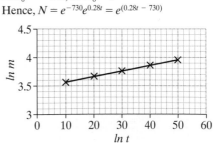

c $a = 32.1$, $k = 0.010$
d 58.5

6.2C

3 & 4

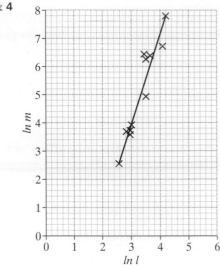

5 $\ln m = -5.3 + 3.1 \ln l$
$m = e^{-5.3}l^{3.1} = 0.005l^{3.1}$

6 255 g – likely to be a bit on the low side. There is quite a
large variation in the table at around 30 cm, but a partridge
would probably be closer in weight to the duck than the
sparrowhawk.

6.2D

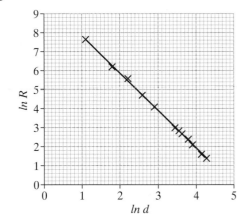

$\ln R = -2.0 \ln d + 9.84$
$R = e^{9.84}d^{-2} = \dfrac{18\,800}{d^2}$ (to 3 s.f.)

6.2E

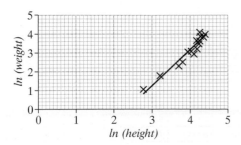

$\ln W = 1.91 \ln H - 4.44$
$W = 0.012H^{1.91}$

6.2F

2

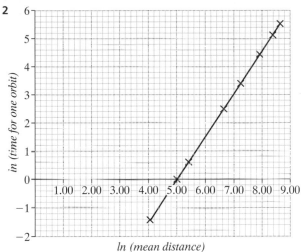

ln (mean distance)

Gradient = 1.5 as expected from Kepler's model in question 1.

6.2G

2 $\ln W = 2.0 \ln h - 3.8$, so $W = 0.022h^2$

6.4 Practice exam questions

1 a 74.8%
   c i Data lies in a straight line.
   d i 0.462   **ii** −0.483%
   e i Light intensity tends to 0.
     ii Light intensity becomes infinite.
     iii Light sources have a finite intensity (often stated on torches for example), but intensities do indeed drop off to zero.

2 d

R (Ohms)	V (millivolts)	1/V
45.3	113	0.00885
49.8	102	0.0098
52.4	96	0.01042
57.6	86	0.01163
62.3	79	0.01266

b

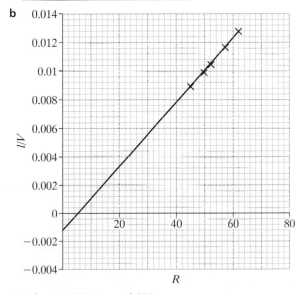

R

c & d $a = 0.0002$, $b = -0.0014$

7 Recurrence relations

7.1 Basic recurrence relations

7.1A
3 $10\,000^{(1/14)} = 1.9307$ to 4 dp.

7.1B
2 £19.21 to nearest pence.
3 It is the initial amount (£40) subtracted from the amount at the end of $(n + 1)$ years, $A_{n + 1} = 1.04A_n$.
4 b i 11 years (£21.58)
   ii 18 years

7.1C
1 $P_{n + 1} = 2P_n$
2 a i Looking at successive 25 year periods.
   ii The population doubles in successive periods.
c

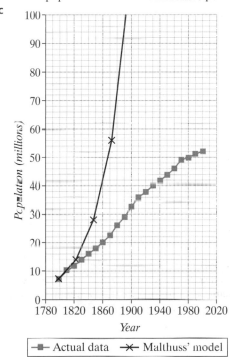

Year

— ■ — Actual data   — ✕ — Malthuss' model

7.2A
1 a =0.015*F2
   b =B3+F2
   c =0.03*C3
   d =50
   e =C3−E3
3 a 11 months
   b £45.81
   c 9.162%

7.2B
Minimum rate: Smile – 11 months (£60.00 interest).
Maximum rate: NextGold – 12 months (122.48 interest).

7.2C

1 a

n	M_n
0	1000
1	1200
2	1440
3	1728
4	2073
5	2489
6	2987
7	3584
8	4301
9	5161
10	6193
11	7432
12	8918
13	10 702
14	12 842
15	15 410
16	18 492
17	22 190
18	26 628
19	31 954
20	38 345

b 4 years

2 a Increasing the value 0.2 increase rate of population growth, decreasing the value 0.2 decreases the rate of population growth or the population may actually decline for negative values > -1.

b Directly proportional.

c

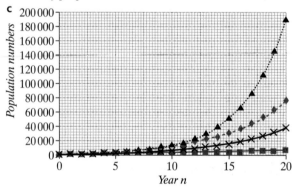

- ✕ Original
- ■ Lower growth
- ▲ Increased growth
- ◆ Higher original population

3 a

n	M_n
0	1000
1	1020
2	1044
3	1073
4	1108
5	1150
6	1200
7	1260
8	1332
9	1418
10	1522
11	1646
12	1795
13	1974
14	2189
15	2447
16	2756
17	3127
18	3572
19	4106
20	4747

b The numbers are greatly reduced by the presence of the owls as modelled.

c 206 mice/year.

d 1000*0.2=500 mice a year to keep the population stable.

7.2D

1 b B2+B2*0.3−25*C2

c 0.01*B2

2 a

Year	Number of mice	Number of owls
0	1000	10
1	1200	10
2	1440	12
3	1728	14
4	2074	17
5	2489	21
6	2987	25
7	3584	30
8	4301	36
9	5161	43
10	6193	52
11	7432	62
12	8918	74
13	10 702	89
14	12 842	107
15	15 410	128
16	18 492	154
17	22 190	185
18	26 628	222
19	31 954	266
20	38 345	320

b The mice numbers are increasing, approximately doubling every 4 years.

7.2E

1 b $E_n = 0.6E_{n-1} + 0.2C_{n-1}$

c

Hour	Car park	Entrance
0	150	150
1	180	120
2	192	108
3	197	103
4	199	101
5	200	100
6	200	100
7	200	100
8	200	100
9	200	100
10	200	100

2 You rarely run out of trolleys at supermarkets and if one place does, then staff will usually try to spread the trolleys available between the two sites.

7.3B

4 $r = 0$: steady population; $r > 0$: population increases without limit exponentially; $r < 0$: population decreases exponentially towards 0.

7.3D

1 a The term is close to 1.
  b The logistic equation approximates the basic model initially.
2 a The term is near 0 (but still positive).
  b The growth is modelled by the logistic equation drops until successive generations are approximately equal: $P_n \approx P_{n-1}$.

7.5 Practice exam question

1 a iii

End of month	Amount owed
0	£640.00
1	£598.00
2	£555.48
3	£512.42
4	£468.82
5	£424.68
6	£379.99
7	£334.74
8	£288.93
9	£242.54
10	£195.57
11	£148.01
12	£99.86
13	£51.11
14	£1.75

  iv £61.75

b i

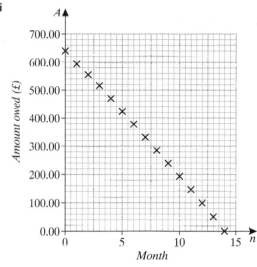

  ii The graph would be stretched in the positive n-direction, showing that it would take longer to clear the debt.
c i $A_{12} = 1.0125^{12}A_0$
  ii 16.08%

Comprehensions

Biorhythms

1 a i $a = -3, b = 3$
    ii $a = -20, b = 20$
2 14 or (41).
3 Period $= \dfrac{360}{90/7} = 28$
4 Stretch in the t direction by scale factor of 7/90.
5 a $t = 2\frac{1}{3}$
  b $t = 16\frac{1}{4}$; half a period later, by symmetry of a sine curve.
6 a $g(t) = \sin\dfrac{360t}{23}$
  b $h(t) = \sin\dfrac{120t}{11}$
7 a $38 = 2 \times 19, 28 = 2 \times 2 \times 7$
  b $\dfrac{28 \times 38}{2} = 532$

Compounding your interest

2 $\dfrac{x-3}{4-3} = \dfrac{200-173}{207-173}$
  $\therefore \dfrac{x-3}{1} = \dfrac{27}{34}$
4 6 years, 9 days

5

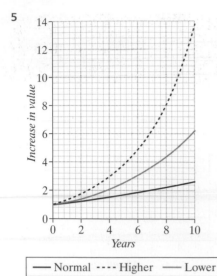

— Normal ---- Higher — Lower

6 100% interest will be given at $(100/n)\%$, n times.

7 3 days, 15 hours, 36 minutes.

Scaling in Nature

1 288 mm.

2 Area of the paper used must be halved, so scale factor of *length* required is $(1/2) = 0.707$ to 3 dps.

3 Scale factor of volume $= 12^3 = 1728$.

4 144 – based on the metabolic rate.

$$\text{specific metabolic rate} = \frac{\text{metabolic rate}}{\text{unit mass}}$$

$$\propto \frac{\text{mass}^{\frac{2}{3}}}{\text{mass}} = \frac{1}{\text{mass}^{\frac{1}{3}}} = \frac{1}{\sqrt[3]{\text{mass}}}$$

7 a 166 days, to nearest day. **b** 9.93%

Making sense of planetary motion

1 a $(1, 1)$ **b** From Figure 4.

2 i and **ii**.

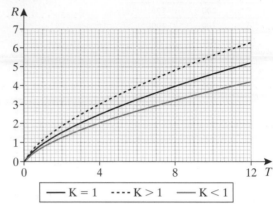

— K = 1 ---- K > 1 — K < 1

3 a i 5.81×10^7 km

  ii 88 days (to nearest day)

  b 2.53×10^{19} km³ day⁻²

4 a 2.40×10^{16} km³ day⁻² **b** 238.71 days

5 Distance covered in one orbit is the circumference of the circle $= 2\pi R$. Speed = distance/time $= 2\pi R/T$.

7 1.01×10^{13} m³ s⁻²

Index